INSTRUCTOR-LED TRAINING

APPROVED COURSEWARE

Microsoft
Outlook 2000
Microsoft Office Application

Expert Skills Student Guide

ActiveEducation

PUBLISHED BY
Microsoft Press
A Division of Microsoft Corporation
One Microsoft Way
Redmond, Washington 98052-6399

Copyright © 2000 by ActiveEducation

All rights reserved. No part of the contents of this book may be reproduced or transmitted in any form or by any means without the written permission of the publisher.

Library of Congress Cataloging-in-Publication Data
Microsoft Outlook 2000 Step by Step Courseware Expert Skills Student Guide / ActiveEducation.
    p. cm.
  Includes index.
  ISBN 0-7356-0982-9 (1 color) -- ISBN 0-7356-0715-X (4 color)
    1. Time management--Computer programs. 2. Personal information
management--Computer programs. 3. Electronic mail systems. I. ActiveEducation
(Firm)

HD69.T54 M539   2000
361.977--dc21   99-044100

Printed and bound in the United States of America.

1 2 3 4 5 6 7 8 9   WCWC   5 4 3 2 1 0

Distributed in Canada by Penguin Books Canada Limited.

A CIP catalogue record for this book is available from the British Library.

Microsoft Press books are available through booksellers and distributors worldwide. For further information about international editions, contact your local Microsoft Corporation office or contact Microsoft Press International directly at fax (425) 936-7329. Visit our Web site at mspress.microsoft.com.

ActiveEducation is a registered trademark of ActiveEducation, Inc. Microsoft, Microsoft Press, NetMeeting, NetShow, Outlook, PowerPoint, Windows, and Windows NT are either registered trademarks or trademarks of Microsoft Corporation in the United States and/or other countries. Other product and company names mentioned herein may be the trademarks of their respective owners.

Unless otherwise noted, the example companies, organizations, products, people, and events depicted herein are fictitious. No association with any real company, organization, product, person, or event is intended or should be inferred.

For ActiveEducation:	For Microsoft Press:
Managing Editor: Ron Pronk	**Acquisitions Editor:** Susanne M. Forderer
Series Editor: Kate Dawson	**Project Editor:** Sandra Haynes
Writer: Holly Freeman	**Proofreader:** Roger LeBlanc
Technical Editor: Sandra L. Knauke	**Production/Layout:** Elizabeth Hansford
Editorial Assistants: Lawrence Coles, Carrice L. Cudworth, Nicole French, Jennifer Jordan, Linda Savell	**Electronic Artist:** Joel Panchot
Indexer: Craig Wise	

Contents

Course Overview v

A Task-Based Approach Using Business Scenarios v • An Integrated Approach to Training vi • Preparation for Microsoft Office User Specialist (MOUS) Certification vi • A Sound Instructional Foundation vi • Designed for Optimal Learning vi • Lesson Features viii • Suggestions for Improvements x

Conventions and Features Used in This Book xi

Using the CD-ROM xiii

System Requirements xiii • If You Need to Install or Uninstall the Practice Files xiv • Using the Practice Files xv • Replying to Install Messages xvii • Copying Outlook Items to Outlook Folders xvii • If You Need Help with the Practice Files xviii

MOUS Objectives xix

Core Skills xix • Expert Skills xx

Taking a Microsoft Office User Certification Test xxiii

Preparing to Take an Exam xxiii • Test Format xxiv • Tips for Successfully Completing the Test xxv • If You Do Not Pass the Test xxvi

Lesson 1   **Customizing Outlook** 1.1

Customizing the Outlook Bar 1.2 • Creating a Shortcut on the Outlook Bar 1.4 • Using the Folder List 1.6 • Assigning Items to a Category 1.9 • Using and Modifying the Master Category List 1.11 • Using and Customizing Outlook Today 1.13 • Importing a Microsoft Access Database into Outlook 1.15 • Exporting Outlook Data to a Microsoft Excel Database 1.19 • Lesson Wrap-Up 1.22 • Lesson Glossary 1.22 • Quick Quiz 1.23 • Putting It All Together 1.23

Lesson 2   **Using Advanced E-Mail Features** 2.1

Customizing the Appearance of Messages 2.2 • Creating and Using Message Templates 2.5 • Adding a vCard to a Message 2.8 • Using the Rules Wizard 2.10 • Tracking When Messages Are Delivered and Read 2.13 • Creating a Personal Address Book 2.16 • Creating a Personal Distribution List 2.18 • Importing Data Between Outlook and Other E-Mail Applications 2.21 • Exporting Data Between Outlook and Other E-Mail Applications 2.24 • Integrating E-Mail with Other Office Applications 2.26 • Setting Up a News Account 2.28 • Viewing Newsgroups and Newsgroup Messages 2.30 • Subscribing to a Newsgroup 2.31 • Lesson Wrap-Up 2.32 • Lesson Glossary 2.32 • Quick Quiz 2.34 • Putting It All Together 2.34

Lesson 3	**Using Advanced Calendar Features**	**3.1**
	Customizing Calendar Options 3.1 • Changing Time Zone Settings 3.5 • Scheduling Online Meetings Using NetMeeting 3.6 • Sharing Calendar Information over the Internet 3.10 • Lesson Wrap-Up 3.12 • Lesson Glossary 3.13 • Quick Quiz 3.14 • Putting It All Together 3.14	
Lesson 4	**Using Advanced Contacts Features**	**4.1**
	Flagging Contacts for Follow Up 4.2 • Sorting Contacts 4.4 • Linking Contacts with Other Outlook Items 4.7 • Using Contacts in a Mail Merge 4.10 • Filtering Contacts for a Mail Merge 4.10 • Performing a Mail Merge 4.12 • Lesson Wrap-Up 4.16 • Lesson Glossary 4.17 • Quick Quiz 4.17 • Putting It All Together 4.18	
Lesson 5	**Using Advanced Tasks Features**	**5.1**
	Creating and Updating Recurring Tasks 5.1 • Creating Tasks While Working in Other Outlook Folders 5.4 • Recording a Task in the Journal 5.5 • Adding Fields to the Task List 5.8 • Lesson Wrap-Up 5.10 • Lesson Glossary 5.11 • Quick Quiz 5.11 • Putting It All Together 5.11	
Lesson 6	**Using Net Folders and Public Folders**	**6.1**
	Sharing a Folder with Others 6.2 • Granting Others Permission to Use Your Folders 6.3 • Granting a Delegate Access to Your Folders 6.5 • Using Net Folders 6.9 • Working Offline 6.14 • Synchronizing Folders 6.16 • Creating a Quick Synchronization Group 6.16 • Synchronizing by Message Size 6.17 • Lesson Wrap-Up 6.18 • Lesson Glossary 6.18 • Quick Quiz 6.19 • Putting It All Together 6.20	
Lesson 7	**Using the Fax Service**	**7.1**
	Setting Up the Fax Service 7.1 • Creating, Sending, and Receiving a Fax 7.6 • Viewing a Fax 7.9 • Lesson Wrap-Up 7.12 • Lesson Glossary 7.13 • Quick Quiz 7.13 • Putting It All Together 7.13	
Appendix	**Creating Forms**	**A.1**
	Quick Reference	**E.1**
	Index	**E.31**

Course Overview

Welcome to the *Step by Step Courseware* series for Microsoft Office 2000 and Microsoft Windows 2000 Professional. This series facilitates classroom learning, letting you develop competence and confidence in using an Office application or operating system software. In completing courses taught with *Step by Step Courseware*, you learn to use the software productively and discover how to make the software work for you. This series addresses core-level and expert-level skills in Microsoft Word 2000, Microsoft Excel 2000, Microsoft Access 2000, Microsoft Outlook 2000, Microsoft FrontPage 2000, and Microsoft Windows 2000 Professional.

The *Step by Step Courseware* series provides:

- A time-tested, integrated approach to learning.
- Task-based, results-oriented learning strategies.
- Exercises based on business scenarios.
- Complete preparation for Microsoft Office User Specialist (MOUS) certification.
- Attractive student guides with full-featured lessons.
- Lessons with accurate, logical, and sequential instructions.
- Comprehensive coverage of skills from the basic to the expert level.
- Review of core-level skills provided in expert-level guides.
- A CD-ROM with practice files.

A Task-Based Approach Using Business Scenarios

The *Step by Step Courseware* series builds on the strengths of the time-tested approach that Microsoft developed and refined for its Step by Step series. Even though the Step by Step series was created for self-paced training, instructors have long used it in the classroom. For the first time, this popular series has been adapted specifically for the classroom environment. By studying with a task-based approach, you learn more than just the features of the software. You learn how to accomplish real-world tasks so that you can immediately increase your productivity using the software application.

The lessons are based on tasks that you might encounter in the everyday work world. This approach allows you to quickly see the relevance of the training. The task-based focus is woven throughout the series, including lesson organization within each unit, lesson titles, and scenarios chosen for practice files.

An Integrated Approach to Training

The *Step by Step Courseware* series distinguishes itself from other series on the market with its consistent delivery and completely integrated approach to learning across a variety of print and online training media. With the addition of the *Step by Step Courseware* series, which supports classroom instruction, the *Step by Step* training suite now provides a flexible and unified training solution.

Print-Based Self-Training in the Step by Step Training Suite

The proven print-based series of stand-alone *Step by Step* books has consistently been the resource that customers choose for developing software skills on their own.

Online Training in the Step by Step Training Suite

For those who prefer online training, the *Step by Step Interactive* products offer highly interactive online training in a simulated work environment, complete with graphics, sound, video, and animation delivered to a single station (self-contained installation), local area network (LAN), or intranet. *Step by Step Interactive* has a network administration module that allows a training manager to track the progress and quiz results for students using the training. For more information, see *mspress.microsoft.com*.

Preparation for Microsoft Office User Specialist (MOUS) Certification

This series has been certified as approved courseware for the Microsoft Office User Specialist certification program. Students who have completed this training are prepared to take the related MOUS exam. By passing the exam for a particular Office application, students demonstrate proficiency in that application to their employers or prospective employers. Exams are offered at participating test centers. For more information, see *www.mous.net*.

A Sound Instructional Foundation

All products in the *Step by Step Courseware* series apply the same instructional strategies, closely adhering to adult instructional techniques and reliable adult learning principles. Lessons in the *Step by Step Courseware* series are presented in a logical, easy-to-follow format, helping you find information quickly and learn as efficiently as possible. To facilitate the learning process, each lesson follows a consistent structure.

Designed for Optimal Learning

The following "Lesson Features" section shows how the colorful and highly visual series design makes it easy for you to see what to read and what to do when practicing new skills.

Lessons break training into easily assimilated sessions. Each lesson is self-contained, and lessons can be completed in sequences other than the one presented in the table of contents. Sample files for the lessons don't depend on completion of other lessons. Sample files within a lesson assume only that you are working sequentially through a complete lesson.

The *Step by Step Courseware* series features:

- **Lesson objectives.** Objectives clearly state the instructional goals for each lesson so that you understand what skills you will master. Each lesson objective is covered in its own section, and each section or topic in the lesson is covered in a consistent way. Lesson objectives preview the lesson structure, helping you grasp key information and prepare for learning skills.

- **Informational text for each topic.** For each objective, the lesson provides easy-to-read, technique-focused information.

- **Hands-on practice.** Numbered steps give detailed, step-by-step instructions to help you learn skills. The steps also show results and screen images to match what you should see on your computer screen. The accompanying CD contains sample files used for each lesson.

- **Full-color illustrations in color student guides.** Illustrated screen images give visual feedback as you work through exercises. The images reinforce key concepts, provide visual clues about the steps, and give you something to check your progress against.

- **MOUS icon.** Each section or sidebar that covers a MOUS certification objective has a MOUS icon in the margin at the beginning of the section. The number of the certification objective is also listed.

- **Tips.** Helpful hints and alternate ways to accomplish tasks are located throughout the lesson text.

- **Important.** If there is something to watch out for or something to avoid, this information is added to the lesson and indicated with this heading.

- **Sidebars.** Sidebars contain parenthetical topics or additional information that you might find interesting.

- **Margin notes.** Margin notes provide additional related or background information that adds value to the lesson.

- **Button images in the margin.** When the text instructs you to click a particular button, an image of the button and its label appear in the margin.

- **Lesson Glossary.** Terms with which you might not be familiar are defined in the glossary. Terms in the glossary appear in boldface type within the lesson and are defined upon their first use within lessons.

- **Quick Quiz.** You can use the short-answer Quick Quiz questions to test or reinforce your understanding of key topics within the lesson.

Lesson Features

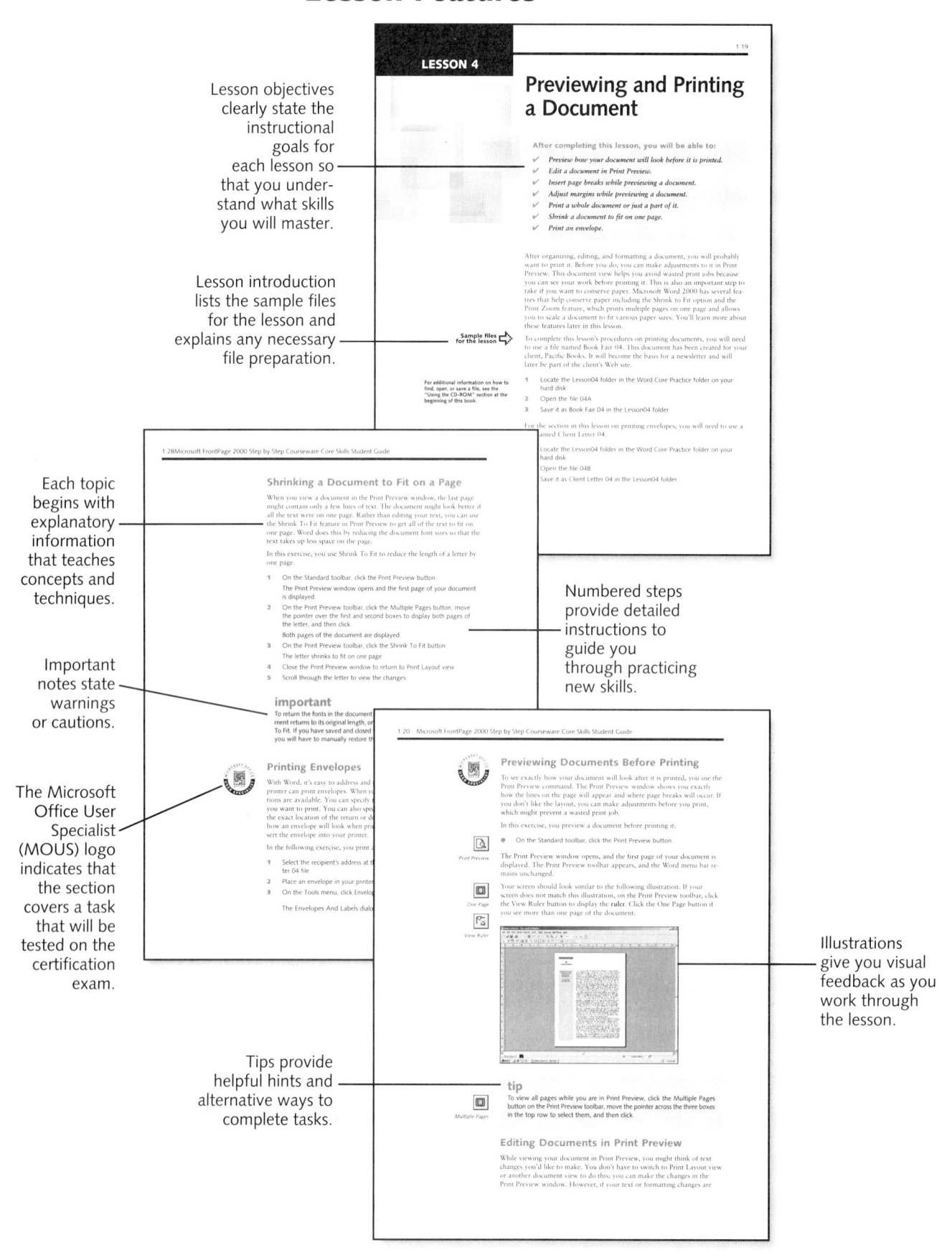

Lesson objectives clearly state the instructional goals for each lesson so that you understand what skills you will master.

Lesson introduction lists the sample files for the lesson and explains any necessary file preparation.

Each topic begins with explanatory information that teaches concepts and techniques.

Important notes state warnings or cautions.

The Microsoft Office User Specialist (MOUS) logo indicates that the section covers a task that will be tested on the certification exam.

Tips provide helpful hints and alternative ways to complete tasks.

Numbered steps provide detailed instructions to guide you through practicing new skills.

Illustrations give you visual feedback as you work through the lesson.

Course Overview   ix

Margin notes provide additional information.

Lesson 4 Previewing and Printing a Document   1.29

To print an envelope of a different size, in the Envelopes And Labels dialog box, click Options. In the Envelope Options dialog box, click the Envelope Options tab. In the Envelope size area, click the appropriate size.

4   In the Envelopes And Labels dialog box, make sure that the recipient's address and the return address are correct. The return address is based on information that you entered when you installed the software. If either address is wrong, type the corrections.

5   Click the Options button, and check the envelope size. The default envelope size is a Size 10 business envelope, but you can click another size in the Envelope Size list.

6   To position the envelope for printing, consult the documentation that came with your printer. Check the preview in the Envelopes And Labels dialog box to see how Word expects the envelope to be loaded into the printer.

7   Click Print to have your printer print the addressed envelope.

tip
To avoid having to add the return address each time you print an envelope, on the Tools menu, click Options. On the User Information tab, type the name and address information that you always want to use as your return address. Click OK.

Lesson Glossary

collate To merge items from two or more sources.
Magnifier A button that alternatively increases or decreases the size of a document.
repaginate To renumber the displayed page numbers in a document.
ruler A bar in the Word window marked with units, used to set indents, margins, and tab stops.
status bar An area along the bottom of a program window.
User information tab An area of the Options dialog box in which you can set your default name, initials, and address.

Lesson Wrap-Up

This lesson covered how to preview documents before printing, how to edit documents in Print Preview, how to print documents, and how to print envelopes in Word 2000.

If you are continuing on to the next lesson:

- On the Standard toolbar, click Save to save changes made to Book Fair 04
- On the File menu, click Close to close the file.

If you are not continuing to other lessons:

- If you want to quit Word for now, on the File menu, click Exit.

Lesson Glossary defines key terms shown in boldface within the lesson.

Lesson Wrap-up covers remaining file administration details to end the lesson.

1:30   Microsoft FrontPage 2000 Step by Step Courseware Core Skills Student Guide

Quick Quiz short-answer questions quiz you on the lesson concepts.

Quick Quiz

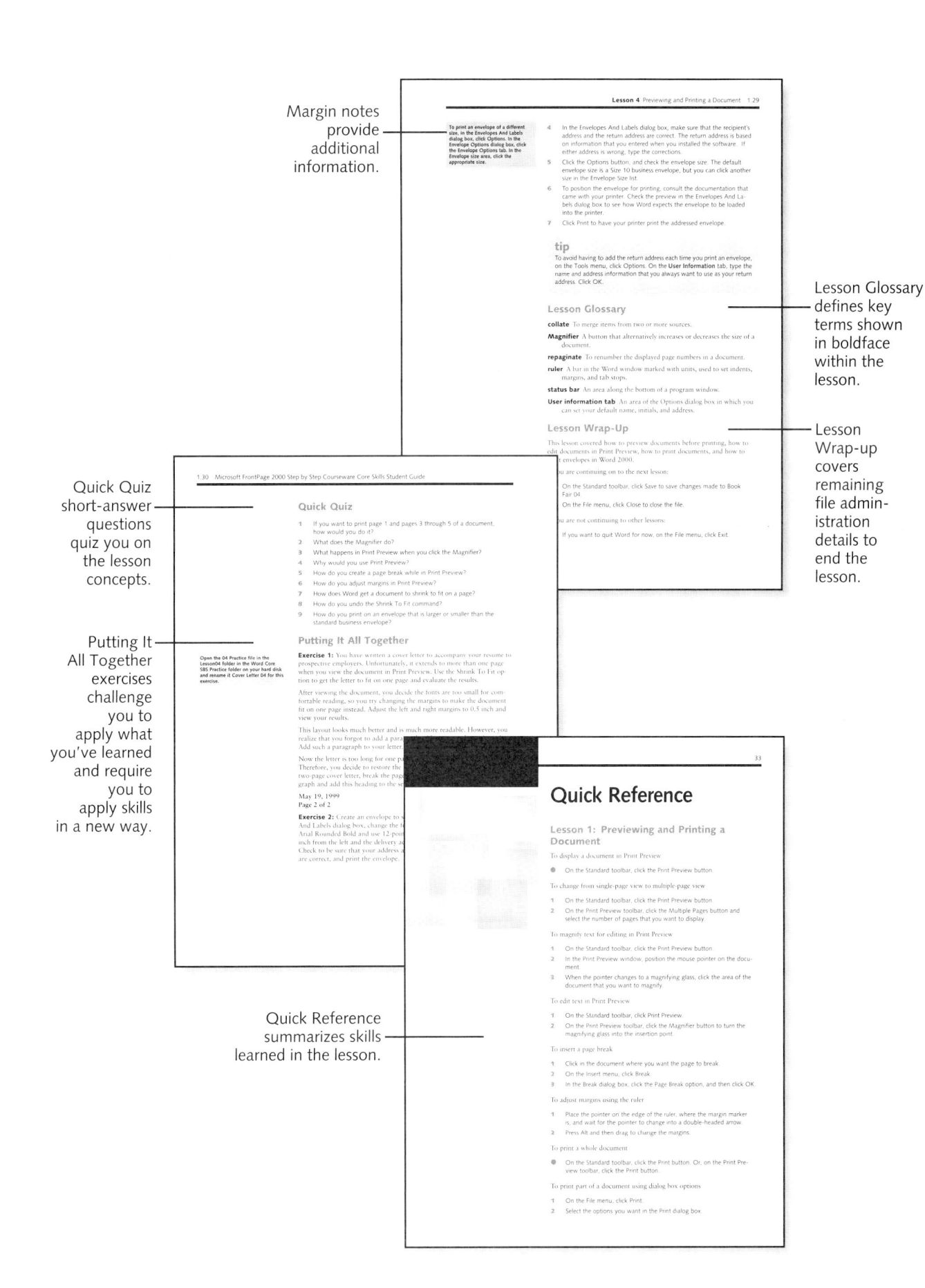

1   If you want to print page 1 and pages 3 through 5 of a document, how would you do it?
2   What does the Magnifier do?
3   What happens in Print Preview when you click the Magnifier?
4   Why would you use Print Preview?
5   How do you create a page break while in Print Preview?
6   How do you adjust margins in Print Preview?
7   How does Word get a document to shrink to fit on a page?
8   How do you undo the Shrink To Fit command?
9   How do you print on an envelope that is larger or smaller than the standard business envelope?

Putting It All Together exercises challenge you to apply what you've learned and require you to apply skills in a new way.

Putting It All Together

Open the 04 Practice file in the Lesson04 folder in the Word Core SBS Practice folder on your hard disk and rename it Cover Letter 04 for this exercise.

Exercise 1: You have written a cover letter to accompany your resume to prospective employers. Unfortunately, it extends to more than one page when you view the document in Print Preview. Use the Shrink To Fit option to get the letter to fit on one page and evaluate the results.

After viewing the document, you decide the fonts are too small for comfortable reading, so you try changing the margins to make the document fit on one page instead. Adjust the left and right margins to 0.5 inch and view your results.

This layout looks much better and is much more readable. However, you realize that you forgot to add a paragraph to your letter. Add such a paragraph to your letter.

Now the letter is too long for one page. Therefore, you decide to restore the two-page cover letter, break the page, and add this heading to the second page:

May 19, 1999
Page 2 of 2

Exercise 2: Create an envelope to send. And Labels dialog box, change the font to Arial Rounded Bold and use 12-point type. inch from the left and the delivery address. Check to be sure that your address and the return address are correct, and print the envelope.

33

Quick Reference

Lesson 1: Previewing and Printing a Document

To display a document in Print Preview

- On the Standard toolbar, click the Print Preview button.

To change from single-page view to multiple-page view

1   On the Standard toolbar, click the Print Preview button.
2   On the Print Preview toolbar, click the Multiple Pages button and select the number of pages that you want to display.

To magnify text for editing in Print Preview

1   On the Standard toolbar, click the Print Preview button.
2   In the Print Preview window, position the mouse pointer on the document.
3   When the pointer changes to a magnifying glass, click the area of the document that you want to magnify.

To edit text in Print Preview

1   On the Standard toolbar, click Print Preview.
2   On the Print Preview toolbar, click the Magnifier button to turn the magnifying glass into the insertion point.

Quick Reference summarizes skills learned in the lesson.

To insert a page break

1   Click in the document where you want the page to break.
2   On the Insert menu, click Break.
3   In the Break dialog box, click the Page Break option, and then click OK.

To adjust margins using the ruler

1   Place the pointer on the edge of the ruler, where the margin marker is, and wait for the pointer to change into a double-headed arrow.
2   Press Alt and then drag to change the margins.

To print a whole document

- On the Standard toolbar, click the Print button. Or, on the Print Preview toolbar, click the Print button.

To print part of a document using dialog box options

1   On the File menu, click Print.
2   Select the options you want in the Print dialog box.

- **Putting It All Together exercises.** These exercises give you another opportunity to practice skills that you learned in the lesson. Completing these exercises helps you to verify whether you understand the lesson, to reinforce your learning, and to retain what you have learned by applying what you have learned in a different way.

- **Quick Reference.** A complete summary of steps for tasks taught in each lesson is available in the back of the guide. This is often the feature that people find most useful when they return to their workplaces. The expert-level guides include the references from the core-level guides so that you can review or refresh basic and advanced skills on your own whenever necessary.

- **Index.** Student guides are completely indexed. All glossary terms and application features appear in the index.

Suggestions for Improvements

Microsoft welcomes your feedback on the *Step by Step Courseware* series. Your comments and suggestions will help us to improve future versions of this product. Please send your feedback to SBSCfdbk@microsoft.com.

Support requests for Microsoft products should not be directed to this alias. Please see "Using the CD-ROM" for information on support contacts.

Conventions and Features Used in This Book

This book uses special fonts, symbols, and heading conventions to highlight important information or to call your attention to special steps. For more information about the features available in each lesson, refer to the "Course Overview" section on page v.

Convention	Meaning
Practice files for the lesson	This icon identifies the section that lists the files that the lesson will use and explains any file preparation that you need to take care of before starting the lesson.
You can also create a new appointment by pressing Ctrl+N.	Notes in the margin area are pointers to information provided elsewhere in the workbook or provide brief notes related to the text or procedures.
2000 New!	This icon indicates a new or greatly improved feature in this version of the software product and includes a short description of what is new.
(MOUS icon) OL2000E.1.4	This icon indicates that the section where this icon appears covers a Microsoft Office User Specialist (MOUS) exam objective. The number below the icon is the MOUS objective number. For a complete list of the MOUS objectives, see the "MOUS Objectives" section on page xix.
tip	Tips provide helpful hints or alternative procedures related to particular tasks.
important	Importants provide warnings or cautions that are critical to exercises.
(save icon) save	When a toolbar button is referenced in the lesson, the button's picture and label are shown in the margin.
Alt+Tab	A plus sign (+) between two key names means that you must press those keys at the same time. For example, "Press Alt+Tab" means that you hold down the Alt key while you press Tab.
Boldface type	This formatting indicates text that you need to type. Or It indicates a glossary entry that is defined at the end of the lesson.

Using the CD-ROM

The CD-ROM included with this student guide contains the practice files that you'll use as you perform the exercises in the book. By using the practice files, you won't waste time creating the samples used in the lessons, and you can concentrate on learning how to use Microsoft Outlook 2000. With the files and the step-by-step instructions in the lessons, you'll also learn by doing, which is an easy and effective way to acquire and remember new skills.

The CD-ROM also includes a Microsoft Word file called Testbank.doc, which provides multiple-choice and true/false questions that you can use to test your knowledge following the completion of each lesson or the completion of the *Microsoft Outlook 2000 Step by Step Courseware Expert Skills* course.

System Requirements

Your computer system must meet the following minimum requirements for you to install the practice files from the CD-ROM and to run Microsoft Outlook 2000.

important

The Outlook 2000 software is not provided on the companion CD-ROM at the back of this book. You should have already purchased and installed Outlook 2000.

- A personal computer running Microsoft Outlook 2000 on a Pentium 75-megahertz (MHz) or higher processor with the Microsoft Windows 95 or later operating system with 24 MB of RAM, or the Microsoft Windows NT Workstation version 4.0 operating system with Service Pack 3 and 40 MB of RAM.
- At least 4 MB of available disk space (after installing Microsoft Outlook 2000 or Microsoft Office 2000).
- Microsoft Excel 95 or later (Lesson 1 only).
- Microsoft Word 97 or later (Lessons 2 and 4 only).
- Microsoft Outlook Express (Lesson 2 only).
- Microsoft Internet Explorer 4 or later and Microsoft NetMeeting or Windows NetMeeting (Lesson 3 only). NetMeeting is an add-on that comes with Internet Explorer and might already be installed on computers with Internet Explorer. To install NetMeeting, start Internet Explorer, point to New on the File menu, and then click Internet Call. Follow the instructions on the screens.

- Microsoft Exchange Server (Lesson 6 and one exercise in Lesson 2 only). For more information on Exchange Server, see the "Configuring Mail Support" sidebar later in this section.
- A modem and fax number (Lesson 7 only).
- A CD-ROM drive.
- A monitor with VGA or higher resolution (Super VGA recommended; 15-inch monitor or larger recommended).
- A Microsoft mouse, a Microsoft IntelliMouse, or other compatible pointing device.
- An Internet or network connection.
- An Internet e-mail account or an e-mail account on a network.

If You Need to Install or Uninstall the Practice Files

Your instructor might already have installed the practice files before you arrive in class. However, your instructor might ask you to install the practice files on your own at the start of class. Also, if you want to work through any of the exercises in this book on your own at home or at your place of business after class, you will need to first install the practice files.

To install the practice files:

1 Insert the CD-ROM in the CD-ROM drive of your computer.

A menu screen appears.

important

If the menu screen does not appear, start Windows Explorer. In the left pane, locate the icon for your CD-ROM, and click this icon. In the right pane, double-click the file StartCD.

2 Click Install Practice Files, and follow the instructions on the screen.

The recommended options are preselected for you.

3 After the practice files have been installed, click Exit.

A folder called Outlook Expert Practice has been created on your hard disk, the practice files have been placed in that folder, and a shortcut to the Microsoft Press Web site has been added to your desktop.

4 Remove the CD-ROM from the CD-ROM drive.

Use the steps on the next page when you want to delete the lesson practice files from your hard disk. Your instructor might ask you to perform these steps at the end of class. Also, you should perform these steps if you have worked through the exercises at home or at your place of business and want to work through the exercises again. Deleting the practice files and then reinstalling them ensures that all files and folders are in their original condition if you decide to work through the exercises again.

To uninstall the practice files:

1 On the Windows taskbar, click the Start button, point to Settings, and then click Control Panel.

2 Double-click the Add/Remove icon.

3 Click Outlook Expert Practice in the list, and click Add/Remove. (If your computer has Windows 2000 Professional installed, click the Remove or the Change/Remove button.)

4 Click Yes when the confirmation dialog box appears.

The steps above will not delete any of the Outlook items or folders that you create during this course. You will need to delete those items manually.

Using the Practice Files

Each lesson in this book explains when and how to use any practice files for that lesson. The lessons are built around scenarios that simulate a real work environment, so you can easily apply the skills you learn to your own work. The scenarios in the lessons use the context of the fictitious Lakewood Mountains Resort, a hotel and convention center located in the mountains of California.

The following is a list of all files and folders used in the lessons.

File Name	Description

Task Items - folder
    Create a project plan for the Pavilion Project
    Create a project team for the Pavilion Project
    Order new office supplies and a chair
    Schedule dentist appointment
	Folder containing the tasks necessary to work through the course.

Contact Items - folder
    Anne L. Paper
    Erik Gavriluk
    Frank Miller
    James C. Wilson
    Jane Clayton
    Ketan Dalal
    Kim Akers
    Lane Sacksteder
    Laura Jennings
    Marta Wolfe-Hellene
    Pat Coleman
    Prasanna Samarawickrama
	Folder containing the contact records necessary to work through the course.

Pavilion	Word file used in Lesson 1.
Expenses	Excel file used in Lesson 1.
New Tasks	Text file used in Lesson 1.
Guests	Access file used in Lesson 1.
LMR Address List	Access file used in Lesson 1.

(continued)

continued

File Name	Description
Salary Increases	Word document used in Lesson 2.
Brochure	Word document used in Lesson 7.
Hiking	Word document used in Lesson 7.

All the files for the lessons appear within the Outlook Expert Practice folder.

On the first page of each lesson, look for the margin icon *Practice files for the lesson*. This icon points to the paragraph that explains which files you will need to work through the lesson exercises.

Configuring Mail Support

To match the exercises in this course, you should set your mail support configuration to Internet Only. To set your mail support to Internet Only:

1. Start Outlook.
2. On the Tools menu, click Options, and click the Mail Services tab. (If you do not have a Mail Services tab, but you do have a Mail Delivery tab, your mail support is already set to Internet Only.)
3. Click the Reconfigure Mail Support button.

    The E-Mail Service Options dialog box appears.
4. In the E-Mail Service Options dialog box, click the Internet Only option, click the Next button, and then follow the instructions on your screen.

    If Outlook does not detect a network card on your computer, it will configure mail support to Internet Only automatically.

For one exercise in Lesson 2 and all of Lesson 6, you will need to use Microsoft Exchange Server, meaning that your mail support configuration should be set up for Corporate or Workgroup.

To set your mail support to Corporate or Workgroup:

1. On the Tools menu, click Options, and click the Mail Delivery tab.
2. Click the Reconfigure Mail Support button.

    The E-Mail Service Options dialog box appears.
3. In the E-Mail Service Options dialog box, click the Corporate Or Workgroup option, click the Next button, and then follow the instructions on your screen.

If you are working through this course (except for the Personal Address Book excercise in Lesson 2 and all of Lesson 6) on a computer that is configured to work with Microsoft Exchange Server, you will probably notice some differences in the appearance of the Folder List and some dialog boxes.

Replying to Install Messages

When you work through some lessons, you might see a message indicating that the feature that you are trying to use is not installed. If you see this message, insert the Microsoft Outlook 2000 CD-ROM or Microsoft Office 2000 CD-ROM 1 in your CD-ROM drive, and click Yes to install the feature.

Copying Outlook Items to Outlook Folders

After you (or your instructor) have installed the practice files, all the files you need for this course will be stored in a folder named Outlook Expert Practice located on your hard disk. To ensure that the lesson exercises work for you in the same way they are described in the workbook, you need to drag the Outlook items in the Task Items folder and the Contact Items folder to the appropriate Outlook folders.

To navigate to these folders and copy the Outlook items to Outlook folders:

1. On the Windows taskbar, click the Start button, point to Programs, and click Microsoft Outlook.

2. Click the Restore button in the top-right corner of the Outlook window.

3. On the Windows taskbar, click the Start button, point to Programs, and click Windows Explorer. (If you are running Microsoft Windows 2000 Professional, click the Start button, point to Programs, point to Accessories, and then click Windows Explorer.)

4. Click the Restore button in the top-right corner of the Windows Explorer window.

    Both the Outlook window and the Windows Explorer window should be visible. If necessary drag the windows' title bars to arrange them side-by-side.

5. In Windows Explorer, navigate to the Outlook Expert Practice folder on your hard disk, and display the contents of the Contact Items folder.

6. Click the first item in the Contact Items folder, hold down Shift, scroll down if necessary, and then click the last item in the Contact Items folder.

7. Drag the selected items to the Contacts shortcut on the Outlook Bar or to the Contacts folder in the Outlook Folder List.

    The contact records appear in the Contacts folder in Outlook.

8. In Windows Explorer, display the contents of the Task Items folder.

9. Click the first item in the Task Items folder, hold down Shift, and then click the last item in the Task Items folder.

10. Drag the selected items to the Tasks shortcut on the Outlook Bar or to the Tasks folder in the Outlook Folder List.

    The tasks appear in the Tasks folder in Outlook.

11. Click the Close button in the top-right corner of the Windows Explorer window and the Outlook window.

If You Need Help with the Practice Files

If you have any problems regarding the use of this book's CD-ROM, you should first consult your instructor. If you are using the CD-ROM at home or at your place of business and need additional help with the practice files, see the Microsoft Press Support Web site at *mspress.microsoft.com/support*.

important

Please note that support for the Outlook 2000 software product itself is not offered through the above Web site. For help using Outlook 2000, rather than this Microsoft Press book, you can visit *www.microsoft.com/support* or call Outlook 2000 Technical Support at (425) 635-7070 on weekdays between 6 A.M. and 6 P.M. Pacific Standard Time. Microsoft Product Support does not provide support for this course.

MOUS Objectives

Core Skills

Objective	Activity
OL2000.1.1	Read mail
OL2000.1.2	Send mail
OL2000.1.3	Compose mail by entering text
OL2000.1.4	Print mail
OL2000.1.5	Address mail by entering text
OL2000.1.6	Use mail features (forward, reply, recall)
OL2000.1.7	Use Address Book to address mail
OL2000.1.8	Flag mail messages
OL2000.1.9	Navigate within mail
OL2000.1.10	Find messages
OL2000.1.11	Configure basic mail print options
OL2000.1.12	Work with attachments
OL2000.1.13	Add a signature to mail
OL2000.1.14	Customize the look of mail
OL2000.1.15	Use mail templates to compose mail
OL2000.1.16	Integrate and use mail with other Outlook components
OL2000.1.17	Customize menu and task bars
OL2000.2.1	Create folders
OL2000.2.2	Sort mail
OL2000.2.3	Set viewing options
OL2000.2.4	Archive mail messages
OL2000.2.5	Filter a view
OL2000.3.1	Navigate within the Calendar
OL2000.3.2	Schedule appointments and events
OL2000.3.3	Set reminders
OL2000.3.4	Print in Calendar
OL2000.3.5	Schedule multiday events
OL2000.3.6	Configure Calendar print options
OL2000.3.7	Customize the Calendar view
OL2000.3.8	Schedule recurring appointments
OL2000.3.9	Customize menu and task bars
OL2000.3.10	Add and remove meeting attendees
OL2000.3.11	Plan meetings involving others
OL2000.3.12	Save a personal or team calendar as a Web page
OL2000.3.13	Book office resources directly (e.g., conference rooms)

Objective	Activity
OL2000.3.14	Integrate Calendar with other Outlook components
OL2000.4.1	Use Outlook Help and Office Assistant
OL2000.4.2	Move items between folders
OL2000.4.3	Navigate between Outlook components
OL2000.4.4	Modify the Outlook Master Categories List
OL2000.4.5	Assign items to a category
OL2000.4.6	Sort information using categories
OL2000.4.7	Use the Office Clipboard
OL2000.5.1	Create, edit, and delete contacts
OL2000.5.2	Send contact information via e-mail
OL2000.5.3	Organize contacts by category
OL2000.5.4	Manually record an activity in a journal
OL2000.5.5	Link activities to a contact
OL2000.5.6	Sort contacts using fields
OL2000.6.1	Create and update one-time tasks
OL2000.6.2	Accept and decline tasks
OL2000.6.3	Organize tasks using categories
OL2000.6.4	Assign tasks to others
OL2000.6.5	Create tasks from other Outlook components
OL2000.6.6	Change the view for tasks
OL2000.7.1	Create and use Office documents inside Outlook 2000
OL2000.8.1	Create and edit notes
OL2000.8.2	Organize and view notes
OL2000.8.3	Customize notes

Expert Skills

Objective	Activity	Page
OL2000E.1.1	Work offline or use remote mail	6.14
OL2000E.1.2	Add a vCard to a message	2.8
OL2000E.1.3	Create reusable mail templates	2.5
OL2000E.1.4	Use mail with Office applications	2.26
OL2000E.2.1	Customize the look of mail	2.2
OL2000E.2.2	Create a Personal Address Book	2.16
OL2000E.2.3	Customize menu and task bars	1.2
OL2000E.2.4	Track when mail messages are delivered or read	2.13
OL2000E.2.5	Create a personal distribution list	2.18
OL2000E.2.6	Create a quick synchronization group	6.16
OL2000E.2.7	Synchronize by message size	6.17
OL2000E.2.8	Organize mail using the Rules Wizard	2.10

MOUS Objective List

Objective	Activity	Page
OL2000E.3.1	Configure Calendar options	3.1
OL2000E.3.2	Share Calendar information with other applications over the Internet	3.10
OL2000E.3.3	Schedule real-time meetings (NetMeeting)	3.6
OL2000E.3.4	Schedule times to watch broadcasts using NetShow	3.9
OL2000E.4.1	Use Net Folders and public folders	6.2, 6.9
OL2000E.4.2	Grant a delegate access to your folders	6.5
OL2000E.4.3	Grant others permission to use your folders	6.3
OL2000E.5.1	Customize and use Outlook Today	1.13
OL2000E.5.2	Configure time zone information	3.5
OL2000E.5.3	Manage favorite Web site addresses	6.13
OL2000E.5.4	Import and export data between Outlook and other mail applications	2.21, 2.24
OL2000E.5.5	Create Outlook forms	A.1
OL2000E.5.6	Create a shortcut to a file on your Outlook Bar	1.4
OL2000E.6.1	Flag contacts for follow up (reminder)	4.2
OL2000E.6.2	Customize Contacts menu and task bars	1.2
OL2000E.6.3	Integrate contacts with other Outlook components	4.7
OL2000E.6.4	Use contacts with Office applications	4.10
OL2000E.7.1	Create and update recurring tasks	5.1
OL2000E.7.2	Customize menu and task bars	1.2
OL2000E.7.3	Record tasks for any Office file with the journal	5.5
OL2000E.7.4	Set delegate access to share tasks with two or more people	6.5
OL2000E.8.1	Import and export data between Outlook and other Office applications	1.15, 1.19
OL2000E.8.2	Use mail merge with Word	4.10
OL2000E.9.1	Receive a fax	7.6
OL2000E.9.2	Create and send a fax from within Outlook 2000	7.6
OL2000E.9.3	Customize a fax	7.9
OL2000E.10.1	Send and receive information through newsreader	2.31
OL2000E.10.2	Set up newsreader	2.28

Taking a Microsoft Office User Specialist Certification Test

The Microsoft Office User Specialist (MOUS) program is the only Microsoft-approved certification program designed to measure and validate your skills with the Microsoft Office suite of desktop productivity applications: Microsoft Word, Microsoft Excel, Microsoft PowerPoint, Microsoft Access, and Microsoft Outlook.

By becoming certified, you demonstrate to employers that you have achieved a predictable level of skills in the use of a particular Office application. Certification is often required by employers either as a condition of employment or as a condition of advancement within the company or other organization. The certification examinations are sponsored by Microsoft but administered through Nivo International.

For each Microsoft Office 2000 application, two levels of MOUS tests are currently or will soon be available: core and expert. For a core-level test, you demonstrate your ability to use an application knowledgeably and without assistance in a day-to-day work environment. For an expert-level test, you demonstrate that you have a thorough knowledge of the application and can effectively apply all or most of the features of the application to solve problems and complete tasks found in business.

Preparing to Take an Exam

Unless you're a very experienced user, you'll need to use a test preparation course to prepare to complete the test correctly and within the time allowed. The *Step by Step Courseware* training program is designed to prepare you for either core-level or expert-level knowledge of a particular Microsoft Office application. By the end of this course, you should have a strong knowledge of all exam topics, and with some additional review and practice on your own, you should feel confident in your ability to pass the appropriate exam.

After you decide which exam to take, review the list of objectives for the exam. This list can be found in the "MOUS Objectives" section at the front of the appropriate *Step by Step Courseware* student guide; the list of MOUS objectives for this book begins on page xix. You can also easily identify tasks that are included in the objective list by locating the MOUS logo in the margin of the lessons in this book.

For an expert-level test, you'll need to be able to demonstrate any of the skills from the core-level objective list, too. Expect some of these core-level tasks to appear on the expert-level test. In the *Step by Step Courseware Expert Skills Student Guide*, you'll find the core skills included in the "Quick Reference" section at the back of the book.

You can also familiarize yourself with a live MOUS certification test by downloading and installing a practice MOUS certification test from *www.mous.net*.

To take the MOUS test, first see *www.mous.net* to locate your nearest testing center. Then call the testing center directly to schedule your test. The amount of advance notice you should provide will vary for different testing centers, and it typically depends on the number of computers available at the testing center, the number of other testers who have already been scheduled for the day on which you want to take the test, and the number of times per week that the testing center offers MOUS testing. In general, you should call to schedule your test at least two weeks prior to the date on which you want to take the test.

When you arrive at the testing center, you might be asked for proof of identity. A driver's license or passport is an acceptable form of identification. If you do not have either of these items of documentation, call your testing center and ask what alternative forms of identification will be accepted. If you are retaking a test, bring your MOUS identification number, which will have been given to you when you previously took the test. If you have not prepaid or if your organization has not already arranged to make payment for you, you will need to pay the test-taking fee when you arrive. The current test-taking fee is $50 (U.S.).

Test Format

All MOUS certification tests are live, performance-based tests. There are no multiple-choice, true/false, or short answer questions. Instructions are general: you are told the basic tasks to perform on the computer, but you aren't given any help in figuring out how to perform them. You are not permitted to use reference material other than the application's Help system.

As you complete the tasks stated in a particular test question, the testing software monitors your actions. An example question might be:

> Customize Outlook Today so that when Outlook starts, Outlook Today appears and displays five days in the Calendar and the tasks for today only. Sort the Tasks list in Outlook Today to sort tasks in ascending order by importance.

The sample tests available from *www.mous.net* give you a clear idea of the type of questions that you will be asked on the actual test.

When the test administrator seats you at a computer, you'll see an online form that you use to enter information about yourself (name, address, and other information required to process your exam results). While you complete the form, the software will generate the test from a master test bank and then prompt you to continue. The first test question will appear in a window. Read the question carefully, and then perform all the tasks stated in the test question. When you have finished completing all tasks for a question, click the Next Question button.

You have 45 to 60 minutes to complete all questions, depending on the test that you are taking. The testing software assesses your results as soon as you complete the test, and the results of the test can be printed by the test administrator so that you will have a record of any tasks that you performed incorrectly. A passing grade is 75 percent or higher. If you pass, you will receive a certificate in the mail within two to four weeks. If you do not pass, you can study and practice the skills that you missed and then schedule to retake the test at a later date.

Tips for Successfully Completing the Test

The following tips and suggestions are the result of feedback received by many individuals who have taken one or more MOUS tests:

- Make sure that you are thoroughly prepared. If you have extensively used the application for which you are being tested, you might feel confident that you are prepared for the test. However, the test might include questions that involve tasks that you rarely or never perform when you use the application at your place of business, at school, or at home. You must be knowledgeable in *all* the MOUS objectives for the test that you will take.

- Read each exam question carefully. An exam question might include several tasks that you are to perform. A partially correct response to a test question is counted as an incorrect response. In the example question on the previous page, you might set Outlook Today to display when Outlook starts, to display five days in the calendar, and the tasks for today only, but forget to sort the Tasks list. This would count as an incorrect response and would result in a lower test score.

- You are allowed to use the application's Help system, but relying on the Help system too much will slow you down and possibly prevent you from completing the test within the allotted time. Use the Help system only when necessary.

- Keep track of your time. The test does not display the amount of time that you have left, so you need to keep track of the time yourself by monitoring your start time and the required end time on your watch or a clock in the testing center (if there is one). The test program displays the number of items that you have completed along with the total number of test items (for example, "35 of 40 items have been completed"). Use this information to gauge your pace.

- If you skip a question, you cannot return to it later. You should skip a question only if you are certain that you cannot complete the tasks correctly.

- Don't worry if the testing software crashes while you are taking the exam. The test software is set up to handle this situation. Find your test administrator and tell him or her what happened. The administrator will work through the steps required to restart the test. When the test restarts, it will allow you to continue where you left off. You will have the same amount of time remaining to complete the test as you did when the software crashed.

- As soon as you are finished reading a question and you click in the application window, a condensed version of the instruction is displayed in a corner of the screen. If you are unsure whether you have completed all tasks stated in the test question, click the Instructions button on the test information bar at the bottom of the screen and then reread the question. Close the instruction window when you are finished. Do this as often as necessary to ensure you have read the question correctly and that you have completed all the tasks stated in the question.

If You Do Not Pass the Test

If you do not pass, you can use the assessment printout as a guide to practice the items that you missed. There is no limit to the number of times that you can retake a test; however, you must pay the fee each time that you take the test. When you retake the test, expect to see some of the same test items on the subsequent test; the test software randomly generates the test items from a master test bank before you begin the test. Also expect to see several questions that did not appear on the previous test.

LESSON 1

Customizing Outlook

After completing this lesson, you will be able to:

✔ *Customize the Outlook Bar.*
✔ *Create a shortcut on the Outlook Bar.*
✔ *Use the Folder List.*
✔ *Assign items to a category.*
✔ *Use and modify the Master Category List.*
✔ *Use and customize Outlook Today.*
✔ *Import a Microsoft Access database into Outlook.*
✔ *Export Outlook data to a Microsoft Excel database.*

You probably already know the basics of Microsoft Outlook: you can send and receive e-mail messages and create and use items such as contacts, tasks, and appointments. The next step is to learn how to organize those items and customize Outlook to fit your needs.

You can customize Outlook to help you locate information faster and save time on tasks. For example, the human resources manager at Lakewood Mountains Resort modified the Outlook Bar so that while she was working in Outlook, she could quickly open employee files created in Microsoft Word, without first having to open Word or Windows Explorer to access the files. She also put related contacts and e-mail messages in different categories so that she could easily find them later. Finally, she set up **Outlook Today** to display her tasks in order of priority. You can customize Outlook to perform these functions and more.

In this lesson, you will learn how to modify the display of the Outlook Bar and create a quick way to access files that you use every day. You will learn how to view the contents of your Outlook folders and your hard disk or floppy disks by using the **Folder List**. You will also learn how to organize items by assigning them to predefined or custom categories and then sorting them so that they are easier to locate. You will learn how to customize the view of your daily tasks and events by using Outlook Today. Finally, you will learn how to **import** and **export** data between Outlook and other Microsoft Office applications to avoid having to reenter data.

To complete the exercises in this lesson, you will need to use the files named Pavilion, Expenses, New Tasks, Guests, and LMR Address List in the Outlook Expert Practice folder that is located on your hard disk.

> Your Outlook folders should already contain the Outlook items (tasks and contact records) that are necessary to complete the exercises in this lesson. If you need to add these items to your Outlook folders, see the "Using the CD-ROM" section at the beginning of this book.
>
> **Practice files for the lesson**

Customizing the Outlook Bar

You can change the Outlook Bar to organize Outlook **shortcuts**. Shortcuts appear as icons on the Outlook Bar on the left side of the program window and offer quick access to files, folders, and programs stored on your hard disk or on a network drive. One way that you can customize the Outlook Bar is by adding a **group** to it. The Outlook Bar is divided into three groups: Outlook Shortcuts, My Shortcuts, and Other Shortcuts (also called Other). These groups contain shortcuts to different Outlook folders (such as Tasks or the Inbox) or files and folders on your computer (such as the My Computer folder). You can add your own group to the Outlook Bar so that you can add shortcuts to folders and files related to specific projects. For example, the grounds manager at Lakewood Mountains Resort is spearheading the creation of a new pavilion and needs to organize various tasks and employees. To make it easier to find files and items related to this project, she created a group called Pavilion Project on the Outlook Bar.

You might have noticed that the Outlook Shortcuts group on the Outlook Bar does not display all the shortcuts at once. You have to click the down arrow at the bottom of the Outlook Bar to display the rest of the shortcuts. To see the shortcuts you saw when you first viewed the group, you click the up arrow at the top of the Outlook Bar. The arrows function like a scroll bar. If you don't want to scroll to access the shortcuts on the Outlook Bar, you can change the Outlook Bar to have it display smaller versions of the icons so that all the shortcuts appear at once.

You can also customize the Outlook Bar by changing its width. Changing the width of the Outlook Bar also changes the size of the viewing area of each folder. To change the width of the Outlook Bar, position the mouse pointer over the right edge of the Outlook Bar. When the mouse pointer changes to a double-headed arrow, drag to the right or left to increase or decrease, respectively, the width of the Outlook Bar.

OL2000E.2.3
OL2000E.6.2
OL2000E.7.2

tip
To customize the toolbars and menus in Outlook, click Customize on the Tools menu. Three tabs appear in the Customize dialog box. You can display additional toolbars as well as create new ones by using the Toolbars tab. You can add buttons to toolbars and commands to menus by dragging commands from the Commands tab on the dialog box to the appropriate position on the toolbar or menu. You can control the display of the menu commands and the appearance of a toolbar by using the Options tab.

In this exercise, you change the size of the icons on the Outlook Bar and the width of the Outlook Bar. You also create a new group called Pavilion Project.

1 If necessary, click the Inbox shortcut on the Outlook Bar.

The contents of the Inbox folder appear.

Lesson 1 Customizing Outlook 1.3

Note that when the icons on the Outlook Bar are small icons, you can see all the folders in the Outlook Shortcuts group at the same time.

Double Arrow

2 Right-click the Outlook Bar, and click Small Icons on the shortcut menu that appears.

The icons on the Outlook Bar appear as small icons.

3 Position the mouse pointer on the right edge of the Outlook Bar.

The mouse pointer appears as a double arrow.

4 Drag the mouse pointer to the right about one inch.

The Outlook Bar gets larger, and you can see less of the Inbox.

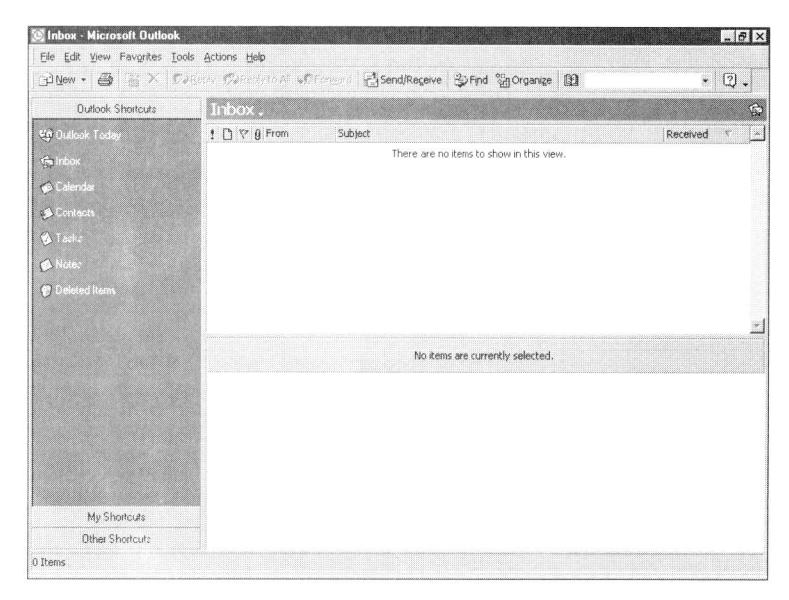

5 Right-click the Outlook Bar, and click Large Icons on the shortcut menu that appears.

The icons on the Outlook Bar are displayed as large icons again.

6 Drag the right border of the Outlook Bar to the left about one inch.

The Outlook Bar gets smaller.

tip

You can hide or display the Outlook Bar. To hide the Outlook Bar, right-click inside the Outlook Bar, and click Hide Outlook Bar on the shortcut menu. To display the Outlook Bar, on the View menu, click Outlook Bar. (You can use the same method to hide the Outlook Bar.)

7 Right-click the Outlook Bar, and click Add New Group on the shortcut menu that appears.

A new group appears at the bottom of the Outlook Bar.

You can delete a group by right-clicking the group and clicking Remove Group on the shortcut menu that appears.

8 Type **Pavilion Project**, and press Enter.

The Pavilion Project group is added to the bottom of the Outlook Bar.

9 On the Outlook Bar, click the Pavilion Project group bar.

The group appears.

You will add a file and folders to this group in the next exercise.

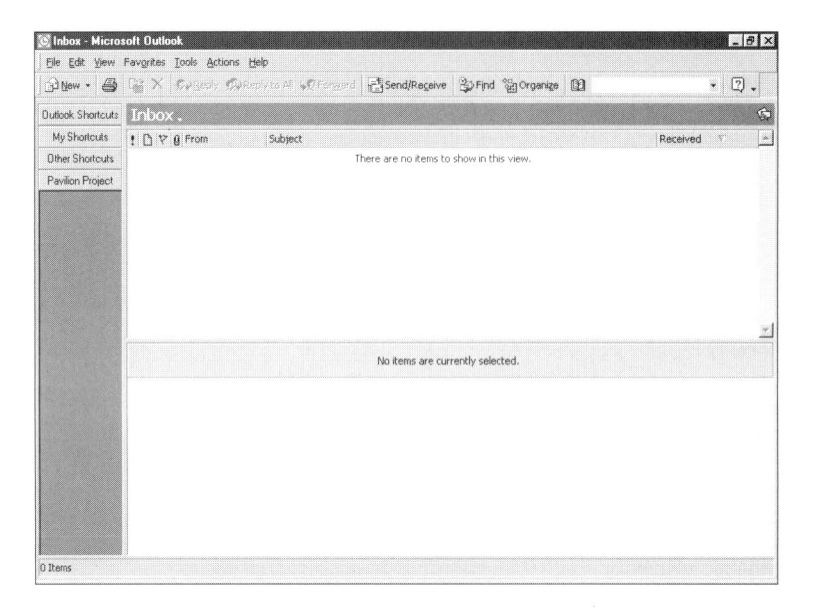

Creating a Shortcut on the Outlook Bar

OL2000E.5.6

You can create shortcuts to items on your computer, such as programs, folders, or files, and add them to any group on the Outlook Bar. Creating shortcuts on the Outlook Bar allows you to open files directly without having to open Windows Explorer or the program the file was created from.

When you click a shortcut, the file, folder, or program that it represents opens. If you are working in a group that you created (such as the Pavilion Project group), you might want to add commonly used Outlook folders such as the Calendar or Tasks to the group. This action lets you access these folders faster while you are working in the group.

In this exercise, you create a shortcut to a file called Pavilion and add it to the Pavilion Project group on the Outlook Bar. You also open the file from within Outlook. Finally, you add the Calendar, Contacts, and Tasks shortcuts to the Pavilion Project group.

1 On the Outlook Bar, click the Other Shortcuts group bar (or the Other group bar).

The Other Shortcuts group (or Other group) appears.

2 On the Outlook Bar, click the My Computer shortcut.

The contents of My Computer appear.

3 In the My Computer pane, double-click the icon for your hard disk.

The contents of your hard disk appear.

4 Double-click the Outlook Expert Practice folder.

The contents of the Outlook Expert Practice folder appear.

5 On the Outlook Bar, click the Pavilion Project group bar.

The Pavilion Project group appears.

Lesson 1 Customizing Outlook 1.5

6 Drag the Pavilion file from the Outlook Expert Practice folder to the Outlook Bar.

A shortcut to the Pavilion file appears in the Pavilion Project group.

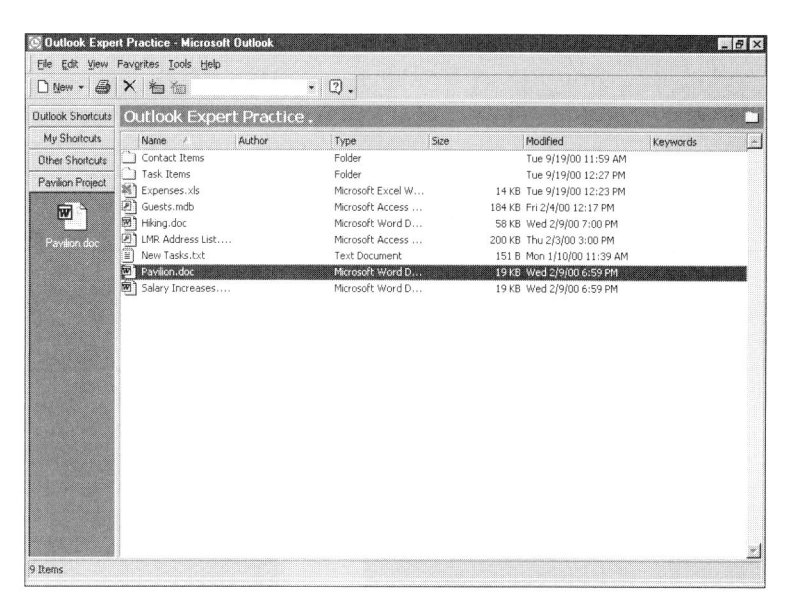

7 On the Outlook Bar, click the Pavilion file shortcut.

The Pavilion file opens in Microsoft Word and the Office Assistant appears.

Close

8 Click the Close button in the top-right corner of the Microsoft Word window.

The Pavilion file closes.

9 Right-click the Outlook Bar, and click Outlook Bar Shortcut on the shortcut menu that appears.

The Add To Outlook Bar dialog box appears.

10 Click the Look In down arrow, and click Outlook.

The Add To Outlook Bar dialog box shows a list of the folders in Outlook.

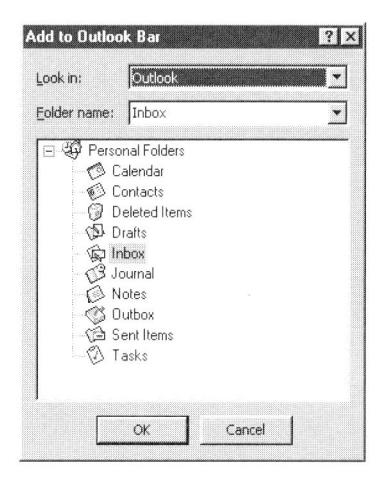

> You can change the order in which the shortcuts appear on the Outlook Bar. Simply drag an icon in the appropriate direction, and release the mouse button when a horizontal line appears.

11 In the list, click Calendar, and click OK.

The Calendar shortcut is added to the Pavilion Project group.

12 Repeat steps 9 through 11 to add the Contacts and Tasks shortcuts to the Outlook Bar.

The Outlook Bar should look similar to the following illustration.

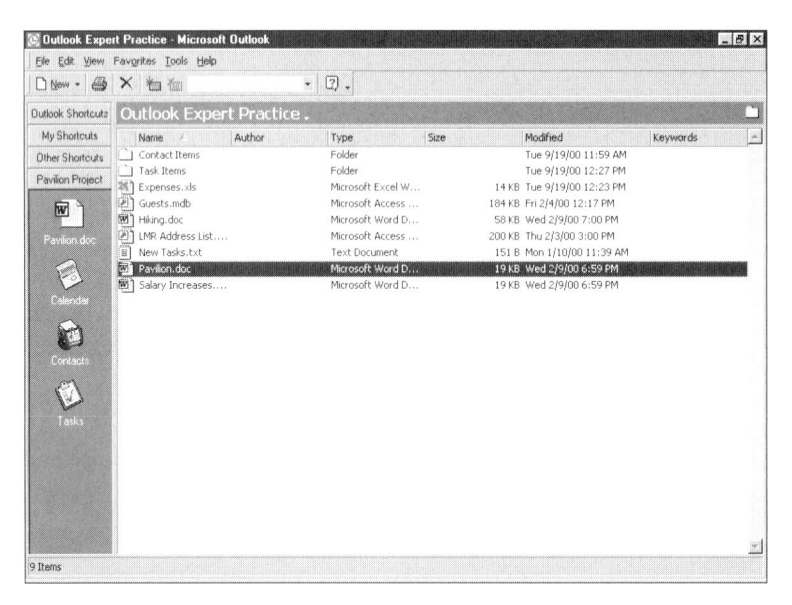

13 On the Outlook Bar, click the Calendar shortcut.

The contents of the Calendar folder are displayed.

14 On the Outlook Bar, click the Contacts shortcut.

The contents of the Contacts folder are displayed.

15 On the Outlook Bar, click the Tasks shortcut.

The contents of the Tasks folder are displayed.

Using the Folder List

In addition to using the Outlook Bar, you can view and access the various components of Outlook as well as the contents of your computer by using the Folder List. The structure of the Folder List is similar to that of Windows Explorer. Simply click an icon in the Folder List to display the contents of a folder or file.

If any of the items on the Outlook Shortcuts or My Shortcuts groups are displayed in the Outlook window, the Folder List displays all the folders in Outlook. A plus sign (+) to the left of a folder indicates that the folder contains additional folders within it. You click the plus sign (+) to display these folders. A minus sign (-) indicates that a folder is completely expanded, and all the contents of the folder are displayed.

Lesson 1 Customizing Outlook 1.7

Folder Banner

Push Pin button

None of the folders in this illustration have a plus sign (+) to the left, meaning that they do not contain subfolders. The minus sign (-) to the left of the Outlook Today folder indicates that its contents are already displayed.

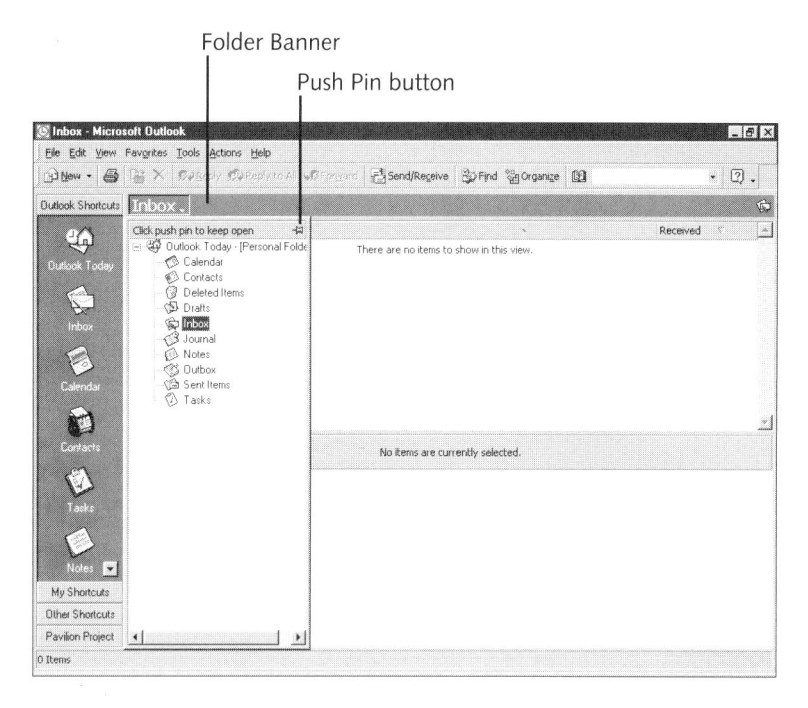

If My Computer or another shortcut in the Other group is selected, the Folder List display changes accordingly. It displays the drive letters and folders contained within the selected item, in a tree-like structure. If your folders have subfolders, you can view them by clicking the plus sign (+) to the left of the folder name.

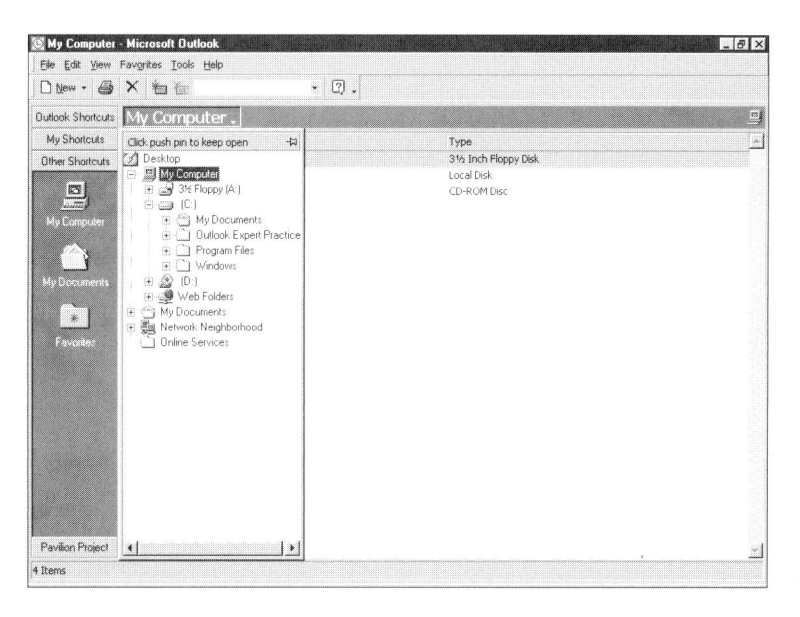

You can display the Folder List in two ways: click the name that appears on the Folder Banner, or click Folder List on the View menu. If you click the folder name in the Folder Banner and then click a folder in the Folder List, the Folder List closes. To keep the Folder List open, you click the Push Pin button in the top-right corner of the Folder List.

1.8　Microsoft Outlook 2000 Step by Step Courseware Expert Skills Student Guide

In this exercise, you use the Folder List to view Outlook items as well as the contents of your hard disk. You then close the Folder List.

If your Folder List is already open, you do not need to perform steps 1 through 3.

1. On the Outlook Bar, click the Outlook Shortcuts group bar, and click the Inbox shortcut.

   The contents of the Inbox appear.

2. On the Folder Banner, click the folder name *Inbox*.

   The Folder List appears.

Push Pin

3. Click the Push Pin button to keep the Folder List open.

4. In the Folder List, click Sent Items.

   The contents of the Sent Items folder appear. Currently there are no items in the Sent Items folder.

5. On the Outlook Bar, click the Other Shortcuts group bar (or the Other group bar), and click the My Computer shortcut.

   The Folder List displays your computer's drives and folders.

Depending on how your computer is configured, your screen might not match the illustration exactly.

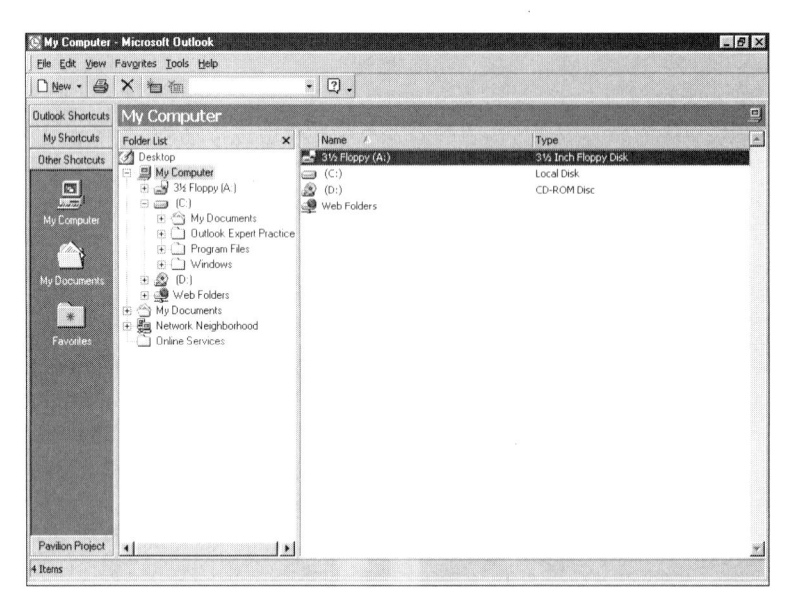

6. If necessary, click the plus sign (+) to the left of the My Computer Icon.

   The folders stored on the computer appear.

7. If necessary, click the plus sign (+) to the left of the hard disk icon.

   The folders stored on the hard disk appear.

8. Click the Outlook Expert Practice folder.

   The contents of the folder appear.

Close

9. In the top-right corner of the Folder List, click the Close button.

   The Folder List closes.

tip

To move items between folders, display the contents of the folder from which you want to move the items, select the items that you want to move, and then drag them to the destination folder in the Folder List.

Assigning Items to a Category

A **category** is a keyword or phrase that you can use to manage messages, tasks, contacts, or other Outlook items so that you can easily locate, sort, filter, or group them. For example, the grounds manager at Lakewood Mountains Resort wants to track all her meetings, contacts, and e-mail messages concerning the planning of the Pavilion Project, so she puts these items in a category called Strategies.

Outlook supplies a ready-made list of categories to which you can assign items, called the **Master Category List**. The following categories are available in the Master Category List.

> You can use this list as is or add your own categories. You will learn how to add a category to the Master Category List in the next exercise.

Available Categories

• Business	• Hot Contacts	• Status
• Competition	• Ideas	• Strategies
• Favorites	• International	• Suppliers
• Gifts	• Key Customer	• Time & Expenses
• Goals/Objectives	• Miscellaneous	• VIP
• Holiday	• Personal	• Waiting
• Holiday Cards	• Phone Calls	

Some of your Outlook items might fit several categories. You can assign an item to as many categories as needed. For example, the grounds manager decided that some of her contacts for a Pavilion Project might also be able to help her with an upcoming Gazebo Project, so she also assigned those contacts to a category called Hot Contacts.

You can assign more than one item to a category at a time. If the items are adjacent to one another, click the first item, hold down Shift, and click the last item in order to select the first item, the last item, and any items in between. You can select nonadjacent items by pressing Ctrl and clicking each item. When the items are selected, you can assign them to a category simultaneously. To see the categories that you assigned items to, you display the folder in the By Category view.

In this exercise, you assign tasks to categories. You also display the tasks in the By Category view. Finally you redisplay the tasks in Simple List view.

1 On the Outlook Bar, click the Outlook Shortcuts group bar, and click the Tasks shortcut.

The contents of the Tasks folder appear.

2 In the Tasks list, click the task *Create A Project Plan For The Pavilion Project*.

3 Press Ctrl, and click the task *Create A Project Team For The Pavilion Project*.

The tasks are selected.

4 Right-click one of the selected tasks, and click Categories on the shortcut menu that appears.

The Categories dialog box appears.

5 Scroll down, and select the Strategies check box.

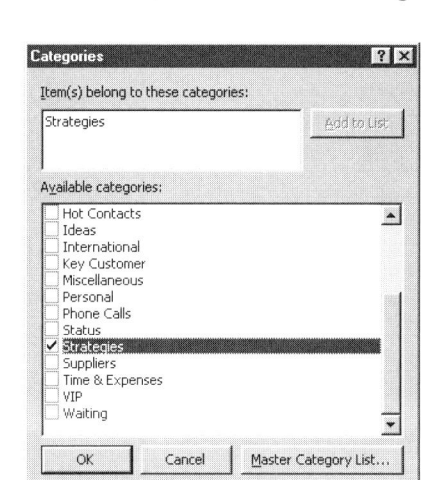

6 Click OK.

The two tasks are assigned to the Strategies category.

7 Right-click the task *Schedule Dentist Appointment*, and click Categories on the shortcut menu that appears.

The Categories dialog box appears.

8 Select the Personal check box, select the Phone Calls check box, and then click OK.

The task is assigned to two categories.

9 On the View menu, point to Current View, and click By Category.

The tasks appear organized by category.

10 Click the plus signs (+) to the left of Categories: Personal (1 Item), Phone Calls (1 Item), and Strategies (2 Items).

The tasks assigned to each category appear.

Note that the task *Schedule Dentist Appointment* appears twice because it was assigned to two categories.

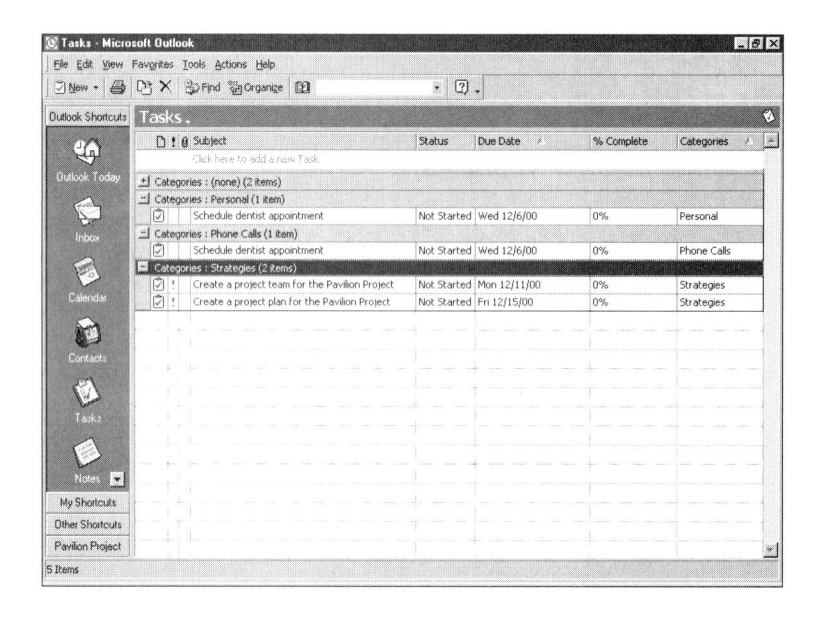

Lesson 1 Customizing Outlook 1.11

> **tip**
> The steps for displaying the contents of the Inbox folder by category are slightly different from the steps for displaying the contents of other folders. If you want to display the contents of the Inbox by category, right-click a blank area of the Inbox window, click Group By, click the Group Items By down arrow, click Categories, and then click OK.

Although the tasks are in Simple List view and don't appear in categories, they are still assigned to the categories. To unassign an item, right-click the item, click Categories, and clear any category check boxes that the item is assigned.

11 On the View menu, point to Current View, and click Simple List.

The Tasks folder appears in Simple List view again.

Using and Modifying the Master Category List

If the Master Category List does not list a category that serves your needs, you can create your own category. The events coordinator at Lakewood Mountains Resort is organizing a company picnic. She wants to create a category called Picnic to track all items dealing with the picnic.

In this exercise, you create a category called Picnic and assign it to contacts.

1 On the Outlook Bar, click the Contacts shortcut.

The contents of the Contacts folder appear.

2 Click the *Jane Clayton* contact.

You might have to scroll through your list of contacts to view and select the needed contacts listed above.

3 Hold down Ctrl, and click the *Erik Gavriluk* and *Prasanna Samarawickrama* contacts.

The contacts are selected.

4 Right-click any selected contact, and click Categories on the shortcut menu that appears.

The Categories dialog box appears.

You can also display the Master Category List by clicking Categories on the Edit menu and then clicking the Master Category List button.

5 Click the Master Category List button.

The Master Category List dialog box appears, with the insertion point already in the New Category box.

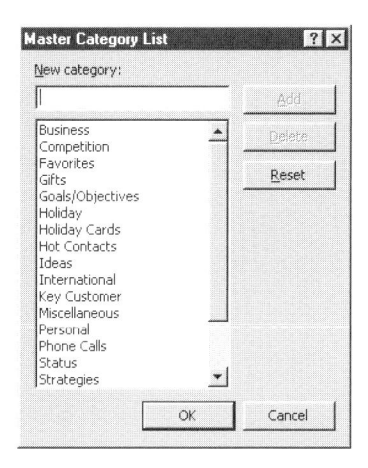

> **tip**
> If you want to return from the Master Category List to the default categories, click the Reset button in the Master Category List dialog box. All categories that you added will be deleted. These changes affect only the Master Category List. If you have items assigned to the deleted categories, they will keep their category assignments. To remove a category assignment from an item, right-click the item, and clear the deleted category's check box in the Categories dialog box.

6 Type **Picnic**, and click the Add button.

The category is added to the Master Category List.

7 Click OK.

The Categories dialog box reappears.

8 Scroll down, select the Picnic check box, and then click OK.

The selected contacts are assigned to the Picnic category.

9 On the View menu, point to Current View, and click By Category.

The contacts are arranged by category.

10 Click the plus sign (+) to the left of the text Categories: Picnic (3 items).

The contacts assigned to the Picnic category appear.

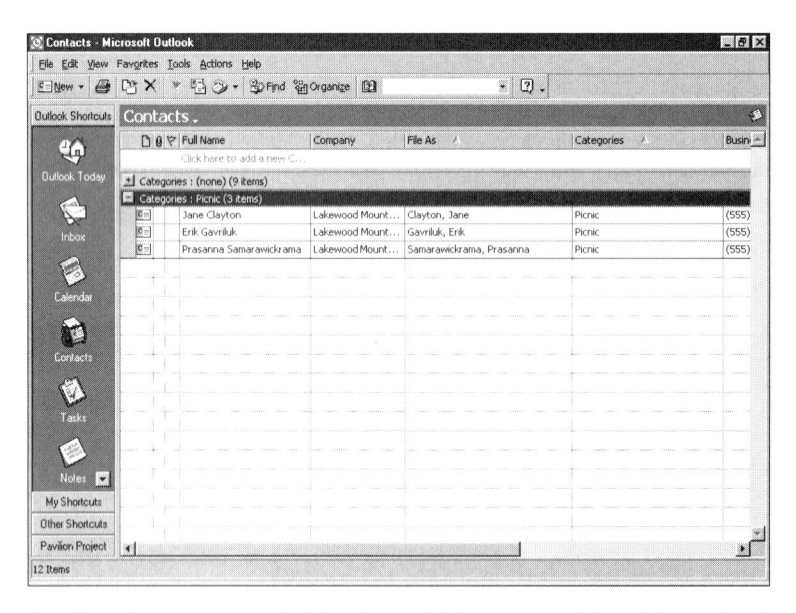

11 On the View menu, point to Current View, and click Address Cards.

The contacts appear in Address Cards view.

Using and Customizing Outlook Today

OL2000E.5.1

Using Outlook Today, you can view a summary of the tasks and appointments for the day as well as the number of new e-mail messages in your Inbox.

The Drafts, Inbox, and Outbox folders appear in Outlook Today by default. You might want to add other folders as well. You can add any additional folders that you've created in the Folder List to Outlook Today. For example, if you created folders for each important project you work on, you can add those folders to Outlook Today so that you can quickly access those folders.

The Outlook Today Calendar automatically displays the events for the current day and the next four days. You can customize the Calendar to display from one to seven days. You can also organize tasks in Outlook Today by selecting options so that you can view all tasks, only the current day's tasks, or tasks with no due date. You can quickly sort tasks by due date, importance, when they were created, or scheduled start date.

You can also choose a style for the Outlook Today page by selecting whether it should be in a one-column or two-column format and whether is has a bright or muted color scheme.

In this exercise, you customize the look of Outlook Today.

1 On the Outlook Bar, click the Outlook Today shortcut.

Outlook Today appears.

2 In the top-right corner of the Outlook Today folder, click the Customize Outlook Today button.

The Customize Outlook Today pane appears.

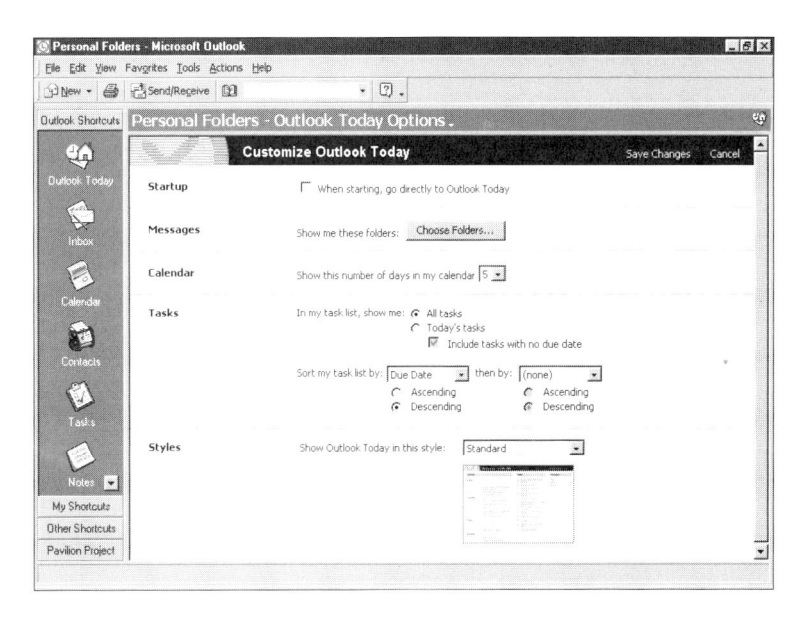

To set Outlook Today as your start page or the first window you view when opening Outlook, select the When Starting, Go Directly To Outlook Today check box.

3 In the Messages section, click the Choose Folders button.

The Select Folder dialog box appears.

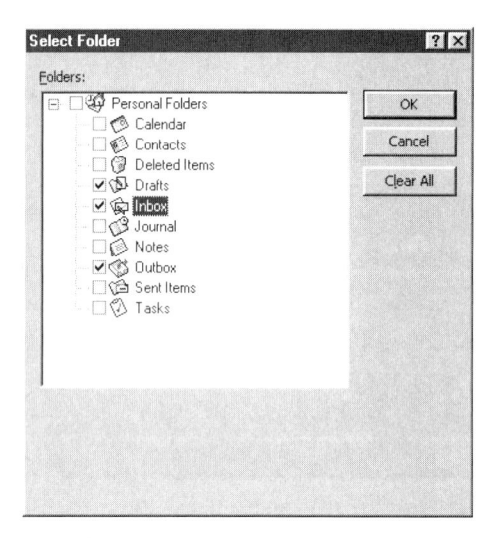

4 Select the Notes and Sent Items check boxes, and click OK.

The number of notes and sent items will appear in Outlook Today.

5 In the Calendar section, click the Show This Number Of Days down arrow, and click 7.

Outlook Today will show your appointments for the next seven days.

6 In the Tasks section, click the Sort My Task List By down arrow, and click Importance.

The tasks displayed in Outlook Today will be organized from the most important task to the least important task.

7 In the Styles section, click the Show Outlook Today In This Style down arrow, and click Winter.

A preview of the Winter style appears. Outlook Today will appear in the colors and layout of the Winter style.

Lesson 1 Customizing Outlook   1.15

8 In the top-right corner of the Customize Outlook Today pane, click Save Changes.

The customized Outlook Today folder appears.

Currently, there are no appointments in the Calendar.

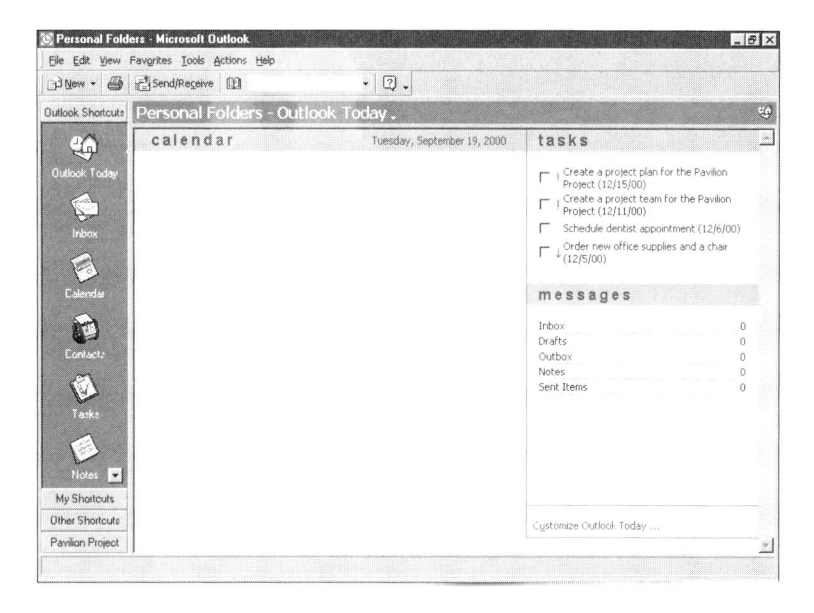

Importing a Microsoft Access Database into Outlook

OL2000E.8.1

If you have created a database of names and addresses in a Microsoft Office application other than Outlook, you can import this information into the Contacts folder in Outlook. (When you import, you bring information from another program into the program you're currently working in.) For example, the marketing director created a database of guests in Microsoft Access. She then decided that it would be useful to also have the contacts in Outlook. To avoid having to retype each contact's information, she imported the Microsoft Access guest information into Outlook.

If the Access field names (such as First name, Street, or City) are not named exactly the same as the field names in the Contacts folder (where you add the contact information), don't worry. The Import And Export Wizard has a feature that lets you **map** your Access field names (which are called values) to similar Outlook field names. Mapping means to pair an application's field names with similar field names in Outlook. For example, you would pair the field name *Zip/Postal* from another application to the field *Business Postal Code* in Outlook. Mapping is not a requirement; however, if you choose not to map values to fields, most likely, not all of the information that you typed in Access will appear in Outlook.

To import from a word processing program such as Microsoft Word, the data must be in a tab-separated or comma-separated format before starting the import process.

In this exercise, you import an Access database of addresses into the Contacts folder.

You must have the Import/Export engine feature installed for this exercise to work. If an alert box appears during the exercise asking if you want to install the feature, insert the Office 2000 or Outlook 2000 CD-ROM, and click Yes.

1.16   Microsoft Outlook 2000 Step by Step Courseware Expert Skills Student Guide

1   On the File menu, click Import And Export.

The Import And Export Wizard appears with the Import From Another Program Or File option already selected.

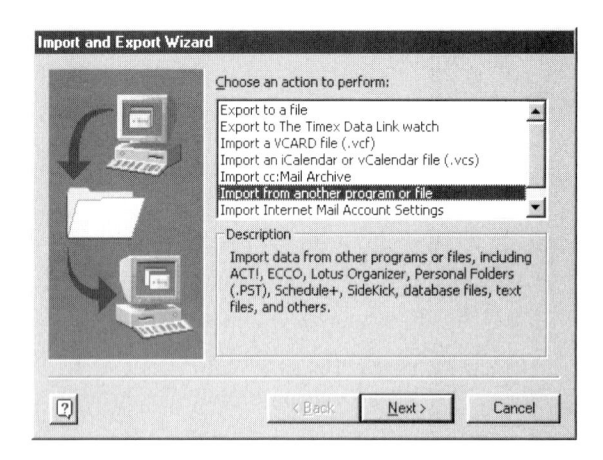

2   Click Next.

The next wizard dialog box appears, asking you to select a file type to import.

> You can also import a Microsoft Excel database into Outlook.

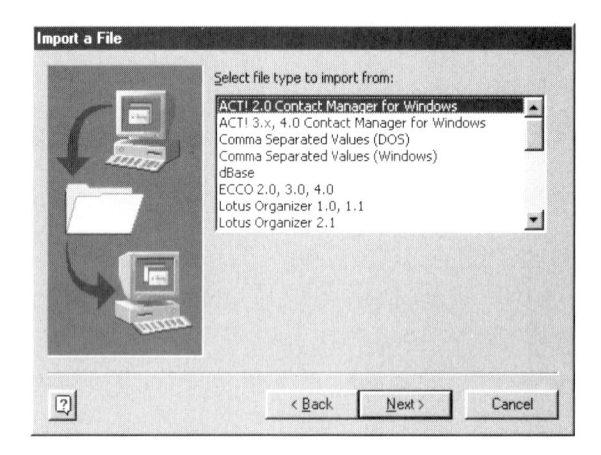

3   Scroll down, click Microsoft Access, and then click Next.

The next wizard dialog box appears, asking you to locate the file to import.

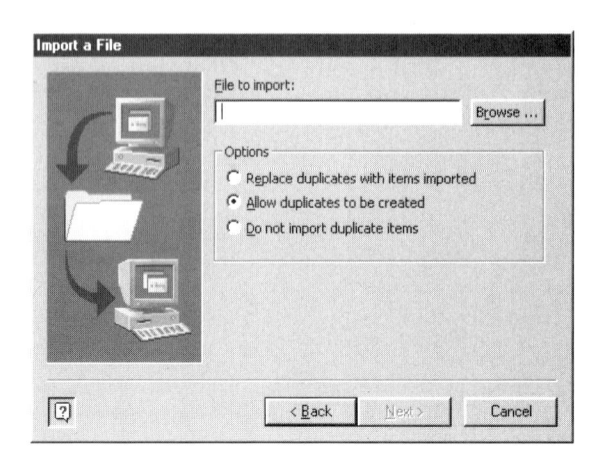

Lesson 1 Customizing Outlook 1.17

4 Click the Browse button.

The Browse dialog box appears.

5 If necessary, click the Look In down arrow, navigate to the Outlook Expert Practice folder on your hard disk, and then double-click the Guests file.

6 Click Next.

The next wizard dialog box appears, asking you to select the Outlook folder in which you want the imported information to appear.

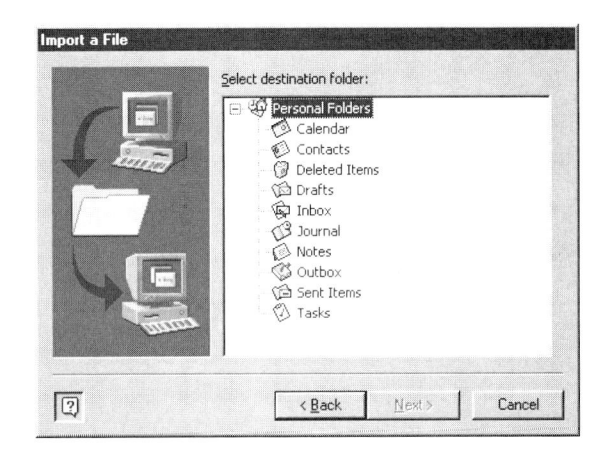

7 If necessary, scroll up, click the Contacts folder, and then click Next.

The final wizard dialog box appears.

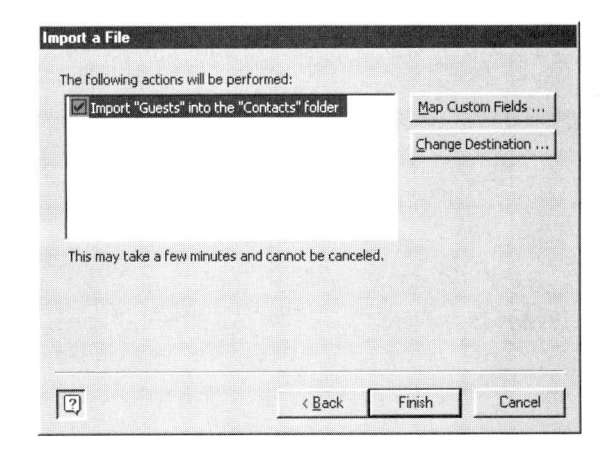

8 Click the Map Custom Fields button.

The Map Custom Fields dialog box appears.

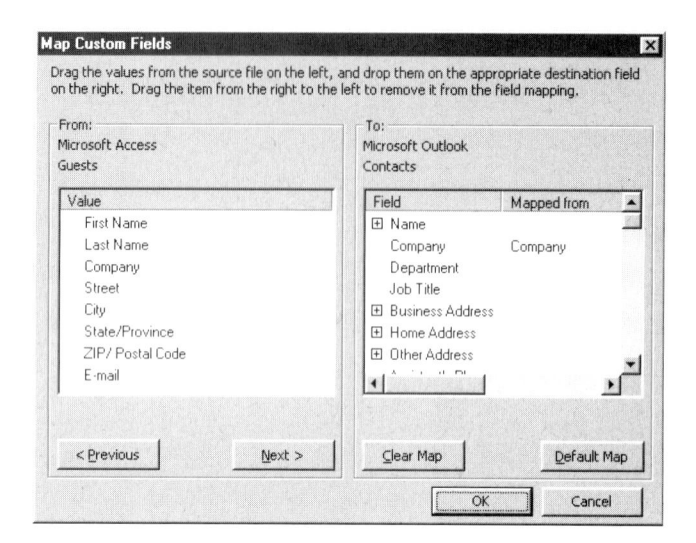

9 In the To section, click the plus sign (+) to the left of the Name field.

The Name field is expanded, showing the elements of the field.

> Notice that the values First Name and Last Name appear under the Mapped From column in the To section. Because the value in the From section and the field in the To section are already the same, you do not have to drag these values onto the name fields.

10 In the To section, scroll down to the Business Address field (so that it appears at the top of the list).

11 In the To section, click the plus sign (+) to the left of the Business Address field.

The Business Address field expands, showing the elements of the field.

12 In the From section, drag the Street value onto the first Business Street field in the To section.

The Street value appears next to the Business Street field, in the Mapped From column.

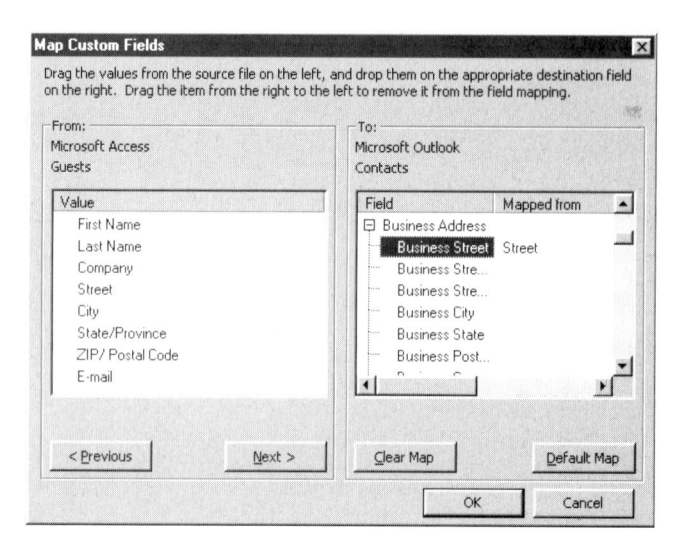

> Outlook tries to "remember" values that have already been mapped to fields. It is possible that the values and the fields already match because someone working through this exercise before you mapped the fields.

13 In the From section, drag the City value onto the Business City field in the To section.

The City value appears next to the Business City field, under the Mapped From column.

14 In the From section, drag the State/Province value onto the Business State field in the To section.

The State/Province value appears next to the Business State field, under the Mapped From column.

15 In the From section, drag the ZIP/Postal Code value onto the Business Post field in the To section.

The ZIP/Postal Code value appears next to the Business Post field, in the Mapped From column.

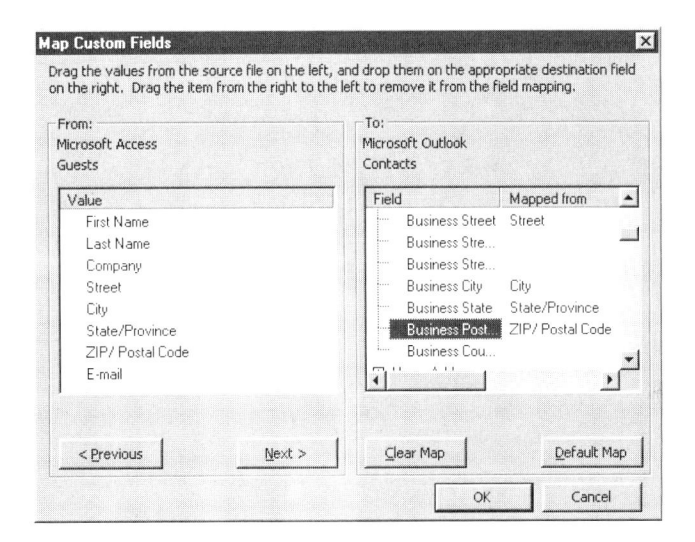

16 In the To section, scroll down until you see the E-Mail field.

The E-Mail field and the Mapped From value are the same, so you don't need to drag the value onto the field.

17 Click OK, and click Finish.

A progress bar appears as the Access files are imported into the Contacts folder.

18 Display the Contacts folder.

The new contacts appear in the Contacts folder.

Exporting Outlook Data to a Microsoft Excel Database

OL2000E.8.1

In addition to importing information into Outlook, you can also export, or move Outlook information out, to other Office applications such as Microsoft Access or Microsoft Excel. Suppose you have been compiling a database of addresses in Excel. If your Excel database did not already contain addresses that you added to Outlook, you could export the Outlook addresses to Excel. When you export data, you must first convert the data to a file that another program can use. For example, if you want to export the contents of your Contacts folder to Excel, you must convert the Outlook information to an Excel file (.xls file). After you perform the export, you can simply navigate to the folder you stored the .xls file in, and then open the file. Excel will start, and the Outlook information you exported will now appear in an Excel database.

You must have the Import/Export feature installed for this exercise to work. If an alert box appears during the exercise asking if you want to install the feature, insert the Office 2000 or Outlook 2000 CD-ROM, and click Yes.

In this exercise, you export the contents of the Contacts folder to an Excel file and save it in the Outlook Expert Practice folder.

important

You must have Microsoft Excel installed on your computer to perform the steps in this exercise.

1 On the File menu, click Import And Export.

The Import And Export Wizard appears.

2 Click Export To A File, and click Next.

The next wizard dialog box appears, asking you to choose a file type for the export.

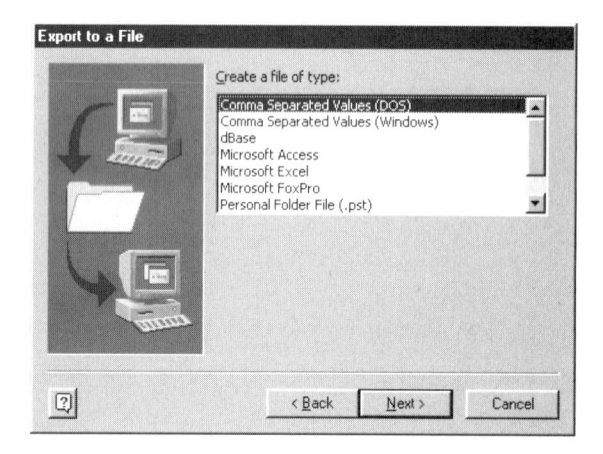

3 Click Microsoft Excel, and click Next.

The next wizard dialog box appears, asking you to choose a folder from which to export. The Contacts folder is already selected.

4 Click Next.

The next wizard dialog box appears, asking you browse to a location in which to save the exported file.

5 Click the Browse button.

The Browse dialog box appears.

6 If necessary, click the Save In down arrow, and navigate to the Outlook Expert Practice folder.

7 Click in the File Name box, delete any existing text, type **[your name]'s Addresses**, and then click OK.

8 Click Next.

The final wizard dialog box appears.

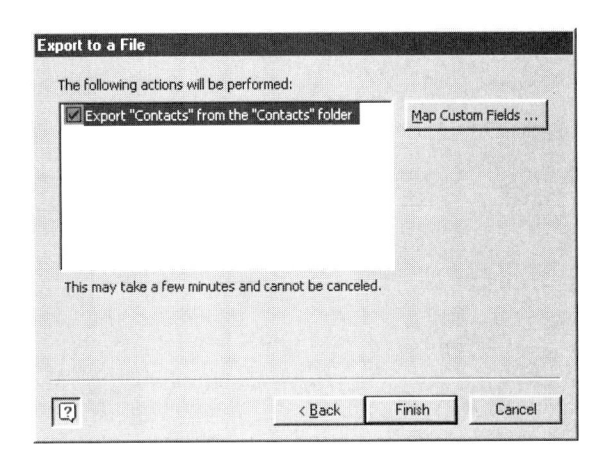

9 Click Finish.

A progress bar appears as the Contact information is exported to an Excel file.

10 Start Windows Explorer, and navigate to the Outlook Expert Practice folder on your hard disk.

11 Double-click the file [your name]'s Addresses.

Excel starts, and the file opens.

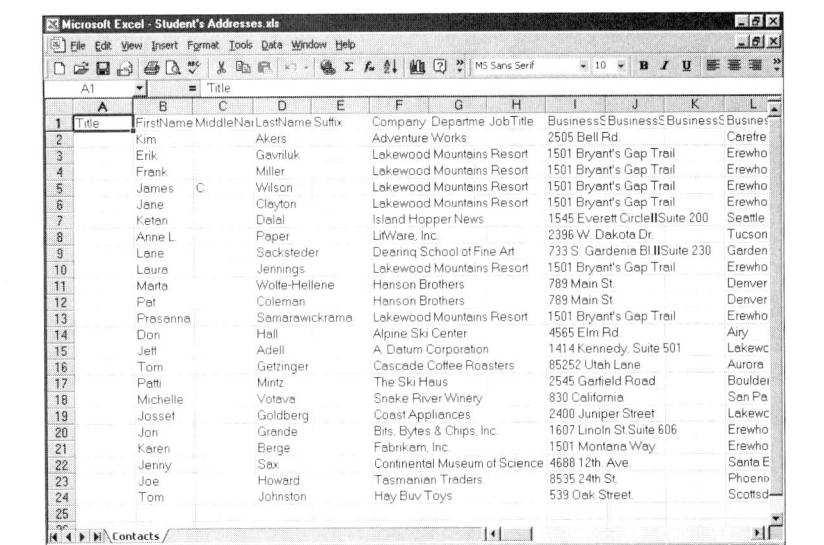

> To delete any columns that you do not need, or that don't contain any information, such as Title and Middle Name, right-click the letter above the column name, and click Delete on the shortcut menu that appears.

Lesson Wrap-Up

This lesson covered how to customize and add shortcuts to the Outlook Bar, how to use the Folder List, how to use categories, how to customize Outlook Today, and finally how to import data into and export data out of Outlook.

If you are continuing to the next lesson:

- In the top-right corner of Excel, click the Close button.
  Excel closes.

If you are not continuing to other lessons:

1. In the top-right corner of Excel, click the Close button.
   Excel closes.
2. In the top-right corner of Outlook window, click the Close button.
   Outlook closes.

Lesson Glossary

category A keyword or phrase that you can use to manage messages, tasks, contacts, or other Outlook items so that you can easily locate, sort, filter, or group them.

export To move information from one program into another.

Folder List A feature in Outlook that displays Outlook folders, or files and folders on your computer. You can display the contents of a folder simply by clicking an icon in the Folder List.

group A set of items with something in common, such as e-mail messages from the same sender or tasks with the same due date.

import To bring information in from one program into another.

map To pair an application's field names with similar field names in Outlook.

Master Category List A ready-made list of categories that you can customize by adding your own categories, and which you use to organize, find, or sort Outlook items.

Outlook Today An Outlook folder that summarizes the current items in specific Outlook folders.

shortcuts In Outlook, icons that appear on the left side of the Outlook window and offer quick access to files, folders, and programs.

Quick Quiz

1 How do you assign a category to an item?
2 How do you create a shortcut to a file?
3 How do you add a category to the Master Category List?
4 How do you use the Folder List to view your computer's files and folders?
5 What is mapping?
6 How do you hide the Outlook Bar?
7 How do you create a new group?
8 How do you set Outlook Today as the default start page?

Putting It All Together

Exercise 1: Create a group called Expenses. Find the Expense file located in your Outlook Expert Practice folder and create a shortcut in the Expenses group. Import the task list called New Tasks into Tasks in Outlook. Hint: You will need to click the Tab Separated Values (DOS) option in the second Import And Export Wizard dialog box.

Exercise 2: Modify Outlook Today as follows: display the Inbox, Drafts, and Outbox in the Outlook Today pane, display two days of events for the Calendar, and display all tasks by due date.

Exercise 3: Import the Access database called LMR Address List into the Contacts folder.

LESSON 2

Using Advanced E-Mail Features

After completing this lesson, you will be able to:

- ✔ Customize the appearance of messages.
- ✔ Create and use message templates.
- ✔ Add a vCard to a message.
- ✔ Use the Rules Wizard.
- ✔ Track when messages are delivered and read.
- ✔ Create a Personal Address Book.
- ✔ Create a personal distribution list.
- ✔ Import data between Outlook and other e-mail applications.
- ✔ Export data between Outlook and other e-mail applications.
- ✔ Integrate e-mail with other Office applications.
- ✔ Set up a news account.
- ✔ View newsgroups and newsgroup messages.
- ✔ Subscribe to a newsgroup.

The office manager at Lakewood Mountains Resort has noticed that the e-mail messages she receives are more specialized than the messages she sends. For example, around holidays, she receives festive messages that have backgrounds and borders. One time she received an important message that, when she deleted it, caused an alert box to appear, asking whether Microsoft Outlook could notify the sender that she had read the message. She has also received a message with a special attachment containing a dialog box that displayed a contact's information, which she could then insert directly into the Contacts folder. Perhaps you have also received such specialized e-mail messages and would like to know how you too can create them. Along with enhancing the appearance of the messages you send, you can use advanced features in Microsoft Outlook, such as tracking the messages you send and receive and organizing your Inbox by using the Rules Wizard. You can also import and export e-mail addresses and send e-mail from Microsoft Office applications such as Microsoft Word and Microsoft PowerPoint.

In this lesson, you will learn how to change the appearance of messages, create and use message templates, and add vCards to messages. You will also learn how to use the Rules Wizard to set rules specifying how messages should be handled when they arrive in your Inbox, track when messages are delivered and read, create a Personal Address Book, and create and use a personal distribution list. Finally, you will learn how to import and export e-mail addresses, send e-mail from Microsoft Word, use a newsreader, and subscribe to a newsgroup.

Practice files for the lesson

Your Outlook folders should already contain the Outlook items (tasks, e-mail messages, and contact records) that are necessary to complete the exercises in this lesson. If you need to add these items to your Outlook folders, see the "Using the CD-ROM" section at the beginning of this book.

To complete the exercises in this lesson, you will need to use a file named Salary Increases in the Outlook Expert Practice folder that is located on your hard disk.

important

To complete some of the exercises in this lesson, you will need to exchange e-mail messages with a class partner. If you don't have a class partner or are performing the exercises alone, you can enter your own e-mail address instead of your class partner's and send the message to yourself.

OL2000E.2.1

Customizing the Appearance of Messages

You can change the appearance of individual messages by changing the default font to a different font color, size, and type using the Formatting toolbar in the message window. You can use three different **text formats** for e-mail messages: **plain text**, **rich text**, and **HTML**. Text formats are standards that specify properties for text such as the font, alignment, and margins. Plain text format is the most commonly used e-mail format because it keeps the e-mail file size small and is transmitted across the Internet quickly. When using plain text format, you cannot use any text or paragraph formatting. When using rich text format, you can use text and paragraph formatting. For example, you can change the font's color, size, and type, add bullets, and change paragraph alignment. However, you cannot add a background or pictures to the message. With HTML format, you can use text and paragraph formatting, and you can add pictures, backgrounds, and Web pages to your e-mail message. Keep in mind that HTML messages are larger than plain text and rich text messages, which means that they will take longer to transmit across the Internet.

It is considered impolite to send HTML messages that take more than 30 seconds to download. Some e-mail applications cannot display HTML messages, so if you're unsure whether your recipient's e-mail program can read HTML messages, it is safer to send the message as plain text or rich text.

When you use HTML format for your messages, you can also apply **stationery** to your messages. Outlook stationery includes borders, backgrounds, font colors and styles, and graphics. It looks like the paper stationery that you can buy in stores. Outlook has many different stationery styles for many different occasions, such as birthdays, birth announcements, holidays, for sale announcements, and more.

Lesson 2 Using Advanced E-Mail Features 2.3

In this exercise, you create and send a message using stationery and a customized font.

1   If necessary, display the Inbox.

New Mail Message

2   Click the New Mail Message button on the Standard toolbar.

A message window appears.

3   In the To box, type your class partner's e-mail address, and press Tab twice.

4   In the Subject box, type **Holiday Party**, and press Enter.

The insertion point moves to the message area.

If HTML is not listed as a command in the message window on the Format menu, click Plain Text first, and click Yes in the alert box that appears. Then, in the message window on the Format menu, click HTML. If you want to switch to Rich Text, and it doesn't appear as a command on the Format menu, follow the same steps (click Plain Text, click Yes, and then click Rich Text on the Format menu). HTML and Rich Text might not appear if your mail format sending option is not set for plain text. (To set your mail format sending option to plain text, on the Tools menu, click Options, click the Mail Format tab, click the Send In This Message Format down arrow, and click Plain Text.)

5   On the Format menu, click HTML.

Notice that the Formatting toolbar is activated and that the font is Arial, and the font size is 10.

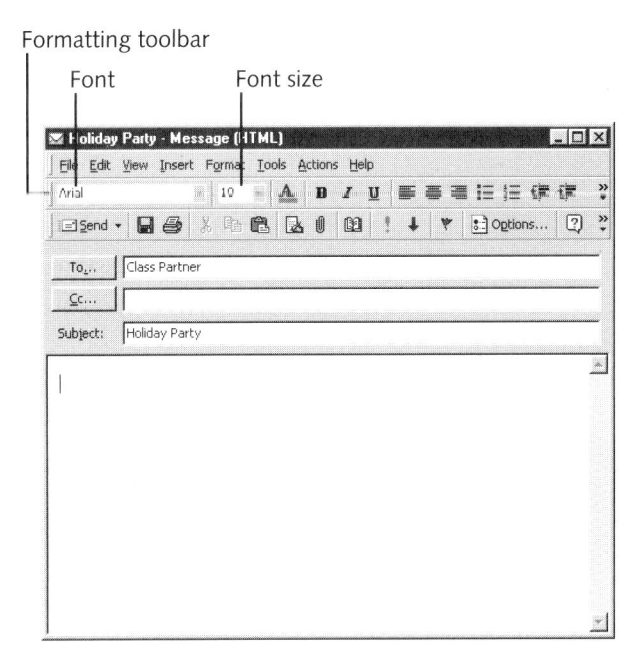

6   On the Formatting toolbar, click the Font down arrow, scroll down, and then click Tahoma.

7   On the Formatting toolbar, click the Font Size down arrow, and click 14.

Font Color

8   On the Formatting toolbar, click the Font Color button.

A color palette appears.

9 Click the Navy square (first row under the Automatic button, second to the last square).

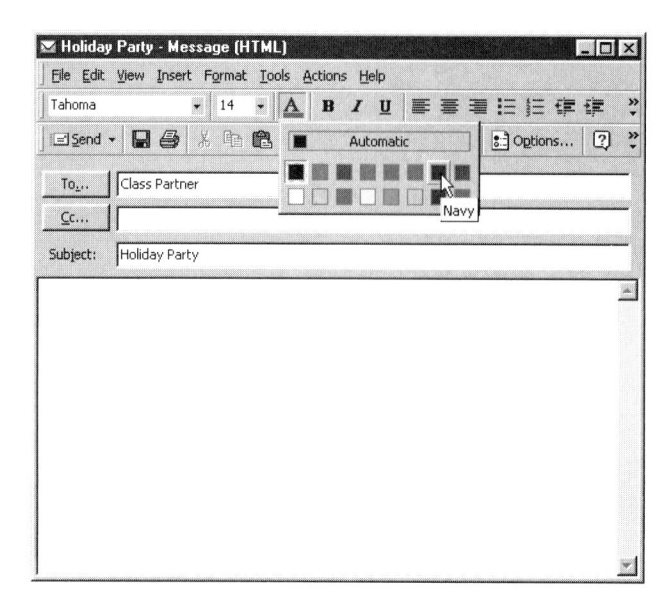

The text that you type in the message window will be displayed in navy, styled in the font Tahoma, and sized at 14 points.

10 On the Format menu, point to Background, and click Picture.

The Background Picture dialog box appears.

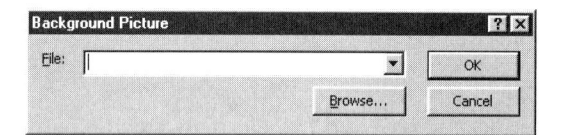

11 Click the File down arrow, scroll down, click Holiday Letter Bkgrd, and then click OK.

The message window now has a holiday background.

Lesson 2 Using Advanced E-Mail Features   2.5

12 Press Enter until the insertion point is below the background picture.
13 Type **You're invited to the company party!**, and press Enter twice.
14 Type **Where: Mom's Kitchen Café**, and press Enter.
15 Type **Day: December 15th**, and press Enter.
16 Type **Time: 5:00 PM.**
17 Select all the text below the text *You're invited to the company party!*
18 On the Standard toolbar, click the Font Color button, click the Red square (second row under the Automatic button, third square), and then click anywhere in the message window.

Font Color

The font is now red. The message window should look similar to the following illustration.

Before you send the message, you can check the spelling by pressing F7 or by clicking Spelling on the Tools menu.

19 On the Standard toolbar in the message window, click the Send button.
20 On the Standard toolbar, click the Send/Receive button, and click the *Holiday Party* message from your class partner in the message list.

The body of the message appears in the Preview Pane.

Creating and Using Message Templates

OC2000E.1.3

If you have a certain message that you send over and over again, you can save it as a **template** so that it can be easily reused. In Outlook, a template is an e-mail message that is used as a pattern to format similar e-mail messages.

The customer service manager at Lakewood Mountains Resort requires that all the customer service representatives send a daily e-mail to him about guest complaints, suggestions, compliments, and how problems, if there were any, were solved. To save time, one of the customer service representatives created a template of the daily e-mail message. He simply typed *Customer Complaints, Customer Suggestions, Customer Compliments,* and *Solutions*, and left space to fill in the actual daily customer comments.

You create templates within a standard message window by saving the message as a template. When you save the message as a template, Outlook saves it in the Templates folder in Windows Explorer by default. Saving templates in the Templates folder is helpful because all templates are stored in one location and are easy to find when needed.

In this exercise, you create and use a message template.

New Mail Message

1. On the Standard toolbar, click the New Mail Message button.

    A message window appears.

2. Click in the Subject box, type **Update**, and then press Enter.

    The insertion point moves to the message area.

3. Type **Customer Complaints:**, and press Enter four times.
4. Type **Customer Suggestions:**, and press Enter four times.
5. Type **Customer Compliments:**, and press Enter four times.
6. Type **Solutions:**.

    The message is created and is ready to be saved as a template.

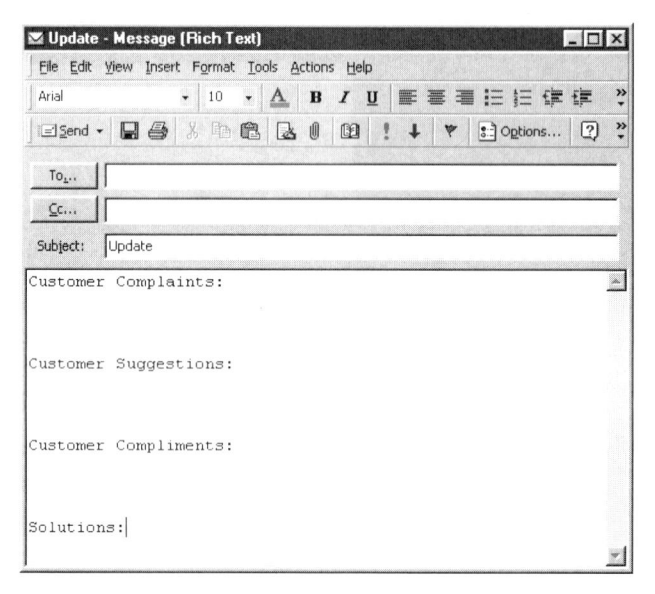

7. On the File menu in the message window, click Save As.

    The Save As dialog box appears.

When you designate a file as an Outlook Template, Outlook automatically saves it to the Templates folder.

8. Click the Save As Type down arrow, and click Outlook Template.
9. Click the Save button.

    The message is now a template.

10. Click the Close button in the top-right corner of the message window, and click Yes in the alert box that appears.

11 On the File menu, point to New, and click Choose Form.

The Choose Form dialog box appears.

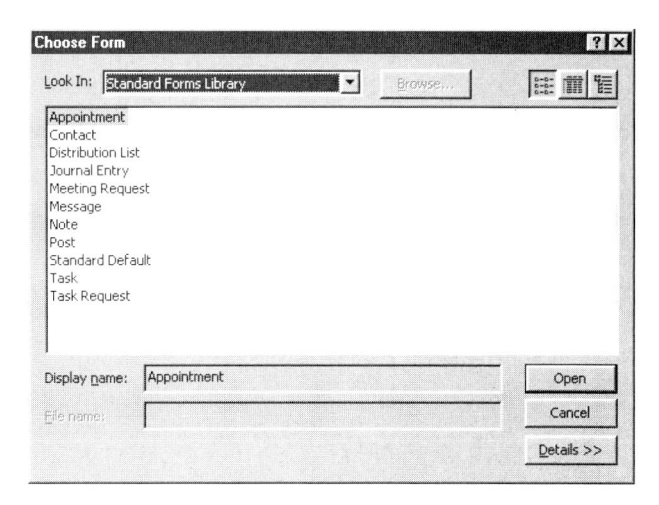

12 Click the Look In down arrow, and click User Templates In File System.

The name of the template that you created appears.

13 Click the Update template, and click Open.

A message box containing the template appears.

14 In the To box, type your class partner's e-mail address.

15 In the message area, click the blank line after the text *Customer Complaints*, and type **None**.

16 Click the blank line after the text *Customer Suggestions*, and type **Customer wants magazines by the hot tub.**

17 Click the blank line after the text *Customer Compliments*, and type **LMR is in a beautiful location!**

18 Click after the text *Solutions*, and press Enter.

19 Type **Put magazines by the hot tub.**

The e-mail message should look similar to the following.

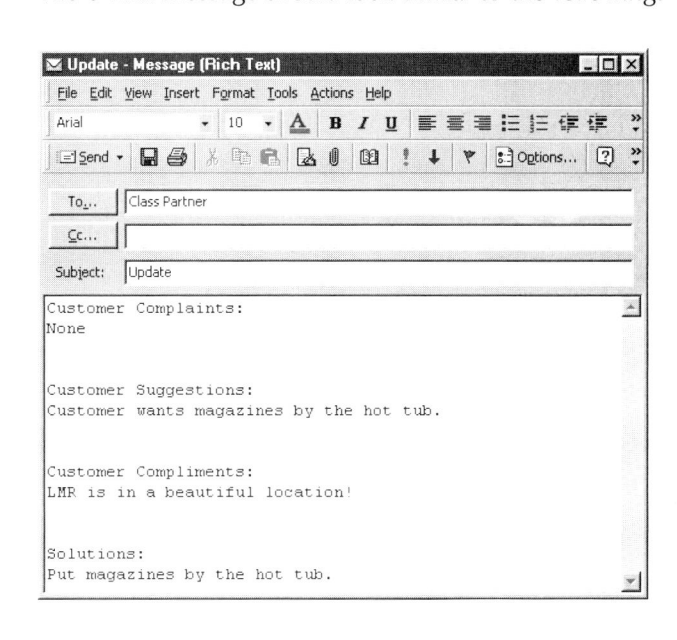

> If you want to make the customer responses stand out from the template text, you can change the text format to Rich Text and use the Formatting toolbar to change the font color of each comment.

20 On the Standard toolbar in the message window, click the Send button.

21 On the Standard toolbar, click the Send/Receive button, and click the *Update* message from your class partner in the message list.

The body of the message appears in the Preview Pane.

Using the Office Clipboard

If you're familiar with Microsoft Word 2000, you've probably used the new **Clipboard**. The Clipboard is an area in your computer's memory that Microsoft Windows reserves to temporarily store content when you cut or copy text and graphics. The Clipboard can hold up to 12 items and can be used to copy data from one application to another. For example, you could copy several blocks of text in a Word document and paste them into the message area for an e-mail message in Outlook. To use the Clipboard in Outlook, you must display the Clipboard toolbar.

To display the Clipboard toolbar:

1 Open an e-mail message.

2 On the View menu, point to Toolbars, and click Clipboard.

To copy text to the Clipboard:

1 Select the text to be copied, and click the Copy button on the Clipboard toolbar.

2 An icon representing the copied item appears on the Clipboard toolbar.

To paste an individual item from the Clipboard:

● Position the insertion point at the desired location, and then click the icon for the item you want to paste.

To paste all items from the Clipboard:

● On the Office Clipboard, click the Paste All button.

Adding a vCard to a Message

You can quickly send contact information over the Internet by attaching a **vCard** to an e-mail message. Think of a vCard as an electronic business card that you can send directly to others' Contacts folders. A major advantage to using vCards is that, when you receive a vCard, you don't have to manually add all the new contact information. You can simply add the vCard to the Contacts folder and all the information is automatically entered for you. For example, the marketing director at Lakewood Mountains Resort likes to send her vCard to new clients so that they can easily add her contact information, such as her phone number, e-mail address, business address, and job title, to their Contacts folders. To send a vCard directly from the Contacts folder, simply right-click the contact that you want to send, and click Forward As vCard. Outlook then opens a new message window with the contact information converted into a vCard and attached to the message.

Lesson 2 Using Advanced E-Mail Features 2.9

If the recipient of a vCard uses Outlook, he or she can view the vCard by opening it as an attachment. If the recipient uses a different e-mail program, the vCard might appear just as text in an e-mail message.

When you receive a vCard as an attachment, you can easily import the information into your Contacts folder by dragging the vCard onto the Contacts shortcut on the Outlook Bar.

In this exercise, you add yourself as a contact, attach a vCard to a message, and read a vCard received in a message.

1 Display the Contacts folder.

New Contact

2 Click the New Contact button.

A contact window appears with the insertion point already in the Full name box.

3 Type your name.

4 Click in the Address box, and type your address.

5 Click in the E-Mail box, and type your e-mail address.

6 On the Standard toolbar in the contact window, click the Save And Close button.

Your contact information appears in the Contacts folder.

If your e-mail is set up for Corporate or Workgroup, you must click the contact record and click Forward As vCard on the Actions menu to forward a contact record as a vCard.

7 Right-click your contact record, and click Forward As vCard on the shortcut menu that appears.

A message window appears with your vCard attached. Notice that the subject is already filled in with the text *FW: [your name]*, meaning that your contact information is going to be forwarded to someone.

8 In the To box, type your class partner's address.

9 Click in the message area, and type **Here's my contact information**.

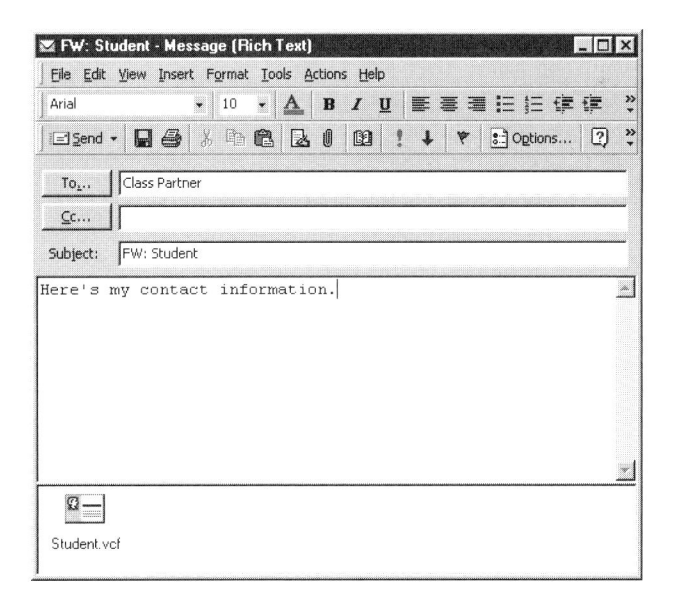

> **If an alert box appears, click the Open It option, and click OK.**

> **In the contact window, you can click the Save And Close button to quickly add the contact information to your Contacts folder.**

10 On the Standard toolbar in the message window, click the Send button.

11 Display the Inbox, and click the Send/Receive button.

Your class partner's vCard message appears in your Inbox.

12 Double-click the message that contains the vCard.

The message window appears.

13 Double-click the vCard attachment.

Your class partner's contact information appears in a contact window.

14 Close the contact window and the message window.

Using the Rules Wizard

OL2000E.2.8

You can organize messages by using the Rules Wizard. You use the Rules Wizard to create **rules** for messages. Rules consist of three elements—**conditions**, **actions**, and **exceptions**—that when combined, process and organize messages in a certain way. Conditions are requirements that must be met for a message, such as messages that you receive must have the word *meeting* in the subject and have an attachment. Actions are what you want Outlook to do with a message, such as delete it, forward it, or move it to a folder upon receipt. Exceptions are provisions for a message that, if met, will exclude a message from being acted upon, such as messages that are received between January 1 and January 7 will not be automatically deleted. When you create a rule, you must describe a condition and an action; however, describing an exception is not required.

The human resources manager at Lakewood Mountains Resort placed an ad in the newspaper for a cook. The ad instructed applicants to e-mail their resumes to her. To quickly separate her general e-mail from the many applicants' e-mail messages, the human resource manager created a rule that would automatically send any messages containing the word *cook* in the message body (condition) to a folder called Cook Position (action), except if the message was marked with high importance (exception).

After a rule is created, you can turn the Rules Wizard on and off (enable or disable the feature) as desired. You can also modify the rules to include different conditions or actions based on what you need at that time. For example, if you created a rule that has an exception that you no longer want, you could remove the exception.

In this exercise, you create a rule that puts messages that have the word *cook* in the subject into a folder you create called *Cook Position*.

Lesson 2 Using Advanced E-Mail Features 2.11

1 On the Tools menu, click Rules Wizard.

The first Rules Wizard dialog box appears.

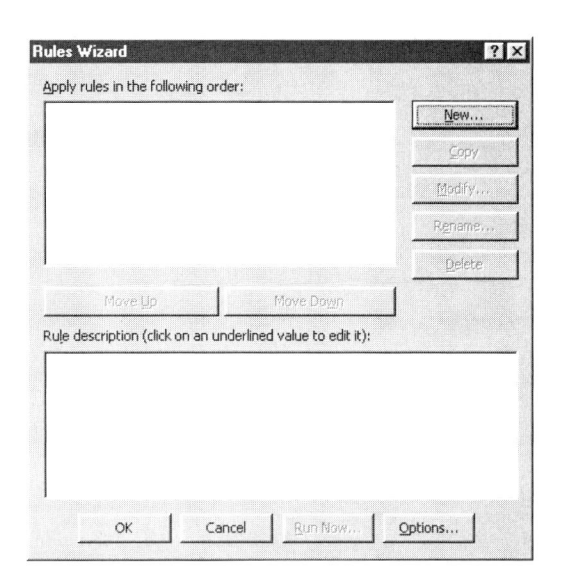

If the Office Assistant appears, asking if you want help, click No, Don't Provide Help Now.

2 Click the New button.

The next wizard dialog box appears with Check Messages When They Arrive already selected.

3 Click the Next button.

The next wizard dialog box appears, asking what conditions you want to set.

4 In the Which Conditions Do You Want To Check list, scroll down, and select the With Specific Words In The Subject check box.

5 In the Rule Description list, click the Specific Words link (indicated by the underlined text).

The Search Text dialog box appears with an insertion point already in the Add New box.

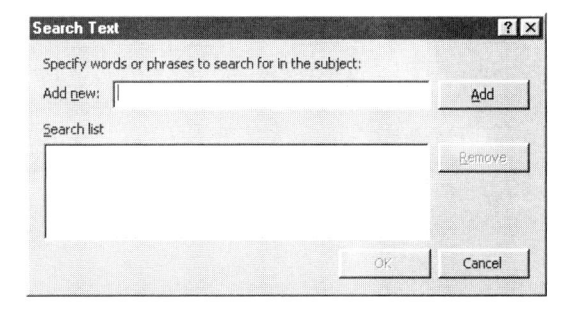

6 Type **cook**.

7 Click the Add button, and click OK.

8 In the wizard dialog box, click Next.

The next wizard dialog box appears, asking what you want to do with the messages.

9 In the What Do You Want To Do With The Message list, select the Move It To The Specified Folder check box.

10 In the Rule Description list, click the Specified link (indicated by the underlined text).

The next wizard dialog box appears, displaying your Outlook folders.

11 Click the New button.

The Create New Folder dialog box appears with the insertion point already in the Name box.

12 Type **Cook Position**, and click OK.

The Add Shortcut To Outlook Bar dialog box appears asking if you want to add a shortcut to the new folder to the Outlook bar.

13 Click Yes.

The folder Cook Position is added to the Outlook Bar and is selected in the Rules Wizard dialog box.

14 Click OK.

15 In the next wizard dialog box, click Next.

The next wizard dialog box appears, asking you to add an exception, if desired.

16 Click Next to choose not to select an exception.

The next wizard dialog box appears, asking you to name the rule. The word *cook* is already inserted in the Please Specify A Name For This Rule box.

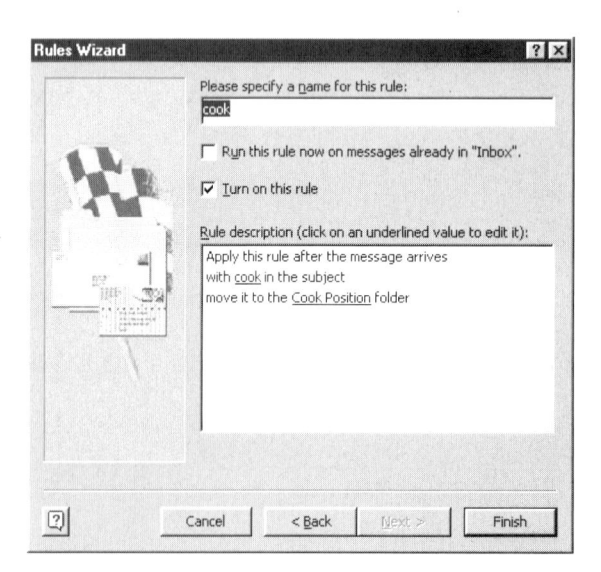

> You can run a newly created rule on messages already in the Inbox. Simply click the Run Now button in the final Rules Wizard dialog box. Select the rule's check box in the Run Rules Now dialog box, and click the Run Now button again.

17 Click Finish.

18 In the final wizard dialog box, click OK.

19 Create a message with the word *Cook* in the Subject box, and send it to your class partner.

20 On the Standard toolbar, click the Send/Receive button.

The message from your class partner is received. Notice that it appears in the Inbox for only a moment before moving to the Cook Position folder.

21 On the Outlook Bar, click the My Shortcuts group bar, and click the Cook Position shortcut.

The contents of the Cook Position folder appear. The Cook e-mail message appears in the Cook Position folder.

22 On the Outlook Bar, click the Outlook Shortcuts group bar, and click the Inbox shortcut.

Tracking When Messages Are Delivered and Read

OL2000E.2.4

Have you ever wondered whether someone read an important message that you sent? With Outlook, you can track what day and time a message was received and read by a recipient. Before you send a message, you can set up Outlook to display an alert box (shown in the following illustration) requesting that the recipient send a **read receipt** (a notice in the form of an e-mail message) verifying the date and time when he or she received and read the message.

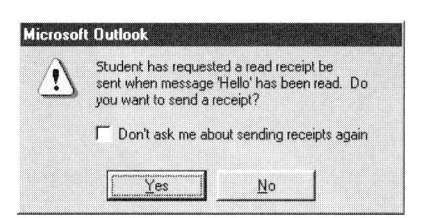

As you can see, the recipient can choose to accept or decline the request. If the recipient accepts, the following e-mail message will automatically be sent to you after the recipient closes or deletes the message.

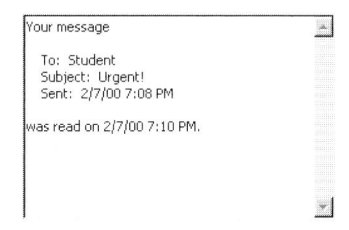

Read receipts verify that the message was received; however, they do not necessarily verify that the message was read. A recipient could delete your message without ever reading it and send a read receipt to you. Even though the recipient didn't read the message, the read receipt would still display a date and time at which the message was read.

It's a good idea to read messages that request read receipts because the information in the message is probably important—so important that the sender needs to make sure that you read it and possibly act upon it after reading it. A dispute might arise if you accept to send a read receipt, but you don't really read the message. The sender will have the advantage in the dispute because he or she will have proof that the message was sent; thus placing the blame solely on you. For example, if the message stated that you were expected to pick up your boss's mother from the airport and you didn't because you really didn't read the message, you have only yourself to blame.

In this exercise, you create a message that requests the recipient to send a read receipt after the recipient reads the message.

New Mail Message

1 On the Standard toolbar, click the New Mail Message button.

A message window appears with an insertion point already in the To box.

2 In the To box, type your class partner's e-mail address, and press Tab twice.

3 In the Subject box, type **Urgent!**

Flag For Follow Up

tip
You can flag a message so that the recipient will perform a particular action, such as call you or reply to you by a specific date. To do so, create a new message, click the Flag For Follow Up button on the Standard toolbar, click the Flag To down arrow, and click a desired flag. If desired, click the Due By down arrow, click a date, and click OK. When the recipient opens the message, a request stating the action will appear in a yellow box under the Standard toolbar of the message window. For example if you clicked Reply in the Flag To list, and clicked the date January 10, 2000 in the Due By calendar, the recipient would receive a message with the request *Reply by Monday, January 10, 2000 10:00 PM*.

4 Click in the message area, and type **Please pick up the boss's mother at the airport at 12:04 P.M., Airways, gate 24.**

Lesson 2 Using Advanced E-Mail Features 2.15

5 On the Standard toolbar in the message window, click the Options button.

The Message Options dialog box appears.

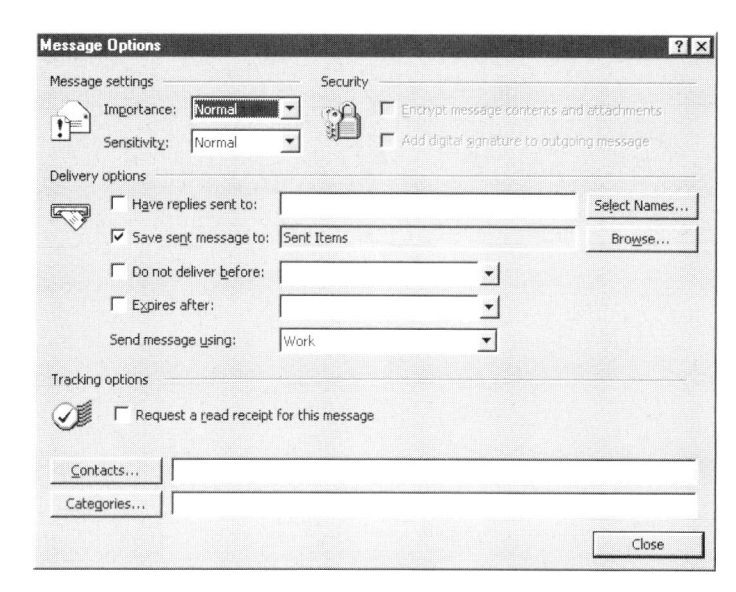

[Screenshot of Message Options dialog box]

6 In the Tracking Options section, select the Request A Read Receipt For This Message check box, and click Close.

7 On the Standard toolbar in the message window, click the Send button.

8 On the Standard toolbar, click the Send/Receive button.

The *Urgent* message from your class partner appears in your Inbox.

9 Double-click the message.

An alert box appears, requesting that you send a read receipt after you read the message.

10 Click Yes.

11 Close the message.

12 On the Standard toolbar, click the Send/Receive button.

The Read: Urgent! message appears in your Inbox.

13 Click the Read: Urgent! message header.

The read receipt message appears in your Inbox. Notice that a read receipt icon appears in the Icon column. The receipt appears in the Preview Pane.

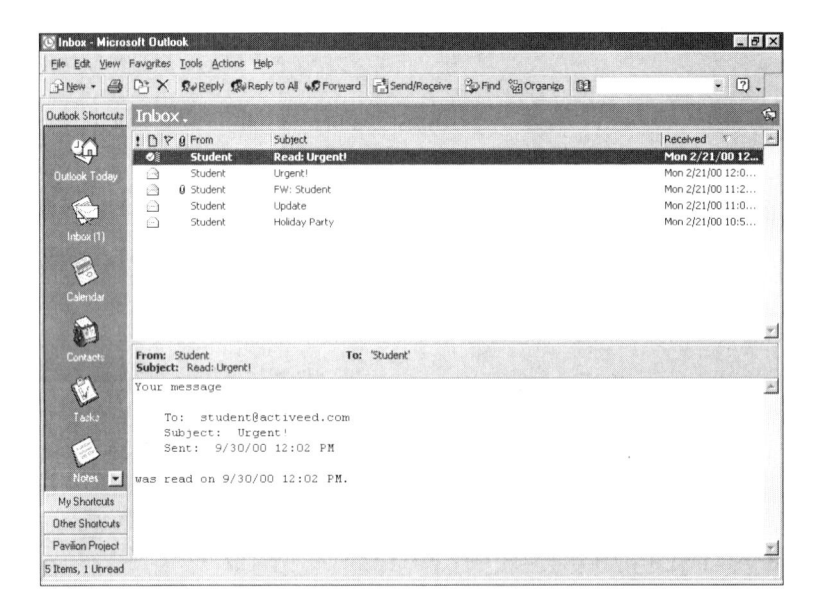

Creating a Personal Address Book

As you know, Outlook has an Address Book that you can use to store the e-mail addresses of your contacts. You alone manage the Address Book. If you use Microsoft Exchange Server, you use the Outlook Address Book. The Outlook Address Book differs from the Address Book in that it contains e-mail addresses of the *all* users on your network and is managed by the system administrator. Because of the likelihood that you will not need to use every e-mail address listed on the server, Outlook offers the **Personal Address Book** for Microsoft Exchange Server users. After you install the Personal Address Book, you can add and remove addresses whenever you want (unlike with the Outlook Address Book).

In this exercise, you add the Personal Address Book to Outlook, add your class partner to it, and then display the Personal Address Book.

important
The options in the following exercise will be available to you only if you use Microsoft Exchange Server. If you do not use Microsoft Exchange Server, please skip to the next section.

1 On the Tools menu, click Services.

The Services dialog box appears.

2 Click the Add button.

The Add Service To Profile dialog box appears.

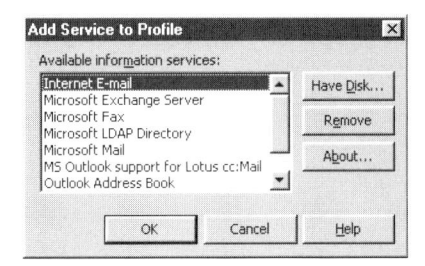

3 Scroll down, if necessary, click Personal Address Book, and then click OK.

The Personal Address Book dialog box appears.

4 Click OK.

An alert box appears, telling you that you need to restart Outlook.

5 Click OK.

6 In the Services dialog box, click OK.

7 Quit Outlook.

8 On the Windows taskbar, click the Start button, point to Programs, and then click Microsoft Outlook to restart Outlook.

9 On the Tools menu, click Services.

The Services dialog box appears.

10 Click the Addressing tab.

11 Click the Add button.

The Add Address List dialog box appears.

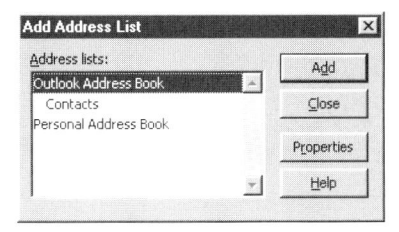

12 Click Personal Address Book.

13 Click the Add button.

14 Click the Close button.

15 Click the Keep Personal Addresses In down arrow, click Personal Address Book, and click OK.

The Personal Address Book is now added to Outlook.

Address Book

16 On the Standard toolbar, click the Address Book button.

The Address Book appears.

17 Click your class partner's name.

Add to Personal Address Book

18 Click the Add To Personal Address Book button.

Your class partner is now also in the Personal Address Book.

19 Click the Show Names From The down arrow.

20 Click Personal Address Book

Your class partner appears in the Personal Address Book.

Close

21 In the top-right corner of the Personal Address Book, click the Close button.

The Personal Address Book closes.

Creating a Personal Distribution List

OL2000E.2.5

To save yourself time sending e-mail, you might want to create a **personal distribution list** for contacts to whom you send the same e-mail message. A personal distribution list is a collection of contacts that have something in common (for example, they all work in a specific department or they all belong to your book club). You use this list to quickly send a message to everyone named in the list. When you want to send a message to the group of people, instead of having to type each person's e-mail address in the To box, you simply add the group's name to the To box. When you send the message, Outlook then sends the message to everyone listed in the distribution list.

important

Do not confuse a personal distribution list with a Personal Address Book. A personal distribution list is a grouping of contacts used for addressing an e-mail message to a group instead of addressing the e-mail message to each person in the group. A Personal Address Book is a custom list of e-mail addresses for Microsoft Exchange Server users.

For example, the human resources manager at Lakewood Mountains Resort created a personal distribution list called Marketing Department so that every time she wants to announce a departmental meeting, she can simply address the message to the name Marketing Department, type the message, and send it.

In this exercise, you create a personal distribution list called Marketing Department. You will then create a message for the group.

Lesson 2 Using Advanced E-Mail Features 2.19

1 On the File menu, point to New, and click Distribution List.

The distribution list window appears with the insertion point already in the Name box.

You can also display the Distribution List window by pressing Ctrl+Shift+L.

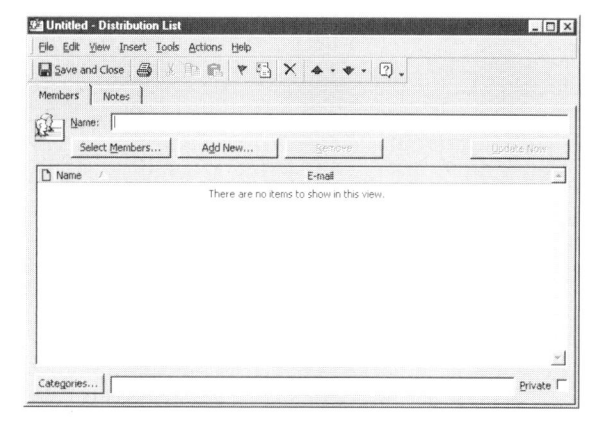

2 Type **Marketing Department**.

3 Click the Select Members button.

The Select Members dialog box appears.

4 Click Erik Gavriluk, and click the Add button.

The *Erik Gavriluk* record moves to the Add To Distribution List section.

To select more than one name at a time, click the first name that you want to add, press Ctrl, and then click the rest of the names. After all names are selected, click the Add button.

5 Click Frank Miller, and click the Add button.

The *Frank Miller* record moves to the Add To Distribution List section.

6 Click the New Contact button.

The Properties dialog box appears with the insertion point already in the First box.

If your e-mail is set up for Corporate or Workgroup, the steps for adding a new contact record will differ slightly. Click the New button, click the In The down arrow, click Contacts, and click OK. Add the contact's information as desired, and click the Save And Close button.

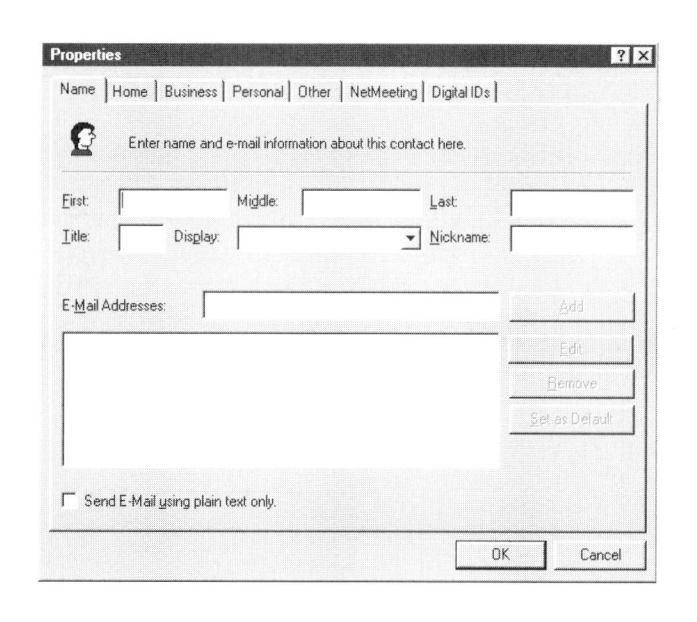

7 Type **Kate**, press Tab twice, and type **Dresen** in the Last box.

8 Click in the E-Mail Addresses box, type **kate@lmr.microsoft.com**, and then click OK.

The *Kate Dresen* contact is selected and added to the Name list.

9 Click the Add button.

The *Kate Dresen* contact moves to the distribution list.

10 Click OK.

11 On the Standard toolbar in the distribution list window, click the Save And Close button.

12 On the Standard toolbar, click the New Mail Message button.

New Mail Message

A message window appears.

13 Click the To button.

The Select Names dialog box appears. Notice that the Marketing Department distribution list is added to the list and appears with a distribution list icon to the left of it.

You might need to scroll down the list to see the Marketing Department distribution list.

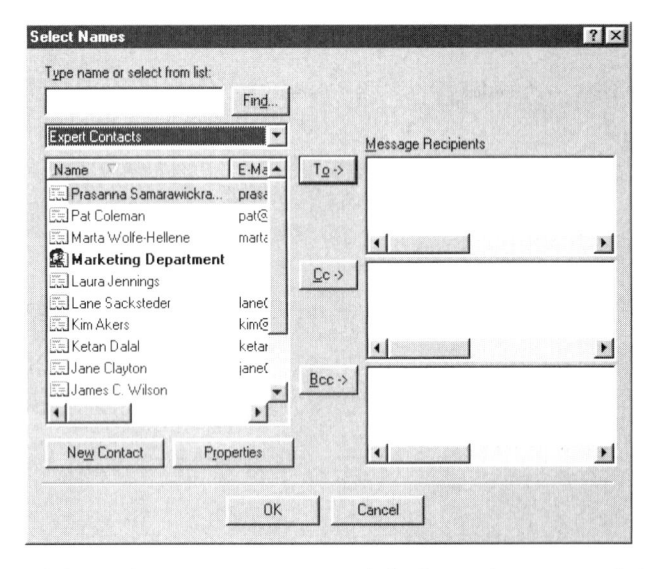

14 Click Marketing Department, click the To button, and then click OK.

The message window reappears with *Marketing Department* now in the To box.

15 Click in the Subject box, type **Meeting**, and press Enter.

The insertion point moves to the message area.

16 Type **A marketing meeting will be held in the auditorium on Tuesday at 2:00.**

The message is ready to be sent; however, you will not send this message because the e-mail addresses are fictitious. If the e-mail addresses were real and you sent this message, each person on the distribution list would receive this message.

Close

17 In the top-right corner of the message window, click the Close button, and click No in the alert box that appears.

The message window closes without saving changes.

Importing Data Between Outlook and Other E-Mail Applications

OL2000E.5.4

You can **import,** or bring in, information from other Office applications. This process is especially useful if you are accustomed to using a different e-mail program, such as Microsoft Outlook Express, and have switched to Outlook. Microsoft Outlook Express is program that is installed with Microsoft Internet Explorer. As in Outlook, you can send and receive e-mail messages and store contact information in Outlook Express; however, you cannot schedule activities, or view a calendar or a journal.

In this exercise, you create a contact in Outlook Express and import the contact into Outlook.

important

You must have Outlook Express installed on your computer to perform the steps in this exercise. You will also need to have the Import/Export engine feature installed for this exercise to work. If an alert box appears during this exercise telling you that this feature is not installed, you will need to insert the Office 2000 or Outlook 2000 CD-ROM to install the feature.

1 On the Windows taskbar, click the Start button, point to Programs, and then click Outlook Express.

Outlook Express starts.

Address Book

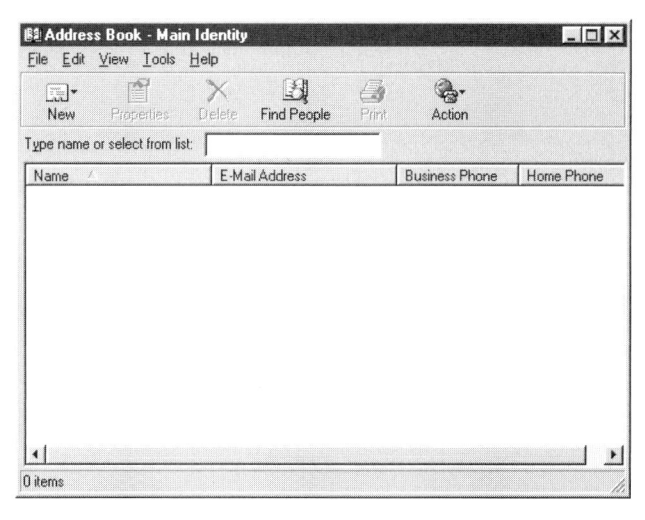

2 On the toolbar, click the Address Book button.

The Address Book window appears.

3 On the Address Book toolbar, click the New button, and click New Contact.

The Properties dialog box appears with the insertion point already in the First box.

4 Type **Lisa**, press Tab twice, and then type **Garmaise**.

5 Click in the E-Mail Addresses box, type **lisa@lmr.microsoft.com**, click the Add button, and then click OK.

6 In the top-right corner of the Address Book window, click the Close button.

Close

The Address book closes.

7 On the Windows taskbar, click the Outlook button.

Outlook reappears.

8 On the File menu, click Import And Export.

The Import And Export Wizard appears.

If the Office Assistant appears asking if you want help with this feature, click No, Don't Provide Help Now.

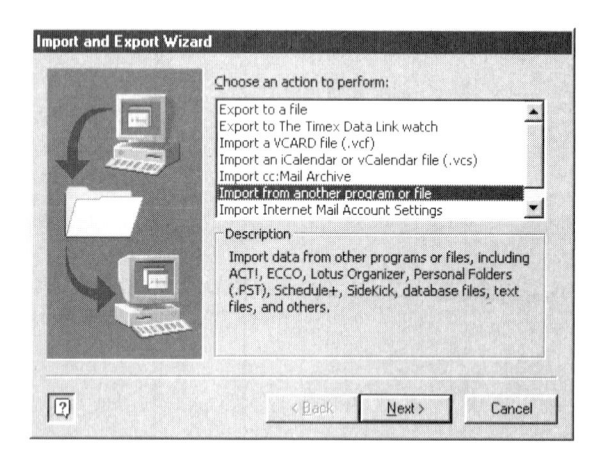

9 Scroll down, click Import Internet Mail And Addresses, and then click Next.

The next wizard dialog box appears, asking you to select the mail application to import from.

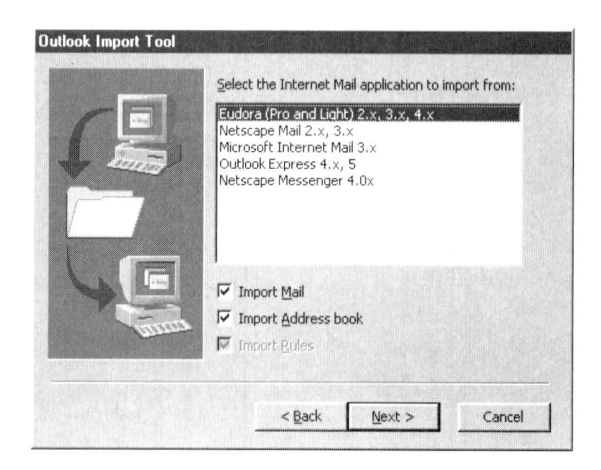

Lesson 2 Using Advanced E-Mail Features 2.23

10 Click Outlook Express 4.x, 5, clear the Import Mail and Import Rules check boxes, and then click Next.

The next wizard dialog box appears. Notice that the Outlook Contacts folder is already selected as the location where the imported files will be stored.

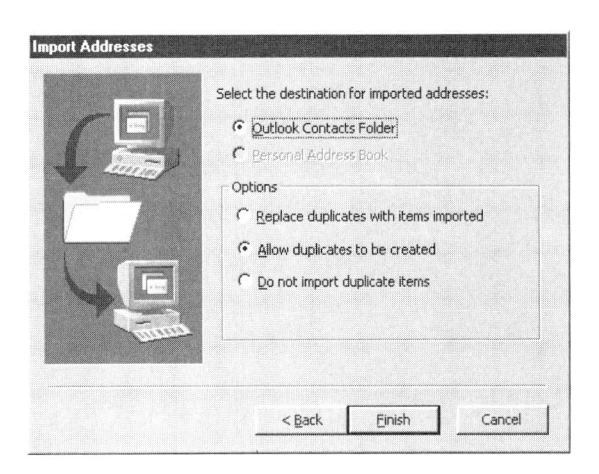

11 Click the Replace Duplicates With Items Imported option, and click Finish.

The Import Progress dialog box briefly appears, showing a progress bar as the file is imported. Then the Import Summary dialog box appears, displaying the results of the import.

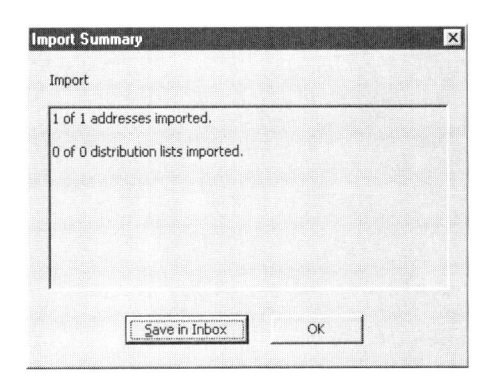

12 In the Import Summary dialog box, click OK.
13 Display the Contacts folder.

The *Lisa Garmaise* contact now appears in your Contacts folder.

Exporting Data Between Outlook and Other E-Mail Applications

OL2000E.5.4

Just as you can import data into Outlook from another e-mail program, you can also **export**, or move, Outlook data into another e-mail program. For example, if you also like to use Outlook Express, you could export your Outlook e-mail addresses into Outlook Express. Performing this export would make these addresses available to you for sending e-mail while you are using Outlook Express. (You wouldn't need to open Outlook to send the e-mail message.)

You use the Import And Export Wizard to export data from Outlook. The wizard will prompt you to choose a file type that the Outlook data will be converted to, such as a comma-separated values text file (.csv file), dBase file, or Microsoft Access file. A **comma-separated values text file** is a text file that takes fields (such as the first name, last name, and address fields in a contact record) and stores them separated by commas. This format can be used to convert Outlook data so that it can be imported into another program such as Outlook Express. After Outlook Express imports such a file, it converts the file into Outlook Express Address Book data.

In this exercise, you export the contents of the Contacts folder to a file, and then import the file into Outlook Express.

dBase and Microsoft Access are database programs.

1 On the File menu, click Import And Export.

The Import And Export Wizard appears.

2 Click Export To A File, and click the Next button.

The next wizard dialog box appears, asking you to choose a file type to create.

3 Click Comma Separated Values (Windows), and click the Next button.

The next wizard dialog box appears, asking you to select a folder that contains the information that you want to export.

4 If necessary, scroll up, click Contacts, and then click the Next button.

The next wizard dialog box appears, asking you to select a location in which to store your exported file.

5 Click the Browse button, and navigate to the Outlook Expert Practice folder on your hard disk.

6 Click in the File Name box, type [your name]**'s Contacts**, and then click OK.

7 In the wizard dialog box, click the Next button.

The final wizard dialog box appears, telling you what actions will be performed.

You must have the Import/Export engine feature installed for this exercise to work. If an alert box appears at this point, insert the Office 2000 or Outlook 2000 CD-ROM to install the feature.

Lesson 2 Using Advanced E-Mail Features 2.25

8 Click the Finish button.

A progress bar appears as the contents of the Contacts folder are exported to a file.

9 On the Windows taskbar, click the Outlook Express button.

Outlook Express reappears.

10 On the File menu, point to Import, and click Other Address Book.

The Address Book Import Tool dialog box appears.

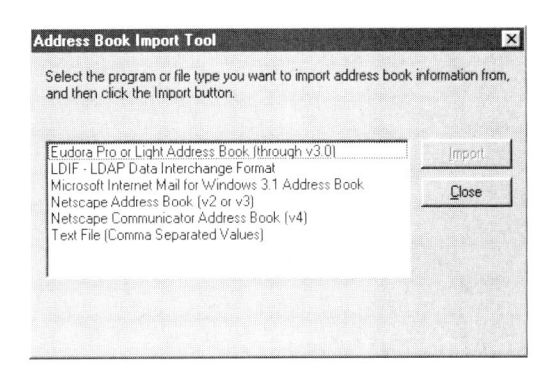

11 Click Text File (Comma Separated Values), and click the Import button.

The CSV Import dialog box appears.

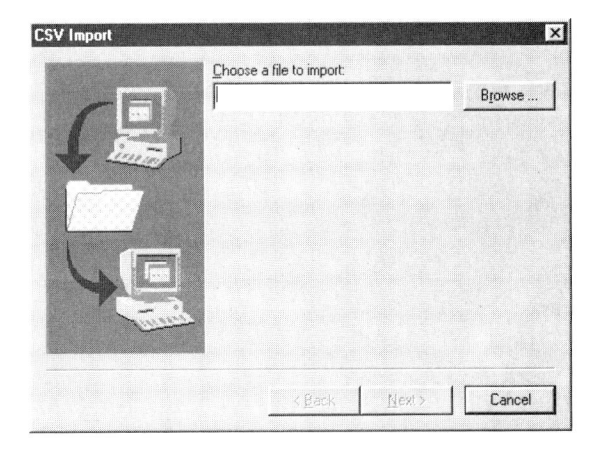

12 Click the Browse button, navigate to the Outlook Expert Practice folder on your hard disk, click the file [your name]'s Contacts, and then click the Open button.

13 In the Comma Separated Values Import dialog box, click the Next button.

The final dialog box appears, asking you to map (match) the Text fields (Outlook fields) to the Address Book fields (Outlook Express) fields.

Notice that the Text fields and Address Book fields already match.

14 Click the Finish button.

The Confirm Replace dialog box appears, telling you that Lisa Garmaise (the contact that you added to the Outlook Express Address Book in the previous exercise) is already present, and asking you if you want to replace the entry.

15 Click No.

An alert box appears telling you that the import process is completed.

16 Click OK, and click the Close button in the Address Book Import Tool dialog box.

Address Book

17 In Outlook Express, click the Address Book button on the toolbar.

The addresses that are in your Contacts folder in Outlook now appear in the Outlook Express Address Book.

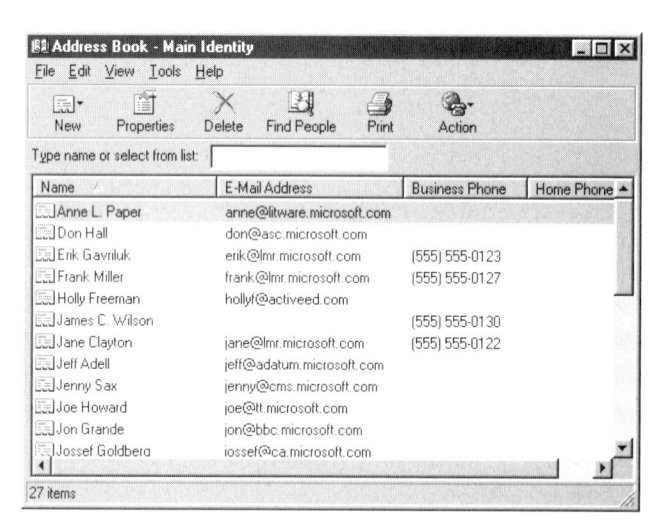

Close

18 In the top-right corner of the Address Book window, click the Close button.

The Address book closes.

19 On the Windows taskbar, click the Outlook button.

Outlook reappears.

Integrating E-Mail with Other Office Applications

OL2000E.1.4

New!

The commands that you click to send an e-mail message will vary slightly from application to application.

With Microsoft Office 2000, you can create e-mail messages within any Office application (Microsoft Word, Microsoft Excel, Microsoft PowerPoint, Microsoft Access, Microsoft PhotoDraw, Microsoft FrontPage, or Microsoft Publisher). This feature saves you time because you no longer need to start Outlook to send an Office file to a recipient; you can send it directly from the application you are working in. Simply create the document, database, table, or presentation as always, and then on the File menu of the Office application, click the appropriate commands to start your default e-mail program. Then fill in the appropriate boxes, and send the e-mail message.

You can also send some Office files without having to attach them to an e-mail message. The Office application converts the document into an e-mail message after you click the E-Mail button on the Standard toolbar in the application. An e-mail header will also appear so that you can address and send the e-mail. The recipient will not have to open an attachment to read your e-mail; however, if the file you sent had a lot of formatting, the recipient's file might not look or function the same way that you had intended. If the file is sent in a format other than as an attachment, the recipient can't edit or save the document as anything other than an e-mail message. For that reason, it is a good idea to send files as attachments so that formatting doesn't get lost in the conversion.

important

You must have Microsoft Word installed on your computer to complete this exercise.

In this exercise, you open a Word document. You then send that document as an e-mail message to your class partner from within Microsoft Word.

1 Display Windows Explorer, navigate to the Outlook Expert Practice folder, and then double-click the file Salary Increases.

The file appears in Microsoft Word.

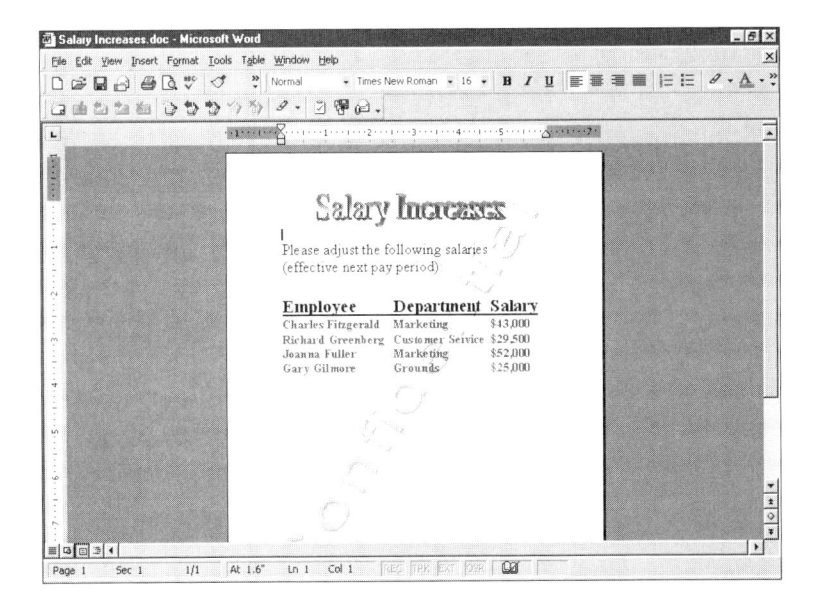

2 On the File menu, point to Send To, and click Mail Recipient (As Attachment).

A message window appears with the file name displayed in the Subject box and an attachment icon of the file displayed in the window.

If Outlook is not specified as your default e-mail manager, a different e-mail program might be used to create the message window in step 2.

3 In the To box, type your class partner's e-mail address.

Your class partner's name appears in the To box.

4 Click in the message area, and type **Here are the salary increases.**

5 On the Standard toolbar in the message window, click the Send button.

The message is sent to your class partner.

6 On the Windows taskbar, click the Outlook button.

Outlook reappears.

7 Display the Inbox folder.

8 On the Standard toolbar, click the Send/Receive button.

The Salary Increases message from your class partner appears in the Inbox.

OL2000E.10.2

Setting Up a News Account

You can send a different kind of e-mail message to a **newsgroup**. A newsgroup is a collection of messages that are constantly being sent and responded to by people within the group. Each newsgroup discusses a specific topic, such as gardening, rock bands, or television programs. The gardener at Lakewood Mountains Resort likes to visit newsgroups that talk about gardening to troubleshoot insect problems and to get tips on how to grow mountain flowers.

Lesson 2 Using Advanced E-Mail Features 2.29

New!

The messages (also called **posts**) appear on a **news server**. A news server is a computer that is maintained by a company, group, or individual, and is configured to accept posts from newsgroups. (Your Internet service provider most likely has a news server you can connect to.) To read these posts, you must use a **newsreader**. A newsreader is an application that you use to send and receive newsgroup posts. Outlook does not come equipped with a newsreader; however, you can access the Microsoft Outlook Express newsreader from within Outlook.

Before you can view newsgroups in a newsreader, you must set up a news account. Setting up a news account is similar to setting up an e-mail account.

You will need to know the following information to set up a news account.

- Your e-mail address
- Your news server name (NNTP server name)
- Your user name
- Your password

Ask your instructor or Internet service provider what your news server name is.

After your news account is set up, Outlook Express downloads the newsgroups from the news server. Because there are thousands of newsgroups, the downloading process might take a few minutes. However, you only have to download once.

In this exercise, you set up a news account.

important

You will need to know your news server name to complete this exercise.

1 On the View menu, point to Go To, and click News.

   Outlook Express appears.

The Folders list looks similar to Outlook's Folder List.

2 If necessary, click the Outlook Express icon in the Folders list.

3 In the Newsgroups section in the Outlook Express pane, click the Set Up A Newsgroups Account link. (You have to do this only once.)

   The Internet Connection Wizard dialog box appears.

4 In the Display Name box, type your name (if necessary), and click Next.

   The next wizard dialog box appears.

5 In the E-Mail Address box, type your e-mail address (if necessary), and click Next.

   The next wizard dialog box appears.

6 Type the news server name, click Next, and then click Finish.

   The Internet Connection Wizard closes, and an alert box appears, asking if you want to download a list of available newsgroups.

You will use the Newsgroup Subscriptions dialog box to view a newsgroup in the next exercise.

7 Click Yes.

   The newsgroups are downloaded, and the Newsgroup Subscriptions dialog box appears.

Viewing Newsgroups and Newsgroup Messages

After you create a news account and download the newsgroups, you can view newsgroups. You use the Newsgroups Subscriptions dialog box to choose a newsgroup to view. The following illustration shows the discussions in a gardening newsgroup.

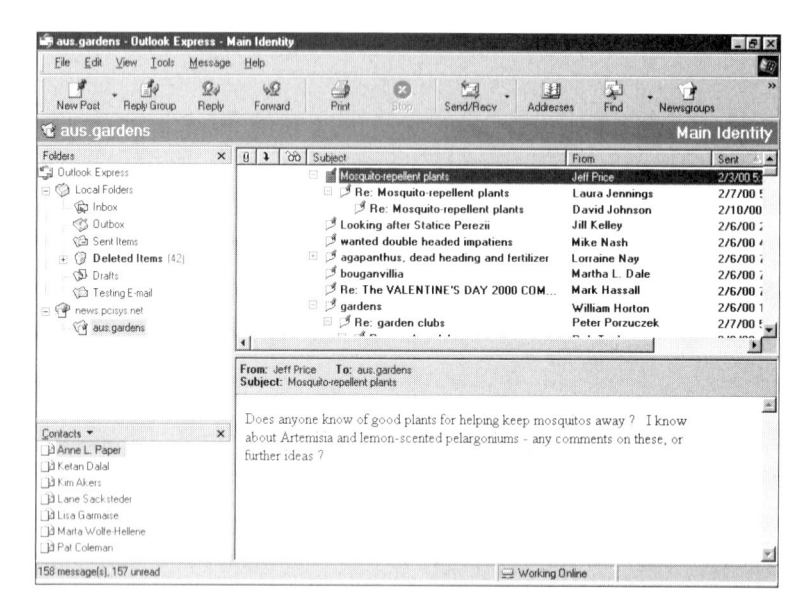

Viewing posts in a newsgroup is similar to viewing e-mail messages. Outlook Express displays the post headers in the message list and posts content in the Preview Pane. Like e-mail messages in Outlook, unread posts appear in bold. Notice the plus and minus signs to the left of the posts in the above illustration. The plus and minus signs indicate the originating message of a message thread. A **thread** includes a message and all of the replies to that message. When you click a plus sign to the left of a post, the responses to that post appear indented under the original post. When you click a minus sign, the responses are hidden.

In this exercise, you view a gardening newsgroup and read various posts.

1 In the Newsgroup Subscriptions dialog box, type **gardens** in the Display Newsgroups Which Contain box.

After a few seconds, the names of newsgroups that discuss gardens appear.

2 Click aus.gardens, and click the Go To button.

The Newsgroup Subscription dialog box closes and the Folders list now displays the newsgroup name. After a few seconds, the posts of the newsgroup appear in the message list.

important

Your Internet service provider's news server might not offer certain newsgroups. If the aus.gardens newsgroup does not appear, choose another.

You can double-click a post to display it in its own message window.

3 Click a post header.

The message body appears in the Preview Pane.

4 Click the plus sign to the left of a post.

The thread expands and shows all posts sent in response to the original post.

5 Click a post that has a minus sign to the left of it.

The thread collapses and responses are hidden.

OL20000E.10.1

tip

Sending posts to newsgroups is similar to sending e-mail messages. To send a message to the newsgroup, click the New Post button on the toolbar, type a subject and a message, and click the Send button. To reply to a post, click the post that you want to reply to and click the Reply Group button (so that the post can be seen by the newsgroup), or click the Reply button (so the post can be seen by only the person who posted it).

Subscribing to a Newsgroup

If you decide that you really like a particular newsgroup, you can **subscribe** to it. In Outlook Express, to subscribe means to add a newsgroup's name to Outlook Express's Folders list. Subscribing makes it easier for you to access a newsgroup. You can subscribe to as many newsgroups as you like. If you find that you rarely visit a newsgroup that you've subscribed to, you can easily unsubscribe from the newsgroup, thus removing it from the Folders list.

In this exercise, you subscribe to the aus.gardens newsgroup, and you unsubscribe to it.

You can also subscribe to a newsgroup by clicking the Newsgroups button on the toolbar to display the Newsgroup Subscription dialog box. Select the newsgroup's name in the list, and click the Subscribe button.

1 In the Folders list, right-click the aus.gardens newsgroup name (or the newsgroup that you chose), and click Subscribe on the shortcut menu that appears.

You are now subscribed to the newsgroup.

2 In the Folders list, right-click the aus.gardens newsgroup (or the newsgroup that you chose), and click Unsubscribe on the shortcut menu that appears.

An alert box appears, asking if you are sure that you want to unsubscribe from the newsgroup.

If an alert box appears, telling you that you are not subscribed to any newsgroups and asking if you would like to see a list of available newsgroups, click No.

3 Click OK.

The newsgroup is no longer listed in the Folders list and is removed from the newsgroup window.

Lesson Wrap-Up

This lesson covered how to create specialized e-mail messages by changing the appearance of messages, creating and using message templates, and adding vCards to messages. You learned how to use the Rules Wizard, track when messages are delivered and read, create a Personal Address Book, and create and use a personal distribution list. You also learned how to import and export e-mail addresses, send e-mail from Microsoft Word, use a newsreader, and subscribe to a newsgroup.

If you are continuing to the next lesson:

Close   **1**   In the top-right corner of Outlook Express, click the Close button.
Outlook Express closes.

Close   **2**   In the top-right corner of Microsoft Word, click the Close button.
Microsoft Word closes.

If you are not continuing to other lessons:

Close   **1**   In the top-right corner of Outlook Express, click the Close button.
Outlook Express closes.

Close   **2**   In the top-right corner of Microsoft Word, click the Close button.
Microsoft Word closes.

Close   **3**   In the top-right corner of Outlook, click the Close button.
Outlook closes.

Lesson Glossary

actions What you want to do with a message, such as delete it, forward it, or move it to a folder upon receipt.

Clipboard An area in your computer's memory that Microsoft Windows reserves to temporarily store content when you cut or copy text and graphics.

comma-separated values text file A text file that takes fields, such as the first name, last name, and address fields in a contact record, and stores them separated by commas.

conditions Requirements that must be met for a message before an action can occur.

exceptions Provisions for a message that, if met, will exclude a message from being acted upon.

export To move information from one program into another.

HTML An e-mail format that allows text and paragraph formatting, pictures, backgrounds, stationery, and Web pages to be transmitted across the Internet.

import To bring information from one program into another.

newsgroup A collection of related messages that are constantly being sent and responded to by people within the group.

newsreader A program used to access newsgroups and view their content.

news server A computer that is maintained by a company, group, or individual and is configured to accept messages from newsgroups.

Personal Address Book A customizable address book designed to store e-mail addresses and distribution lists for Microsoft Exchange users.

personal distribution list A grouping of contacts (who have something in common) used for addressing an e-mail message to a group instead of addressing the e-mail message to each person in the group.

plain text The most commonly used e-mail format, which does not allow any text or paragraph formatting to be transmitted across the Internet. This keeps the e-mail file size down so that the message can be sent across the Internet quickly.

posts Messages that appear in a newsgroup, which you can read or send.

read receipt A notice in the form of an e-mail message, verifying the date and time the recipient received and read the message.

rich text An e-mail format for text and paragraph formatting (such as font color, font size, type bullets, and paragraph alignment) that is transmitted across the Internet, but does not let you add backgrounds or pictures to the message.

rules The conditions, actions, and exceptions that combine to process and organize messages in a certain way.

stationery A combination of font styles and background formats that can be applied to a message when it is in HTML format.

subscribe To add a newsgroup to the Folder List in Outlook Express.

template In Outlook, an e-mail message that can be used as a pattern to format similar e-mail messages.

text formats Standards that specify properties for text such as the font, alignment, and margins.

thread In newsgroups, a post and every response to that post.

vCard An electronic business card that is created from contact information stored in Outlook and that can be attached to messages so that the information can be sent to other users.

Quick Quiz

1. How do you mark a message for a read receipt?
2. How do you access the Outlook Express newsreader from Outlook?
3. How do you display the Personal Address Book?
4. How do you send a vCard?
5. How do you unsubscribe from a newsgroup?
6. How do you save a message as a template?
7. What are the three available mail formats for Outlook messages?

Putting It All Together

Exercise 1: Using stationery, create a birthday e-mail message for a friend. Make the font size of the text 18, and change the font color to a color that appeals to you. Save the message as a template, and use the template to create a birthday e-mail message for your class partner. Request a read receipt and then send the message.

Exercise 2: Create a personal distribution list called Managers. Add the following names to the list: Erik Gavriluk, Frank Miller, Jane Clayton, and Laura Jennings. Create a rule that takes messages that arrive in your Inbox marked with high importance and flags them for follow-up within one day of receipt.

LESSON 3

Using Advanced Calendar Features

After completing this lesson, you will be able to:

✔ *Customize Calendar options.*
✔ *Change time zone settings.*
✔ *Schedule online meetings using NetMeeting.*
✔ *Share Calendar information over the Internet.*

When you first began using the Microsoft Outlook Calendar, you probably just typed in a few appointments and scheduled a few meetings. As you continue to use the Calendar, however, you might want to make use of more of its features or you might want to customize it to fit the way you work. For example, you might prefer to display the time slots in the Appointment Area with a different color. Or you might want to change the Appointment Area so that the start and end times match the times when you come in and leave work. And as you view different menus, you might wonder about some of the more advanced features that are represented on the menus, such as online meetings. In this lesson, you will learn how to customize Calendar options and change time zone information, how to schedule online meetings with Microsoft **NetMeeting**, and how to share Calendar information with others over the Internet or over an intranet.

Practice files for the lesson

No practice files are required to complete the exercises in this lesson.

important

To complete some of the exercises in this lesson, you will need to exchange e-mail messages with a class partner. If you don't have a class partner or are performing the exercises alone, you can enter your own e-mail address instead of your class partner's and send the message to yourself.

OL2000E.3.1

Customizing Calendar Options

By default, the Outlook Calendar displays a Monday through Friday, 8:00 A.M. to 5:00 P.M. work week. However, this work week might not fit your work schedule. For example, your work week might start on a Tuesday and end on Saturday. Also, the Calendar doesn't automatically show holidays from different countries, different time zones, or the numbers of the weeks (1 through 52). However, you can change any of these options to reflect your work environment. The table on the following page details some of the Calendar options you can change by using the Calendar Options dialog box.

important

To see all the options mentioned in the following table, you must set your e-mail service options to Corporate or Workgroup. (On the Tools menu, click Options, click the Mail Delivery tab, and click the Reconfigure Mail Support button. In the dialog box, click the Corporate Or Workgroup option, click the Next button, and then follow the screen prompts.)

Calendar Option	Description
Sun, Mon, Tue, Wed, Thu, Fri, Sat	Depending on which check boxes you select, displays the selected days as working days in Work Week view. This is useful if the days that you work are other than Monday through Friday. If your work schedule changes, you can select a different set of check boxes.
First day of week	Arranges the Calendar so that the specified day is the first day of the work week.
First week of year	Specifies whether you want the first week of the year to start on January 1, the first four-day week, or the first full week.
Start time	Specifies what time you begin your work day.
End time	Specifies what time you end your work day.
Show week numbers in the Date Navigator	Displays the numbers of the weeks of the year from 1 to 52 to the left of each week in the Date Navigator.
Always use local	Opens the Calendar from your computer rather than from a network server Calendar.
Background color	Changes the background color for the time slots in the Appointment Area.
Time Zone	Displays a time zone from a country you specify. If you have customers or associates who work in a different time zone, you can set the Appointment Area so that it displays the times for your time zone along with the corresponding times for a second time zone.
Add Holidays	Display holidays from a country you specify. If you have customers or associates who work in a different country, you can display holidays for that country so that you know when they will be out of the office.
Free/Busy Options	Lets other people know when you are available for meetings. Also lets you set how much information you want to share.

In this exercise, you create a work week that starts on Wednesday and ends on Sunday. You also set the daily start time to 2:00 P.M. and the end time to 10:00 P.M. You then change the color of the Appointment Area. Finally, you set up Outlook to show holidays from the United Kingdom.

Lesson 3 Using Advanced Calendar Features   3.3

Notice that the default work week is Monday through Friday, 8:00 A.M. to 5:00 P.M.

1   Display the Calendar.
2   On the Standard toolbar, click the Work Week button.
    The Calendar is displayed in Work Week view.
3   On the Tools menu, click Options.
    The Options dialog box appears with the Preferences tab visible.
4   Click the Calendar Options button.
    The Calendar Options dialog box appears.

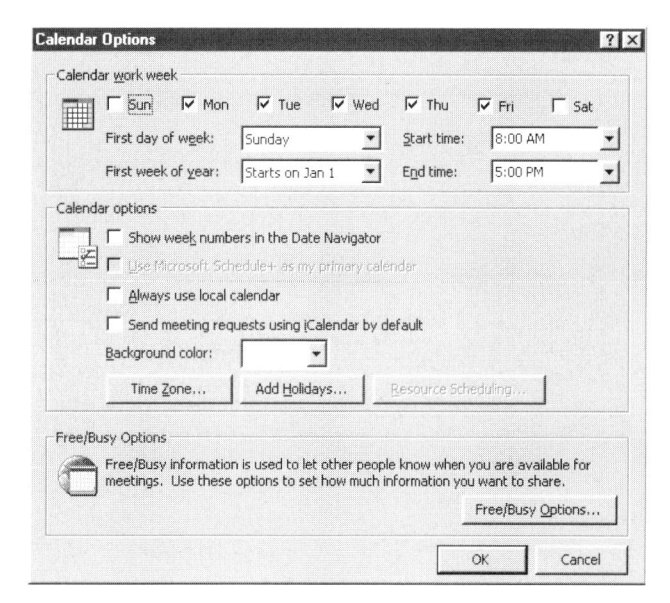

5   Select the Sun check box, clear the Mon and Tue check boxes, and then select the Sat check box.
    The new workdays are selected.
6   Click the First Day Of Week down arrow, and click Wednesday.
    Wednesday is now specified as the first day of the work week.
7   Click the Start Time down arrow, scroll down, and then click 2:00 PM.
8   Click the End Time down arrow, scroll down, and then click 10:00 PM.
    The start and end time of each work day is specified.
9   Click the Background Color down arrow, and click a blue section.
    The background of the Calendar will now be blue.
10 Click the Add Holidays button.
    The Add Holidays To Calendar dialog box appears.

> You can select holidays for as many countries as you want.

11 Select the United Kingdom check box, clear the United States check box, and then click OK.

A progress bar might appear while the holidays from the United Kingdom are added to the Calendar.

12 In the Calendar Options dialog box, click OK.

13 In the Options dialog box, click OK.

The new options that you specified are activated. Notice that the time slots in the Appointment Area are now blue and that the days Wednesday through Sunday appear as the work week days.

tip

If you decide that you no longer want to see holidays for a specific country, you can quickly delete the holidays from the Calendar. On the View menu, point to Current View, and click Events. Click the Location column heading to sort by country, select all holidays for the country that you want to remove, and then press Delete.

14 On the Standard toolbar, click the Day button.

The Calendar is displayed in Day view.

15 Using either the left or right arrow in the Date Navigator, display the day May 1, 2000, and click it.

The Calendar displays the United Kingdom's May Day Bank Holiday.

> You can also display the current date by right-clicking the Appointment Area of the Calendar and clicking Go To Today.

16 On the Standard toolbar, click the Go To Today button.

The current day is displayed.

Scheduling Multiday and Recurring Events

Events are items on your Calendar that are important to remember, but they do not necessarily need to have time blocked out for them. Some examples of events include birthdays and anniversaries. Multiday events might include vacations and conventions. To set up a multiday event, right-click the Appointment Area of the Calendar, and on the shortcut menu, click New All Day Event. In the event window, click the Start Time down arrow, and click the first day of the event. Click the End Time down arrow, and click the last day of the event. Type a subject, and select the rest of the event information as desired. Click the Save And Close button.

Frequently, events that you schedule occur again at a specific time interval, such as birthdays. Making a birthday a recurring event will ensure that you are reminded each year for a specified number of years. To create a recurring event, right-click the Appointment Area of the Calendar, and on the shortcut menu, click New Recurring Event. In the Appointment Recurrence dialog box, set the desired recurrence options, and then click OK. Enter the rest of the event data, and click the Save And Close button.

Lesson 3 Using Advanced Calendar Features   3.5

Changing Time Zone Settings

OL2000E.5.2

You can change the time zone used by Outlook if you move to a different location or if the current time zone is incorrect. When you change the time zone in Outlook, you are changing it for all other programs as well—just as if you had changed the time zone by using the Date/Time Properties dialog box in Microsoft Windows. You can also add a second time zone to the Calendar, which is useful if you frequently work with people in a different time zone or country, or if you are planning a business trip and want to view the time difference.

For example, reservation agents at Lakewood Mountains Resort frequently phone guests to confirm upcoming reservations. Lakewood Mountains Resort is located in California and has many visitors from France. So reservation agents have set up France as an additional time zone so that they can make sure they call guests at reasonable hours.

In this exercise, you add the time zone for Paris to your Calendar as a second time zone.

1   On the Tools menu, click Options.

    The Options dialog box appears.

2   Click the Calendar Options button.

    The Calendar Options dialog box appears.

3   Click the Time Zone button.

    The Time Zone dialog box appears.

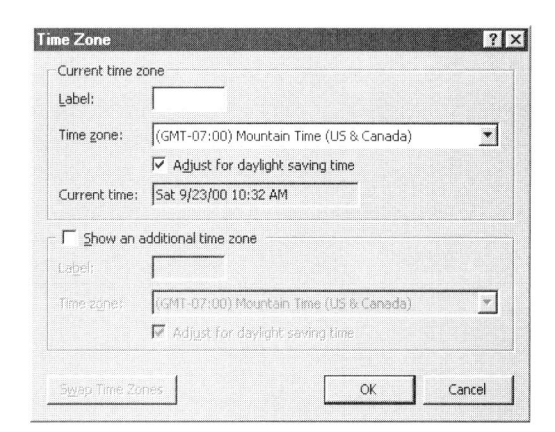

The settings in your Time Zone dialog box might be different than those in the illustration shown here, depending on where you are taking this class.

If you decide you no longer want to show an additional time zone, simply clear the Show An Additional Time Zone check box.

4   Select the Show An Additional Time Zone check box.

5   In the Show Additional Time Zone section, click in the Label box, and type **France**.

6   Click the Time Zone down arrow, scroll down, click the line (GMT + 01:00) Brussels, Copenhagen, Madrid, Paris, and then click OK.

7   In the Calendar Options dialog box, click OK.

8 In the Options dialog box, click OK.

The time zone information for France now appears in the Calendar.

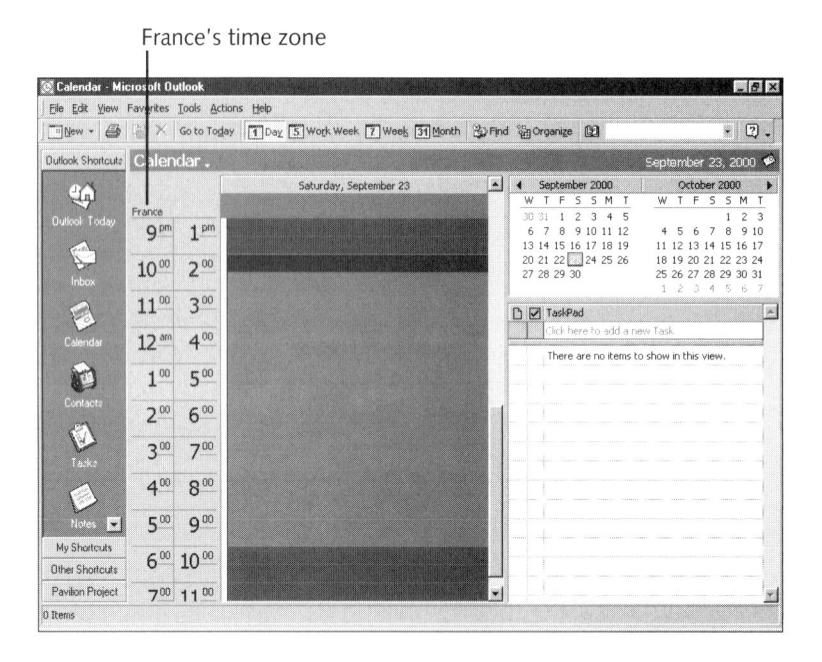

France's time zone

Scheduling Online Meetings Using NetMeeting

OL2000E.3.3

In addition to using Calendar to schedule meetings with participants who can attend a meeting in person, you can also schedule an online meeting for those whom you know will not be able to attend the meeting in person. For example, the Lakewood Mountains Resort is planning to host a seminar for the hotel industry on how to attract international guests. The guest relations manager at Lakewood Mountains Resort has a business associate in Ireland whom she knows would like to attend this seminar, but who won't be able to make the trip from Ireland to California. As an alternative, she invited her associate to attend the conference via an online meeting.

To conduct such a meeting, you can use Microsoft NetMeeting. NetMeeting is an add-on program that comes with Microsoft Internet Explorer. Using NetMeeting, you can conduct meetings over the Internet or over an intranet. NetMeeting supports two-way communication among meeting participants by using sound and video. To communicate in this way, you must have a sound card, speakers, a microphone, and a video camera installed on your computer. If you do not have the following items, you can still exchange information by typing messages in a **chat window** (a window used to exchange typed messages instantaneously), drawing on an electronic **Whiteboard** (a blank screen that simulates marker boards used in classrooms or conference rooms), or sharing files and applications.

Lesson 3 Using Advanced Calendar Features 3.7

You can schedule an online meeting within Outlook. The steps for scheduling an online meeting are similar to the steps for scheduling a normal meeting using the Calendar. Simply follow the same steps you would for a normal meeting and then specify that the meeting will be held online using NetMeeting. You can set up a reminder in Outlook to remind each attendee before the meeting is about to occur. When it is time for the meeting, the organizer will start by opening the meeting request, and then clicking Start Meeting on the Actions menu. Other participants join the meeting by opening the meeting in the Calendar and clicking Join Meeting on the Actions menu.

important

You must be set up for NetMeeting before you begin this exercise. To set up NetMeeting, start Internet Explorer 5. Then on the File menu, point to New, and click Internet Call. Follow the steps in the wizard.

In this exercise, you schedule an online meeting with your class partner using NetMeeting.

1 In the Calendar, display next Thursday. (Remember: The calendar runs from Wednesday to Sunday now.)

Remember to click the 5:00 P.M. time slot for your time zone—not France's.

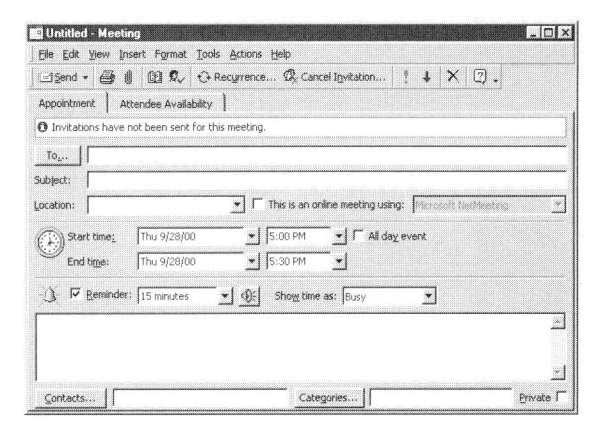

2 In the Calendar, click the 5:00 P.M. time slot.

3 On the Standard toolbar, click the down arrow to the right of the New Appointment button.

4 Click Meeting Request.

The meeting window appears.

You can also display the meeting window by right-clicking the time at which the meeting is to begin (in the Appointment Area) and clicking New Meeting Request on the shortcut menu.

5 Click the To button.

The Select Attendees And Resources dialog box appears.

6 Scroll to see your class partner's name if necessary, and click your class partner's name.

7 Click the Required button, and click OK.

The meeting request will be sent your class partner.

8 Click in the Subject box, and type **Environmental NetMeeting**.

9 Select the This Is An Online Meeting Using check box.

The meeting window expands, showing more options. Notice that Microsoft NetMeeting already appears in the This Is An Online Meeting Using box.

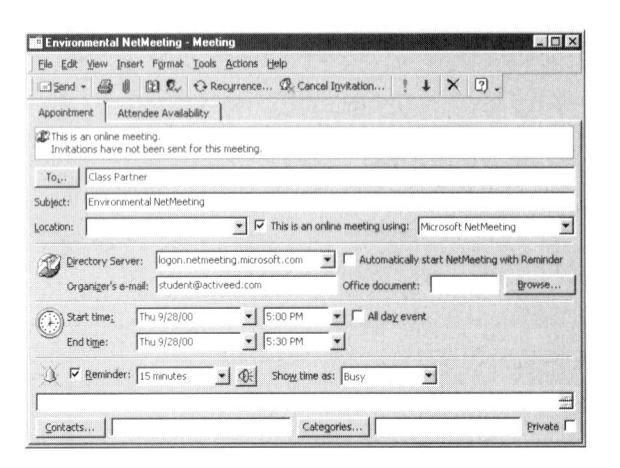

> If you select the Reminder check box and the Automatically Start NetMeeting With Reminder check box, Outlook will remind you and the attendees that you have fifteen minutes (or any other time you specify) before NetMeeting automatically starts.

10 Click the second End Time down arrow, and click 7:00 PM (2 Hours).

11 On the Standard toolbar in the meeting window, click the Send button.

The NetMeeting request is sent to your class partner. The meeting is displayed in your Calendar.

Using NetMeeting

To actually participate in a NetMeeting, you must first start NetMeeting and then set up NetMeeting by entering your personal information in the NetMeeting dialog box. You start NetMeeting by right-clicking an online meeting, which is not currently selected, in the Calendar and then clicking Start NetMeeting. (If you don't have an existing meeting in the Calendar, you can access NetMeeting by starting Internet Explorer 5. Then on the File menu, point to New, and click Internet Call.)

You can also use an **ILS** (Internet Locator Service) **directory** to start a NetMeeting (an ILS directory lists users who are currently connected to a particular computer that serves as a contact point for NetMeeting participants) or you can use an **IP address** to start a NetMeeting. (An IP address uses numbers and dots to identify your computer on an internal, local-area network and on the Internet. You must know both your IP address and a meeting participant's IP address.)

To start a NetMeeting using an ILS directory:

1 If necessary, go to ils.microsoft.com. (In NetMeeting, on the Call menu, click Log On To Microsoft Internet Directory.)

2 On the Call menu, click Directory, select the person you're calling from the list, and then click the Call button.

(continued)

continued

To start a NetMeeting using an IP address:

1   Exchange IP address information with your contact. (To find your IP address, start NetMeeting and then, on the Help menu, click About Windows NetMeeting. Your IP Address will be listed at the bottom of the About Windows NetMeeting dialog box after the text IP Addresses.)

2   Type your contact's IP address in the Address text box, and click the Place Call button. Your contact will have to answer the call.

Place Call

To find out more information about how to set up and use NetMeeting, use the online Help in Outlook and search for *NetMeeting*.

Scheduling Appointments to Watch Broadcasts Using NetShow

OL2000E.3.4

NetShow is a specification developed by Microsoft that transfers multimedia content over the Internet in a steady, continuous stream. NetShow is a broadcast of content from an Internet or intranet site in either audio or video format. By using NetShow, you can watch broadcasted presentations, listen to radio programs, or watch distance learning training seminars at home or at the office. NetShow is useful if you want to create your own broadcast and show it to someone with Internet access. For example, the customer service manager at Lakewood Mountains Resort created a NetShow about how to handle difficult customers. New employees watch this NetShow as part of their training.

As part of the setup process for scheduling a NetShow broadcast, you must provide the Web address where the broadcast will occur. As with NetMeeting, you schedule NetShow broadcasts using the Calendar. You can send reminders to attendees, and you can have the broadcast start automatically.

You can see a list of NetShows by typing NetShow in the search box at the top of the MSN home page (*www.msn.com*).

The organizer of a NetShow meeting and the meeting attendees can start or view the broadcast by opening the meeting in the Calendar, and then clicking the View NetShow button on the Standard toolbar.

To schedule a NetShow:

1   To the right of the New Appointment button, click the down arrow, and click Meeting Request.

2   Click the To button.

3   Select attendees, clicking the Required button after each one, and click OK.

4   In the Subject box, type the meeting subject.

(continued)

continued

5 Select the This Is An Online Meeting Using check box, click the This Is An Online Meeting Using down arrow, and click NetShow Services.

6 In the Event Address box, type the Web address of the NetShow.

7 Click the first Start Time down arrow, and click a start date. Click the second Start Time down arrow, and click a time.

8 Click the first End Time down arrow, and click an end date (if necessary). Click the second End Time down arrow, and click an end time.

9 On the Standard toolbar in the meeting window, click Send.

Sharing Calendar Information over the Internet

OL2000E.3.2

Outlook has a component called **iCalendar** (Internet Calendaring), which allows you to send meeting requests and receive responses from invitees outside your company's network. For example, the events coordinator at Lakewood Mountains Resort sent a meeting request to her son's English teacher to schedule a time to discuss her son's performance.

important
iCalendar won't work properly if you send a meeting request to a recipient who uses a mail program that does not have iCalendar.

When you send a meeting request over the Internet, Outlook sends an iCalendar attachment that contains the meeting information. When an invitee receives a meeting request, he or she can open or save the attachment to his or her hard disk, and then either accept or decline the invitation. If the invitee accepts, he or she can then add the meeting to his or her own Calendar.

In this exercise, you create a meeting and send the meeting as an iCalendar attachment to your class partner. Then you accept a meeting request that your class partner sends to you.

1 Display next Wednesday in Day view.

2 In the Calendar, click the 7:00 P.M. time slot.

3 On the Standard toolbar, click the down arrow to the right of the New Appointment button, and click Meeting Request.

   A meeting window appears.

Lesson 3 Using Advanced Calendar Features   3.11

4 Click the To button.

The Select Attendees And Resources dialog box appears.

5 If necessary, scroll down until you see your class partner's name, and then click your class partner's name.

6 Click the Required button, and click OK.

The meeting request will be sent to your class partner.

7 Click in the Subject box, and type **Ski Club Meeting**.

8 Click in the Location box, and type **Lakewood Mountains Resort Lounge**.

9 Click the second End Time down arrow, and click 8:00 P.M. (1 Hour).

10 In the meeting window, on the Actions menu, click Forward As iCalendar.

A message window appears. Your class partner's e-mail address is already inserted, and the iCalendar appears as an attachment.

11 Click the Send button.

The meeting request will be sent to your class partner.

Close

12 In the top-right corner of the meeting window, click the Close button.

An alert box appears, asking whether you want to save changes.

13 Click No.

Normally you would click Yes in the alert box so that the meeting would appear in your Calendar, but because your class partner is going to send this same meeting request to you, you need your Calendar to be open on this day for this exercise to work properly. Otherwise, when you open the iCalendar attachment from your partner, a meeting window will appear, alerting you that you already have a meeting on that day (the meeting *you* tried to schedule). Normally you would not see this result. By clicking No, you will be able to be both the meeting organizer and the invitee.

14 Display the Inbox, and on the Standard toolbar, click the Send/Receive button.

A meeting request from your class partner appears in the Inbox.

15 Open the attachment in the Ski Club Meeting message.

A window appears.

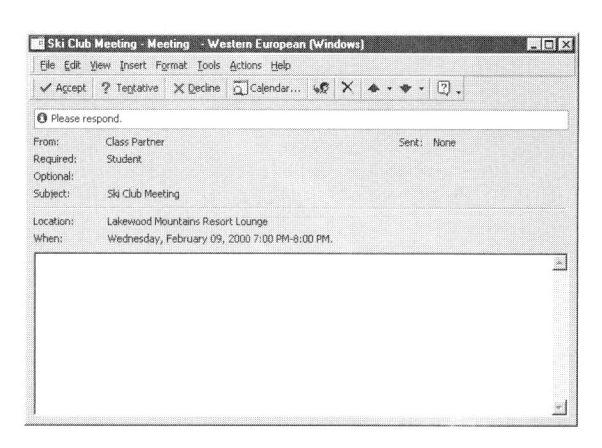

You can also click the Tentative button if you think that you might be able to attend the meeting, or click the Decline button if you can't attend the meeting. If you want to quickly look at your Calendar to see if you are available, you can click the Calendar button.

16 On the Standard toolbar, click the Accept button.

An alert box appears, informing you that the meeting will be added to your Calendar and asking whether you want to include comments with your response. The Send The Response Now option is already selected.

After the response is sent, the meeting organizer can see who has responded to the meeting by double-clicking the meeting in the Calendar, clicking the Attendee Availability tab, and clicking the Show Attendee Status option.

17 Click OK, and click the Send/Receive button.

An e-mail message appears in your Inbox stating that your class partner has accepted.

18 Display the Calendar.

19 In the Calendar, display next Wednesday.

The meeting appears in your Calendar.

Using the Calendar on the Web

You can save a Calendar as a Web page if you want to make it available publicly or to everybody on an intranet. This can be especially useful if your organization uses an intranet to share documents as Web pages, because you can make your Calendar available to everybody even if some people on the intranet do not use Outlook. For example, the events coordinator at Lakewood Mountains Resort saved a Web calendar that details the schedule for an employee volleyball tournament. Now all employees who want to view the schedule can simply type the calendar's Web address in their Web browser.

When you save the Calendar as a Web page, Outlook converts the Calendar to **HTML**. HTML is a markup language used to display documents on the Internet. Before you save your Calendar as a Web page, you must schedule the appointments that you want to display.

To save a calendar as a Web page:

1 Add appointments to the Calendar, as necessary.

2 On the File menu, click Save As Web Page to display the Save As Web Page dialog box.

3 In the Duration section, specify a start date and end date.

4 In the Options section, specify any additional options.

5 In the Calendar Title box, select the current text, and type a title for the Calendar.

If an alert box appears telling you that you need to install the feature that will publish the Calendar to the Web, click Yes and insert the Microsoft Office 2000 or Microsoft Outlook CD-ROM into the disk drive.

6 Click the Browse button to navigate to a location in which to store the file, type a file name (don't add spaces in the file name) in the File Name box, and then click Select.

7 Click Save.

Lesson Wrap-Up

This lesson covered how to customize different Calendar options and how to change a time zone or add a second time zone; how to schedule online meetings with NetMeeting; how to schedule appointments to watch or listen to broadcasts using NetShow; and how to share Calendar information over the Internet.

If you are continuing to the next lesson:

- On the Standard toolbar, click the Go To Today button.
  The current day appears in the Calendar.

If you are not continuing to other lessons:

- In the top-right corner of the Outlook window, click the Close button. Outlook closes.

Lesson Glossary

broadcast In NetShow, information that is transmitted via audio or video to a listening or viewing audience via the Internet.

chat window In NetMeeting, a window that you can use to type messages and to view messages that you've received. In a chat window, messages are sent and received instantly, just as if you were having a phone conversation.

events Activities that have a 24-hour or longer duration, such as a birthday, seminar, or vacation.

HTML A markup language that is used by Web browsers to format and display content on Web sites.

iCalendar (Internet Calendaring) A component of Outlook and an Internet standard format that lets you send meeting requests over the Internet to people outside your company's network.

ILS directory A list of users who are currently connected to a particular computer that serves as a contact point for NetMeeting participants.

IP address An identifier made up of numbers and dots (such as 192.161.255.0) used to identify a computer on a network and used by NetMeeting to identify a user's computer during a NetMeeting.

multimedia A presentation of text, graphics, video, animation, and sound, or any combination of these.

NetMeeting An add-on program, supplied with Internet Explorer, that you can use to conduct meetings over the Internet or over an intranet by using text messages, sound, and video, or all of these elements.

NetShow A specification developed by Microsoft that transfers multimedia content over the Internet in a steady, continuous stream.

Whiteboard A blank screen used in NetMeeting that simulates marker boards used in classrooms or conference rooms. You can use the mouse pointer to draw on the Whiteboard.

Quick Quiz

1. What is multimedia?
2. Why are NetMeetings used?
3. What is NetShow?
4. What is an event?
5. When you save a Calendar as a Web page, what does Outlook convert the Calendar information to?
6. What do you use iCalendar for?
7. What is one way you can customize the Calendar?

Putting It All Together

Exercise 1: Modify the following Calendar options: change the work week to go from Tuesday through Friday, 9:00 A.M. to 7:00 P.M.; designate Tuesday as the first day of the work week; change the background color to yellow; and display a second time zone labeled Tokyo. (Select the appropriate time zone.)

Exercise 2: Invite your class partner (or a friend if you are not in class) to an online meeting to discuss some of the features of NetMeeting; the meeting will be held the second Tuesday of next month from 1:00 P.M. to 2:00 P.M. Using iCalendar, invite your instructor (or a second friend) to a canned food drive meeting, which will be held in the parking lot the first Thursday of next month from noon to 12:15 P.M.

LESSON 4

Using Advanced Contacts Features

After completing this lesson, you will be able to:

✔ Flag contacts for follow up.
✔ Sort contacts.
✔ Link contacts with other Outlook items.
✔ Use contacts in a mail merge.
✔ Filter contacts for a mail merge.
✔ Perform a mail merge.

Once you start creating contact records in Microsoft Outlook, your Contacts folder can grow to be pretty large, making it difficult to locate specific contacts quickly. Fortunately Outlook has several features that make it easy for you to organize and manage contacts. One way to manage contacts is to **flag**, or mark with a flag icon, certain contacts to indicate that some follow-up action relating to the contact needs to be taken. For example, after listening to all her voice mail messages, the marketing manager at Lakewood Mountains Resort flags the contact records for the people she needs to call back. By flagging these contacts, she won't have to write down reminders. In fact, Outlook will provide a visual reminder on the screen when she needs to return a call.

Another way to manage your contacts is to organize, or **sort**, the contacts by certain categories, such as job title, company, or mailing address, among others. You can also sort contacts in ascending or descending order so that you can quickly locate them. You can even sort contacts by Follow-Up Flag. You can also manage your contacts by linking them to other Outlook items, such as other contacts, tasks, or e-mail messages. For example, you could link contact information for a manager with contact information for the manager's assistant. Another way to organize contacts is by filtering them. When you **filter** contacts, Outlook displays only contacts that meet criteria that you specify. You can filter contacts to quickly locate a contact or to perform a **mail merge**, in which you use your contacts to quickly create form letters, mailing labels, or envelopes.

In this lesson, you will learn how to flag contacts for follow up. You will also learn how to sort and link contacts and how to filter contacts prior to performing a mail merge. You will also learn how to merge filtered contacts with mailing labels and envelopes.

Your Outlook folders should already contain the Outlook items (tasks, e-mail messages, and contact records) that are necessary to complete the exercises in this lesson. If you need to add these items to your Outlook folders, see the "Using the CD-ROM" section at the beginning of this book.

Practice files for the lesson

No practice files are required to complete the exercises in this lesson.

OC2000E.6.1

If you do not mark a flag as completed by the due date, Outlook displays the flagged contact information in red text.

Flagging Contacts for Follow Up

When you flag a contact, you can also specify the kind of follow-up action you will take, along with a due date and time for the follow-up action. You can specify whether you're flagging a contact to remind yourself to make a phone call, arrange a meeting, send an e-mail message, send a letter, or perform some other action. If you're performing an action not listed in Outlook, you can type in your own description, such as *Send flowers*. For example, the human resources manager at Lakewood Mountains Resort wants to remind herself to arrange a meeting with a contact, so she flags the contact. When she next looks at her list of contacts, a flag and the text *Arrange meeting* will appear below the contact's name. If she decides to include a due date and time, Outlook will display an on-screen reminder at the designated time.

Outlook displays flagged contacts differently, depending on the view you currently have selected. In Address Cards and Detailed Address Cards views, flagged contacts appear with the text *Flag for Follow Up: [description of the action that you are supposed to perform]*. In all other views, a red flag icon appears in the Flag Status column to the left of the contact.

After you have completed a follow-up activity, you can mark the flag as complete. By marking a flag as complete, you can keep a record of completed items related to a contact. You can also clear a flag if you have performed the action and no longer need to keep a record of the action performed.

In this exercise, you flag contacts to remind yourself to call Ketan Dalal by tomorrow and to send flowers to Anne L. Paper by next Monday. You also create a past due flag to send Lane Sacksteder a birthday card. You then mark a flag as complete.

1 Display the Contacts folder.

Flag For Follow Up

2 Click the contact *Ketan Dalal*, and click the Flag For Follow Up button on the Standard toolbar.

The Flag For Follow Up dialog box appears.

You can also display the Flag For Follow Up dialog box by right-clicking the contact and clicking Flag For Follow Up on the shortcut menu.

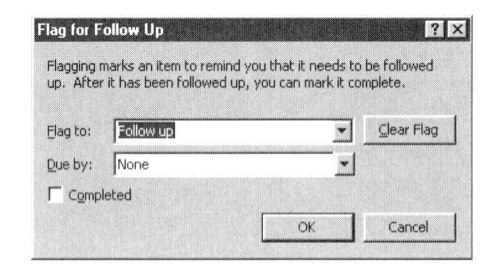

3 Click the Flag To down arrow, and click Call.

4 Click the Due By down arrow, click tomorrow's date, and then click OK.

The text *Follow Up Flag: Call* appears under the contact's name.

5 Double-click the contact *Ketan Dalal*.

The contact window appears with a *Call by [Date]* message.

6 Close the contact window.

7 Click the contact *Anne L. Paper*, and click the Flag For Follow Up button on the Standard toolbar.

Flag For Follow Up

The Flag For Follow Up dialog box appears.

8 In the Flag To box, type **Send flowers**.

9 Click the Due By down arrow, click Monday of next week, and then click OK.

The text *Follow Up Flag: Send flowers* appears under the contact's name.

10 Double-click the contact *Anne L. Paper*.

The contact window appears with a *Send flowers by [Date]* message.

11 Close the contact window.

12 Click the contact *Lane Sacksteder*, and click the Flag For Follow Up button on the Standard toolbar.

Flag For Follow Up

The Flag for Follow Up dialog box appears.

13 In the Flag To box, type **Send birthday card**.

14 Click the Due By down arrow, click Tuesday of last week, and then click OK.

An alert box appears, telling you that no reminder will be set because the specified date and time are in the past.

15 Click OK.

The text *Follow Up Flag: Send birthday card* appears under the contact's name. The *Send birthday card* text and the contact information appear in red, indicating that the action is past due.

16 Double-click the contact *Lane Sacksteder*.

The contact window appears with a *Send birthday card by [Date]* message.

17 Close the contact window.

18 Right-click the contact *Ketan Dalal*, and click Flag Complete on the shortcut menu that appears.

You can remove a flag by right-clicking the contact and clicking Clear Flag on the shortcut menu.

19 Double-click the contact *Ketan Dalal*.

The message in the contact window has changed to describe the date the action was due and when it was completed.

20 Close the contact window.

Sorting Contacts

In Lesson 1, you sorted contacts in the By Category view. You probably noticed that when you displayed contacts (or the contents of any other Outlook folder) by category, the contact records were displayed in a table (rows and column) format. The views Phone List, By Company, By Location, and By Follow-Up Flag also display contact records in table format. The following figure is in By Follow-Up Flag view. Notice that the row under the banner displays column headings. If you position the mouse pointer over a column heading, a ScreenTip appears and displays the text *Sort By: [name of column]*—for example, *Sort By: Flag Status* (as shown below). If you click the column heading, Outlook will display the contacts related to the column in ascending or descending order.

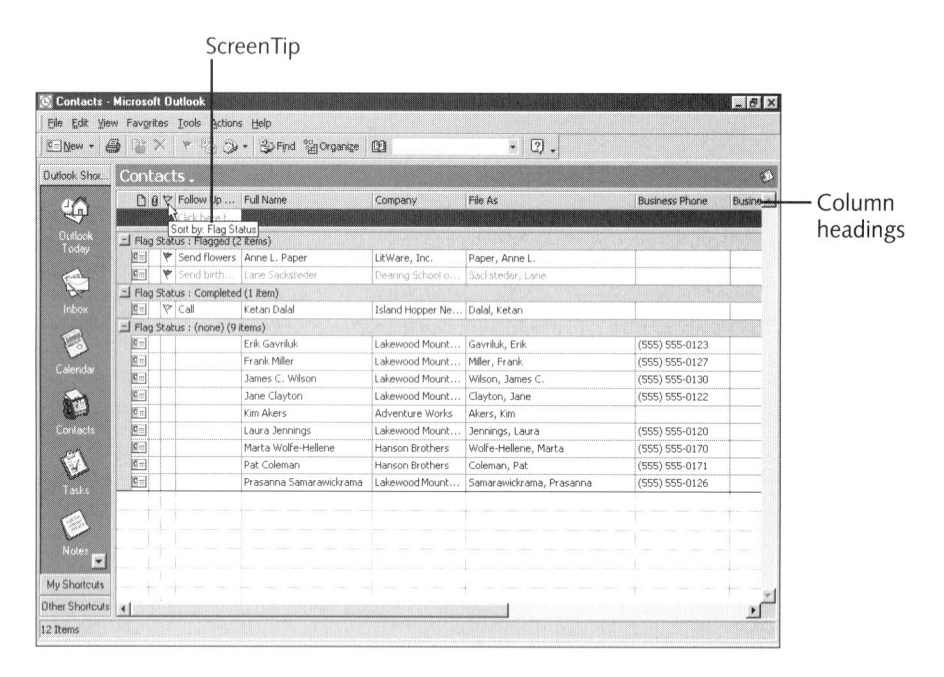

Address Cards view (the default) and Detailed Address Cards view do not display contact records in a table format. Consequently, you sort the contacts in these views differently. Because there are no column headings in these views, you must use the Sort dialog box to sort the contact records.

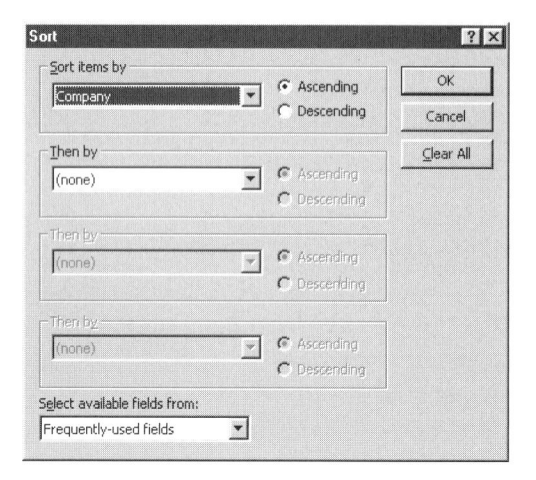

Lesson 4 Using Advanced Contacts Features 4.5

You can also use the Sort dialog box in any view to sort contact records using multiple criteria. For example, the marketing director at Lakewood Mountain Resort wanted to find a contact that she knew didn't have an e-mail address and knew that the contact's last name started with the letter "R." To find this contact, she sorted the contacts by e-mail address in ascending order. This sort displayed all the contacts without an e-mail address at the top of the contact list but in no particular order. She then sorted the contacts by last name in descending order, which caused the contacts without e-mail addresses to appear in alphabetical order. This two-level sort brought the marketing director's target contact closer to the top of the contact list.

In this exercise, you sort contacts in the By Follow-Up Flag view. You then sort the contacts in Address Cards view.

1 On the View menu, point to Current View, and click By Follow-Up Flag.

The contacts appear in By Follow-Up Flag view with current flagged items first, completed flagged items next, and unflagged items last.

Note that the flag for the completed activity is now gray and that the flags for activities that have not been completed are red.

Sort By: Flag Status

The Flag Status column heading is located under the Contacts banner and looks like a flag. If you rest the mouse pointer on the column heading, a ScreenTip will appear that contains the name of the column.

2 Click the Sort By: Flag Status column heading (indicated by the flag icon).

The records are sorted so that unflagged items appear first, completed items next, and current flagged items are last.

3 Click the Sort By: Flag Status column heading again.

The flagged records appear at the top of the list and are sorted by flag status.

4 Click the Sort By: Company column heading (indicated by the word *Company*).

The contacts remain sorted by flag. Within each flag group, the contacts are sorted in ascending order by company.

> When you sort records using File As, the records are sorted by the contents of the File As box in the contact record. By default, the records are usually sorted by last name when you use File As to sort.

5 Click the Sort By: File As column heading (indicated by the words *File As*).

The flagged records remain at the top of the list, and the contacts are sorted in ascending order by last name.

6 On the View menu, point to Current View, and click Address Cards.

The contacts appear in Address Cards view.

7 Right-click any blank area in the Contacts folder, and click Sort on the shortcut menu that appears.

The Sort dialog box appears.

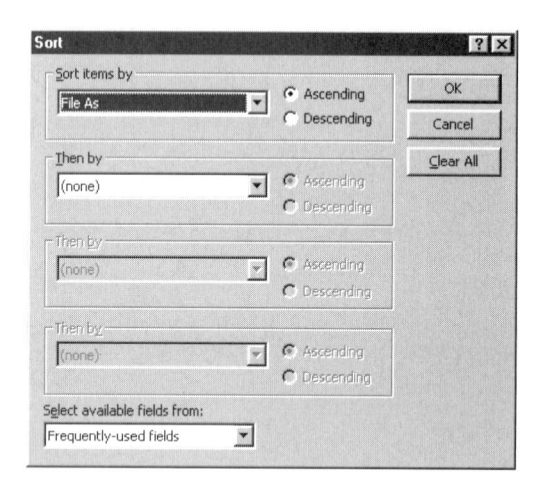

8 Click the Sort Items By down arrow, scroll up, and then click E-mail.

9 In the Sort Items By section, click the Descending option, and click OK.

The contacts are sorted in descending order by e-mail address. The contacts that do not have e-mail addresses appear at the end of the list. These contacts are in descending order by last name.

> You can clear all the current sort options by clicking the Clear All button in the Sort dialog box.

10 Right-click any blank area in the Contacts folder, and click Sort on the shortcut menu that appears.

The Sort dialog box appears.

11 Click the Then By down arrow, if necessary scroll down, and then click File As.

12 In the Then By section, click the Ascending option, and click OK.

The contacts that do not have e-mail messages are sorted by last name in ascending order.

Lesson 4 Using Advanced Contacts Features 4.7

Linking Contacts with Other Outlook Items

OL2000E.6.3

You can create a relationship between, or **link,** a contact record and any Outlook item such as another contact record, a task, or an e-mail message. When you link a contact, you can:

- Designate who is responsible for completing an item
- Designate who will be affected by an item
- Create relationships between items

Another way to integrate contacts with other Outlook components is to add a vCard to a message; vCards are discussed in Lesson 2, "Using Advanced E-Mail Features."

For example, at the beginning of the week, the office manager at Lakewood Mountains Resort linked the contact record for Marta Wolfe-Hellene at Hanson Brothers to the contact record for Marta's assistant. She also linked Marta to the tasks *Get quote on lobby couch* and *Ask when dining tables will be delivered*. At the end of the week, before she called Marta, she displayed her contact window to remind her of the activities she had linked her to. She saw that she had linked her to two tasks and a contact. When she called, she was unable to reach Marta, so she double-clicked her assistant's name in Marta's contact window. The assistant's contact window appeared, and she then called the assistant to ask her the questions instead.

After you link a contact, you can click the Activities tab in the contact window to view the items to which the contact is linked. In the following illustration, the contact *Marta Wolfe-Hellene* is linked to the contact for her assistant Pat Coleman and is also linked to the task *Get quote on lobby couch* and the task *Ask when dining tables will be delivered.*

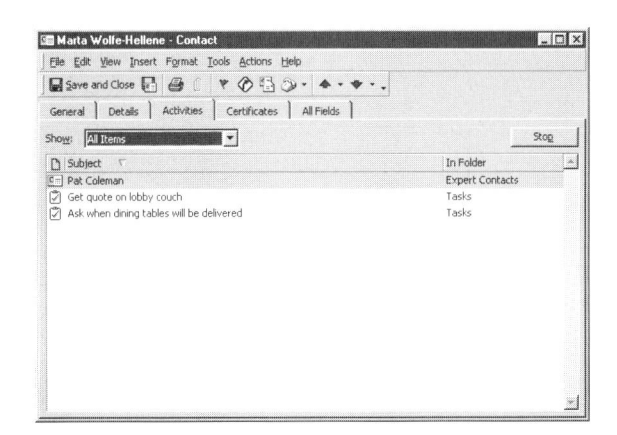

In this exercise, you create two tasks and link a contact to them. You also link a contact to another contact. You then view the items that the contact is linked to on the Activities tab in the contact window.

1 Display the Tasks folder.

2 Click in the box that contains the text *Click Here To Add A New Task*, type **Get quote on lobby couch**, and then press Enter.

The task is created, and the insertion point remains in the first box under the Subject column.

3 Type **Ask when dining tables will be delivered**, and press Enter.

The task is created.

4 Display the Contacts folder.

5 Right-click the contact *Marta Wolfe-Hellene*, point to Link on the shortcut menu that appears, and then click Items.

The Link Items To Contact dialog box appears.

> By default, the Link Items To Contact dialog box shows the contents of the Inbox in the Items list.

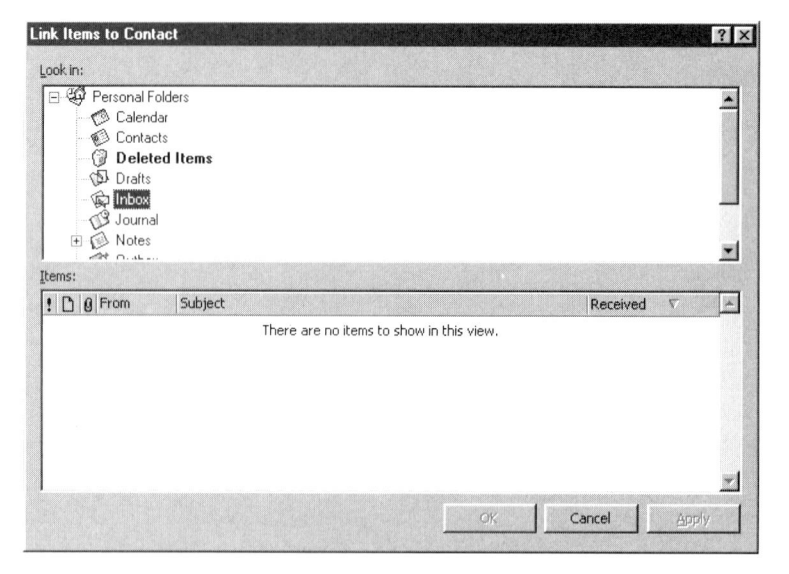

6 In the Look In list, scroll down and click Tasks.

Your tasks appear in the Items list.

7 In the Items list, click the task *Get quote on lobby couch*, and then click the Apply button.

The contact is linked to the task.

8 In the Items list, click the task *Ask when dining tables will be delivered*, and then click the Apply button.

The contact is linked to the task.

> You can select multiple items by pressing Ctrl and clicking all the items to which you want to link the contact.

9 In the Look In list, scroll up and click Contacts.

Your contacts appear in the Items list.

10 In the Items list, click the contact *Pat Coleman*, and then click the Apply button.

The contact *Pat Coleman* is linked to the contact *Marta Wolfe-Hellene*.

> Outlook also links the contact *Marta Wolfe-Hellen* to the contact *Pat Coleman*.

11 Click OK.

The dialog box closes, and the Contacts folder reappears.

Lesson 4 Using Advanced Contacts Features 4.9

12 Double-click the contact *Marta Wolfe-Hellene*.

The contact window opens. Notice that the contact *Pat Coleman* appears in the Contacts box in the bottom of the window.

If you double-click a contact in the Contact box, Outlook displays that contact's window.

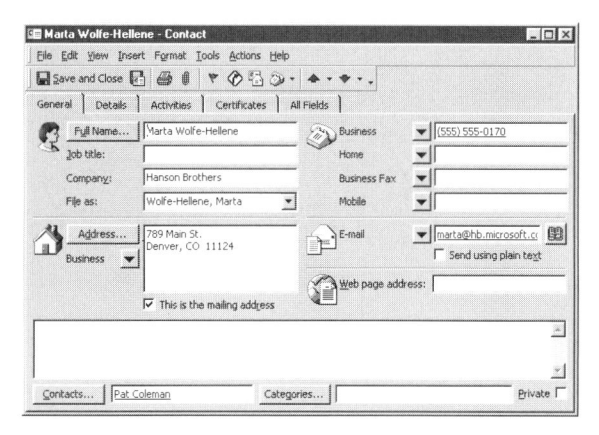

13 In the contact window, click the Activities tab.

Outlook searches for the items to which the contact is linked. The contact and the two tasks appear on the Activities tab.

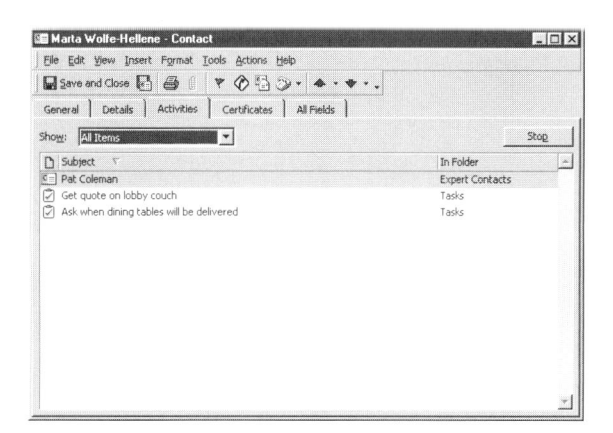

14 Close the contact window.

tip

Using the Find feature, you can locate a contact in Outlook by entering a full or partial name. On the Standard toolbar, click in the Find A Contact box, type the desired name or partial name, and then press Enter. If Outlook finds more than one contact, the Choose Contact dialog box appears. Click the name of the contact in the Choose Contact dialog box, and click OK. The contact window of the contact that you wanted to find will then open. You can also click the Find A Contact down arrow on the Standard toolbar, and click the name of a contact for which you previously searched.

OL2000E.6.4
OL2000E.8.2

Using Contacts in a Mail Merge

Your contact records collectively form a database that you can use to perform a mail merge, in which you merge and print your contact records onto letters, labels, or envelopes. To create form letters, you need three items: a **main document**, a **data source**, and at least one **field** within the data source. The main document is a file that contains fixed text, such as the body of the form letter. The data source contains records, such as the information for each contact in your Contacts folder. A field is a single item in a record—such as a first name, last name, street address, or home phone. When you prepare a main document for a mail merge, you place codes representing each field into the main document. The codes tell Outlook which fields to insert from the data source into the main document and in which locations.

For example, the marketing director at Lakewood Mountains Resort created a form letter offering a room discount to any guest who stayed at the resort on his or her birthday. After creating the body of the letter in Microsoft Word, the marketing director inserted contact field codes into the form letter, such as the First Name field after the word *Dear*, and the Birthday field after the text *Because your birthday was on*. When she performed the mail merge, Word created a personalized letter for each contact.

If you're creating merge documents that contain *only* fields from the data source, you don't need to create a main document first. For example, in Outlook you can create mailing labels and envelopes without having to create a main document; Word creates the mailing label or envelope document for you when you perform the mail merge. This document formats the records from the data source as you specify. For example, if you perform a merge to create mailing labels, each page of the merge document displays the records just as they will look when they print on the mailing label sheets. If you will be printing addresses on envelopes, the merge document displays the records as they will appear on the printed envelopes.

Filtering Contacts for a Mail Merge

When performing a mail merge, you'll probably want to merge only some contact records. Outlook allows you to filter the contact records so that only those records that you want to include in the merge appear in the Contacts folder. Records that do not appear still exist; however, they won't be included when you perform the mail merge. You can remove the filter later so that you can see all your contact records.

For example, during summer months, the temperatures at Lakewood Mountains Resort are much cooler than in Arizona. So the marketing manager decides to create and send a "beat-the-heat" form letter to prospective guests who live in Arizona, inviting them to cool off at the resort. In Outlook, she applies a filter to her contacts so that contact records appear only if the State field in a record is *AZ*.

There are three ways to filter records before you begin a mail merge. You can:

- Use the Filter dialog box to filter contacts.

■ Filter contacts by holding down the Alt key, and then clicking each contact record that you want to include.

■ Filter contacts by creating a custom folder that contains only those contacts that you want to merge, and display this folder before you perform the merge.

The first approach is the most efficient if your Contacts folder contains several dozen or even hundreds of contact records. The second approach is a quick way to filter records if you have only a few records in your Contacts folder. The third approach is useful if you want to use the same set of contact records for more than one mail merge. With this approach, you won't have to filter the records before performing future mail merges because all the desired records are already stored in the same folder. You can also specify that you want to store the selected contacts in a separate folder when you perform the mail merge the first time. In other words, you don't have to create the folder yourself or move the selected records into the new folder.

You use the Mail Merge Contacts dialog box to select the fields that you want to use in the merge. This dialog box provides a list of more than 100 fields from which to choose, such as Manager's Name, Birthday, and Anniversary. For many mail merges, you'll need only a few of these fields. For instance, to create mailing labels, you need to include only name and address fields. If you want to avoid having to scroll through all the fields in the Mail Merge Contacts dialog box, you can also add or remove fields directly in your Contacts folder by clicking the Contact Fields In Current View option in the Mail Merge Contacts dialog box.

In this exercise, you filter your contacts so that only contacts from California appear. You then hide fields that you won't need for the mailing labels (which you will create in the next exercise).

1 Right-click a blank area of the Contacts folder, and click Filter in the shortcut menu that appears.

The Filter dialog box appears with the insertion point already in the Search For The Words box.

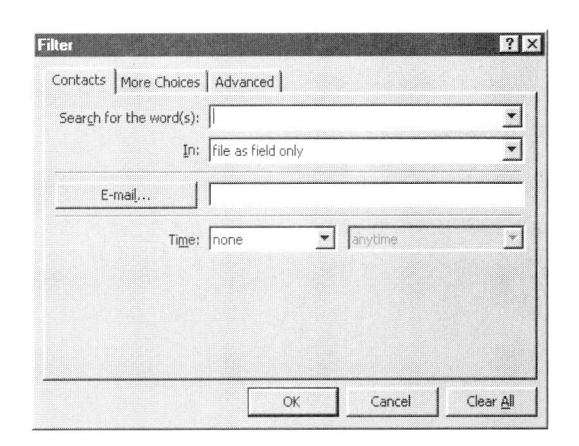

2 Type **CA**, click the In down arrow, and then click Address Fields Only.

3 Click the More Choices tab.

If you select the Match Case check box, Outlook will find only contact information that contains the uppercase letters *CA*. Outlook will ignore any words that contain the letters *ca* if either one of the letters is in lowercase such as Cathy or cable.

4 Select the Match Case check box, and click OK.

Only the records for contacts from California appear.

5 Right-click a blank area of the Contacts folder, and click Show Fields on the shortcut menu that appears.

The Show Fields dialog box appears.

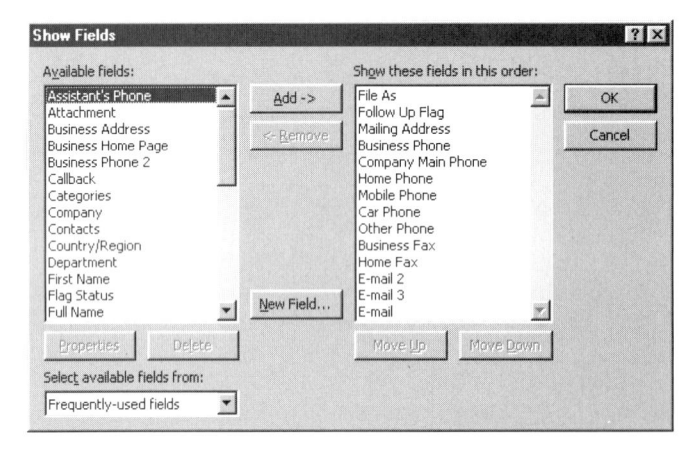

6 In the Show These Fields In This Order list, click Follow Up Flag, and click the Remove button.

The Follow Up Flag field moves to the Available Fields list.

To select more than one field to remove, press Ctrl, click each undesired field, and then click the Remove button.

7 Repeat step 6 to remove the rest of the fields in the Show These Fields In This Order list except Mailing Address.

8 In the Available Fields list, scroll down, click Full Name, click the Add button, click the Move Up button, and then click OK.

Only the Full Name and Mailing Address fields for each contact record are available for merging.

Performing a Mail Merge

To create mailing labels, you use the Mail Merge Contacts dialog box to start the mail merge process.

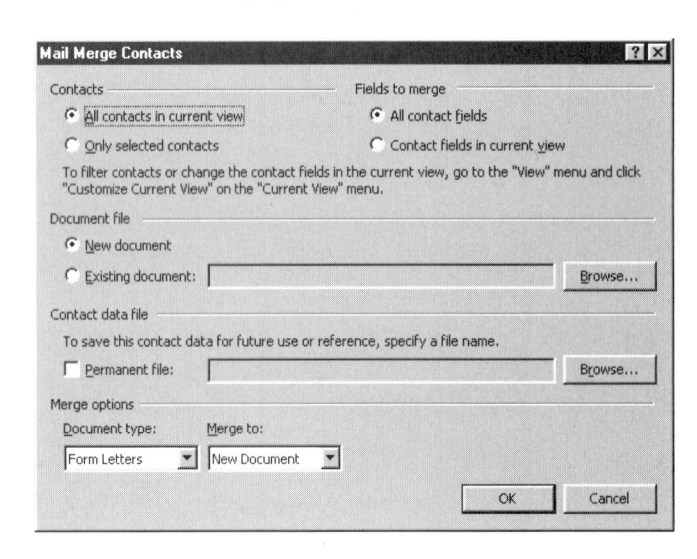

You can select from numerous options in the Mail Merge Contacts dialog box. So before you perform a mail merge, you should understand how all the options affect the results of a mail merge. The following table explains the options that you can choose in the Mail Merge Contacts dialog box.

Option	What It Does Description
All contacts in current view	All the contacts in your current view will be included in the mail merge. If you filter your contacts or put contacts in a custom folder, only the visible contacts will be merged.
Only selected contacts	Only the contacts that you select will be included in the mail merge. You can select multiple nonconsecutive contacts by pressing Ctrl and then clicking the desired contacts. If you select any contacts, this option will already be selected for you.
All contact fields	Outlook will allow you to select from among more than 100 fields to include in the merged document.
Contact fields in current view	Outlook will export only those fields that are displayed in the current view. If you are creating mailing labels, you would probably want to choose this option so that you don't have to locate a few fields from among the entire list of fields.
New document	Microsoft Word will create a new document as a result of the merge. You would use this option to create mailing labels or envelopes.
Existing document	Merges the data into a main document or other existing document. You would select this option if you were merging a data source with a form letter document.
Permanent file	Selected records will be copied to a separate folder so that you can perform this same merge without having to filter records again.
Document type	Lets you create the following document types: form letters, mailing labels, envelopes, or catalogs.
Merge to	Specifies the type of mail merge you want to perform. You can create a merge in a new file, you can create a merge that will be automatically printed, you can merge to an e-mail form letter, or you can merge to a Fax form.

4.14 Microsoft Outlook 2000 Step by Step Courseware Expert Skills Student Guide

In this exercise, you use the contacts that you filtered in the previous exercise to create mailing labels.

1 On the Tools menu, click Mail Merge.

The Mail Merge Contacts dialog box appears.

Note that All Contacts In Current View is already selected.

Note that New Document is already selected.

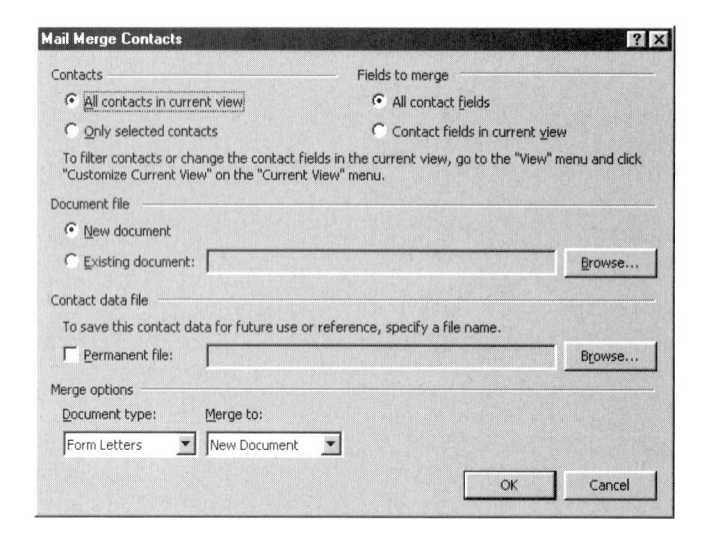

2 In the Fields To Merge section, click the Contact Fields In Current View option.

3 In the Merge Options section, click the Document Type down arrow, click Mailing Labels, and then click OK.

Microsoft Word starts, and the Office Assistant appears telling you that Outlook has created a Mail Merge document.

4 Click Complete Setup.

The Mail Merge Helper dialog box appears.

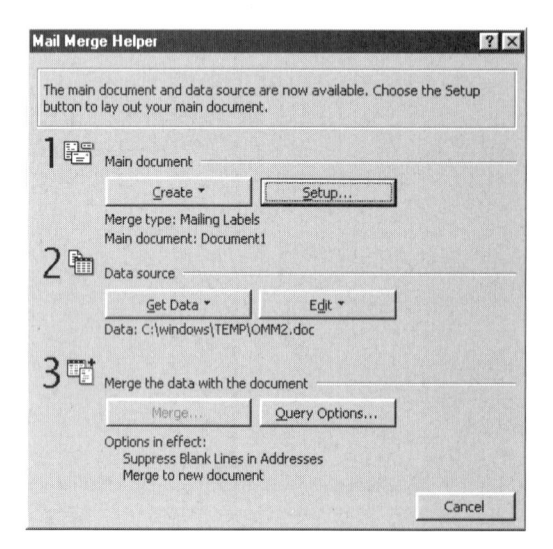

Lesson 4 Using Advanced Contacts Features 4.15

5 Click the Setup button.

The Label Options dialog box appears.

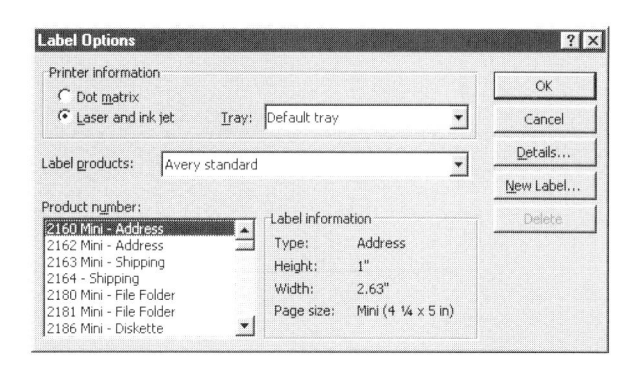

To quickly display the product numbers that begin with the number eight, click in the product number list and type 8.

6 In the Product Number list, scroll down, click 8460 – Address, and then click OK.

The Create Labels dialog box appears.

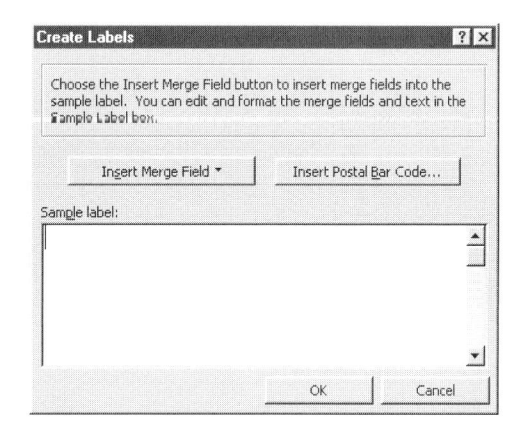

7 Click the Insert Merge Field button, and click Full_Name.

The Full_Name field appears in the Sample Label section.

8 Press Enter.

9 Click the Insert Merge Field button, and click Mailing_Address.

The Mailing_Address merge field appears in the Sample Label section.

10 Click OK.

11 In the Mail Merge Helper dialog box, click the Merge button.

The Merge dialog box appears.

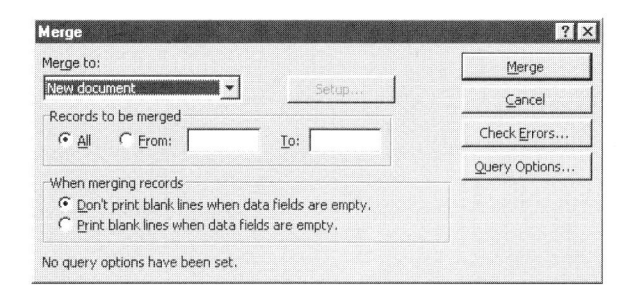

12 Click the Merge button.

The Merge dialog box closes, and the labels appear in a new Word document.

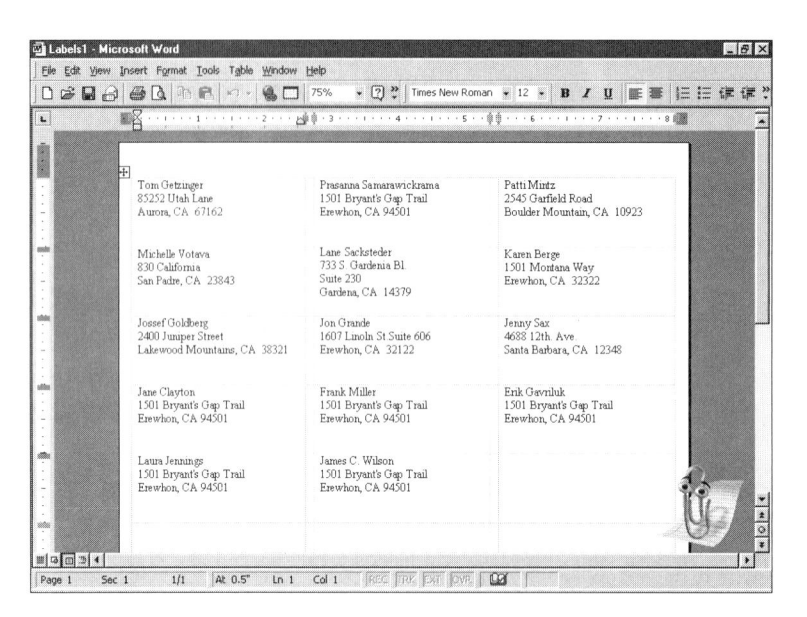

You would normally put label sheets in the printer prior to printing the labels, but for this classroom exercise, you will print the labels on a blank sheet of 8-1/2-by-11-inch paper.

Print

13 On the Standard toolbar, click the Print button.

14 Close all open Microsoft Word documents without saving changes.

tip

You can quickly generate a letter in Word for a selected contact in Outlook. Begin by selecting the desired contact. On the Actions menu, click New Letter To Contact. The Microsoft Word Letter Wizard will start. In the Letter Wizard dialog boxes, you can select a format and add any other special information to the letter.

Lesson Wrap-Up

This lesson covered how to flag contacts for follow up, how to sort and filter contacts, and how to merge contacts with form letters and envelopes.

If you are continuing to the next lesson:

1 Right-click any blank area of the Contacts folder, and click Filter on the shortcut menu that appears.

2 In the Filter dialog box, click Clear All, and click OK.

If you are not continuing to other lessons:

1 Right-click any blank area of the contacts folder, and click Filter on the shortcut menu that appears.

2 In the Filter dialog box, click Clear All, and click OK.

3 In the top-right corner of the Outlook window, click the Close button. Outlook closes.

Close

Lesson Glossary

data source A place where records and fields that can be used in a mail merge, such as each contact in the Contacts folder, are kept.

field A single item of data in a record, such as a first name, last name, or street address.

filter To restrict records to just those that meet specific criteria.

flag To mark a contact for a follow-up action.

link A relationship between a contact and one or more other Outlook items.

mail merge A process that integrates contacts (the data source) with a main document or a new document to create form letters, mailing labels, and envelopes.

main document A file that contains fixed text, such as the body of a form letter, and field codes that indicate which fields should be inserted from a source document and where the fields will go.

sort The process of organizing Outlook items alphabetically, numerically, or by flag status.

Quick Quiz

1 What is one way to quickly locate contacts?

2 What happens when you filter contacts?

3 Can you sort contacts by clicking column headings while in Address Cards view? Explain your answer.

4 How can you limit the number of contacts used in a mail merge?

5 What does flagging mean?

6 When you have completed the follow-up action specified by a flag, what should you do to the flag?

7 What is a mail merge?

Putting It All Together

Exercise 1: View the detailed address cards for all your contacts, sort them by business address and then by last name. Flag the contact Kim Akers to remind you to send him a get well card tomorrow.

Exercise 2: Using the contacts in the current view, perform a mail merge using the Full_Name, Company, and Business_Address merge fields to create size 10 envelopes. When you are finished, close all open Word windows without saving.

LESSON 5

Using Advanced Tasks Features

After completing this lesson, you will be able to:

✔ Create and update recurring tasks.
✔ Create tasks while working in other Outlook folders.
✔ Record a task in the Journal.
✔ Add fields to the task list.

As you become increasingly familiar with Microsoft Outlook, you will discover that Outlook provides several advanced features that extend the capabilities of the basic program. This lesson focuses on how some of these features can be used for tasks and the Journal.

For recurring activities, such as submitting a biweekly status report to your manager, you can set Outlook to automatically insert recurring tasks into your task list. And for your convenience, you can create tasks within other Outlook folders. To keep track of Microsoft Office documents that you create, you can use the Outlook Journal to view the date and time a document was created and where a document is located. If you like, you can track other Outlook items, such as tasks, in the Journal as well. To quickly view details of tasks, you can add the Notes column to the task list. If you understand how to use these and other Outlook features, you're on your way to becoming a true Outlook expert.

In this lesson, you will learn how to create and update recurring tasks, and how to create tasks within other Outlook folders. You will also learn how to record tasks in the Journal and how to display notes in the task list.

Your Outlook folders should already contain the Outlook items (tasks, e-mail messages, and contact records) that are necessary to complete the exercises in this lesson. If you need to add these items to your Outlook folders, see the "Using the CD-ROM" section at the beginning of this book.

Practice files for the lesson

OL2000E.7.1

No practice files are required to complete the exercises in this lesson.

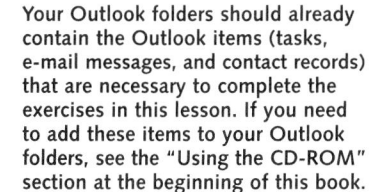

Creating and Updating Recurring Tasks

If you want to be reminded of a task that you perform on a regular basis, such as submitting a monthly report to your manager, or a recurring task that you will perform for a specific period, such as watering your neighbor's plants once a week while she's on a month-long vacation, you don't need to add the task to your task list repeatedly; you can set the task so that it automatically recurs on the days you specify. **Recurring tasks** repeat on specified days for a specific amount of time. For example, the restaurant manager at Lakewood Mountains Resort sends biweekly updates to the accounting department about any dinners that he decided to make complementary for visiting VIPs. To remind himself to do this, he created a recurring task called Comp Update.

You can create recurring tasks from scratch by setting recurrence options at the time the task is created. You can also turn an existing task into a recurring task by opening it and setting the recurrence options. The recurrence can be set to run indefinitely or for a specified period.

Each time you complete a recurring task, you can update the Tasks folder by marking the task as complete. After you mark a recurring task as complete, the task will appear marked out, and the next recurrence of the task will appear, displaying the next due date that you specified when you set up the recurrence options.

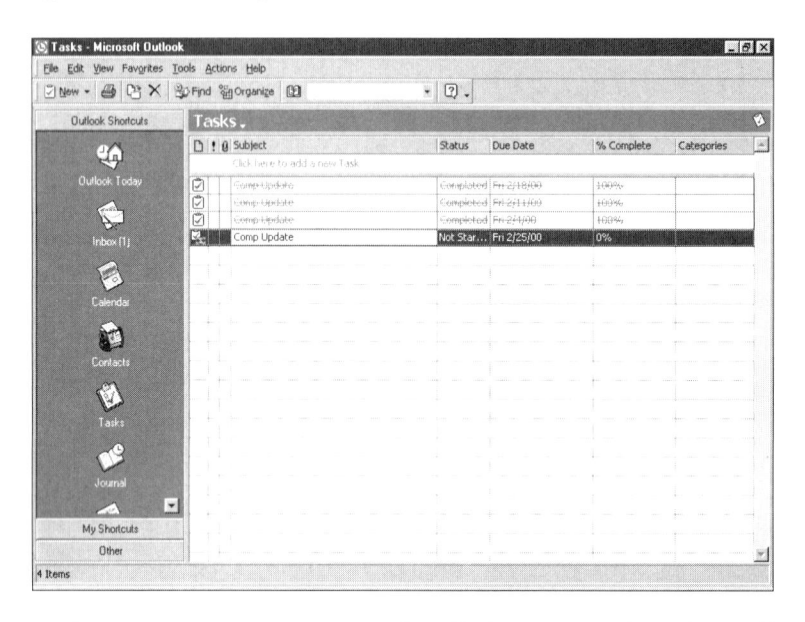

In this exercise, you create a task called Comp Update that will recur every other Friday, and then you update a recurring task.

1 Display the Tasks folder.

2 On the Standard toolbar, click the New Task button.

New Task

A task window appears, with the insertion point already in the Subject box.

3 Type **Comp Update**.

4 Click the Start Date down arrow, and click next Friday.

You make an existing task a recurring task by double-clicking the task, clicking the Recurrence button, selecting the recurrence pattern, clicking OK, and clicking the Save And Close button.

5 On the Standard toolbar, click the Recurrence button.

The Task Recurrence dialog box appears.

The dates that appear in your Task Recurrence dialog box might differ from those shown in the illustration, depending on when you take the class.

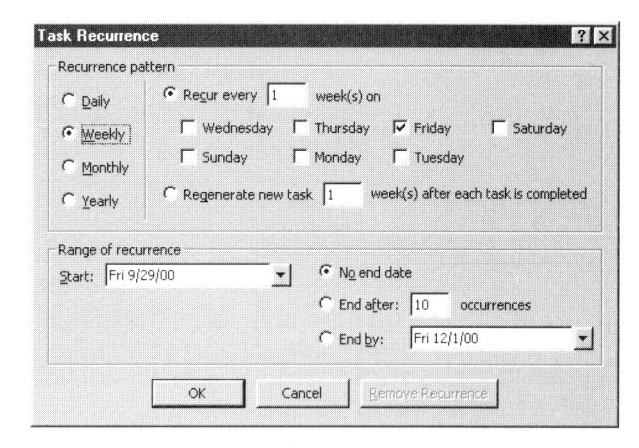

6 In the Recur Every box, select the number 1 and type **2**.

7 Verify that only the Friday check box is selected, and click OK.

A message appears in the task window explaining that the task will be due every two weeks on Friday.

8 On the Standard toolbar, click the Save And Close button.

The recurring task appears in the task list.

You can delete a recurring task by clicking the task and clicking the Delete button on the Standard toolbar. In the alert box, you can click Delete All to delete all recurrences, or you can click Delete This One to delete only the selected task.

9 On the View menu, point to Current View, and click Detailed List.

The task list switches to Detailed List view.

10 In the Comp Update task, click the text *Not Started*.

A down arrow and list appear.

11 Click Completed.

12 Click a blank area of the task list.

The message appears with a line through it and another Comp Update task appears with a due date two weeks later than the previous due date.

13 In the % Complete field of the new task, delete the text *0%*, type **5**, and then press Enter.

The task is updated, and the Status field of the new task now displays the text *In Progress*.

Creating Tasks While Working in Other Outlook Folders

Outlook lets you create tasks within different Outlook folders. You probably already know that you can create a task in the Calendar by typing a task on the TaskPad. You can also create a task for a specific contact in the Contacts folder. Being able to create tasks while you're working in different Outlook folders makes it easy for you to get the most out of the Tasks feature. For example, the human resources manager at Lakewood Mountains Resort scheduled an appointment to meet with an employment recruiter to help her find an employee for the night desk. She also needed to prepare a job description for the position. So after she scheduled the appointment in the Calendar, she created a task to prepare a job description on the Calendar's TaskPad.

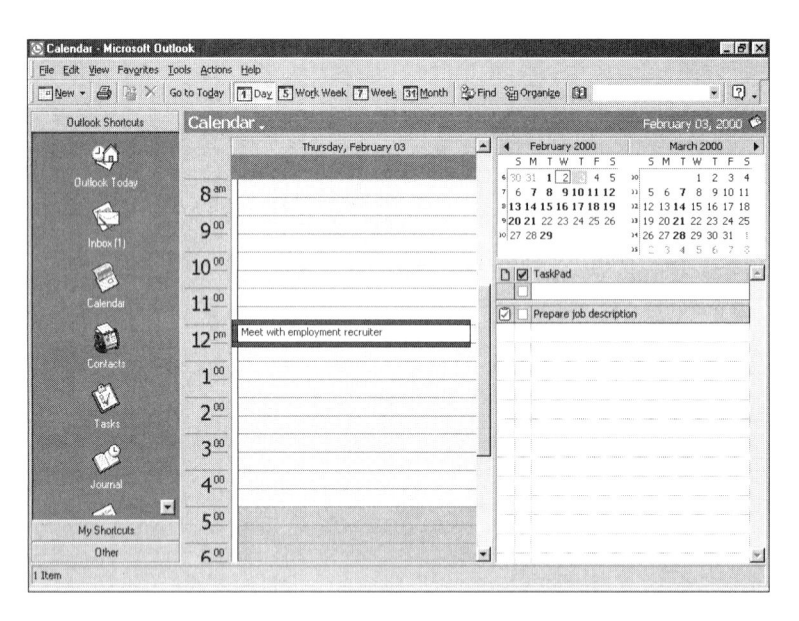

In this exercise, you create a new task while you're in the Calendar. You also create a task for a contact in the Contacts folder.

1 Display the Calendar.

2 On the TaskPad, click in the box that contains the text *Click Here To Add A New Task*.

The text in the box disappears.

3 Type **Create job description**, and press Enter.

The task is created.

4 Display the Tasks folder.

The task *Create job description* also appears in the task list.

> You can also create a task from an appointment. Drag the desired appointment to the Tasks shortcut on the Outlook Bar. Enter the desired task information, and click the Save And Close button.

5 Display the Contacts folder.

6 Right-click the contact *Frank Miller*, and click New Task For Contact.

A task window appears, with an insertion point already in the Subject box.

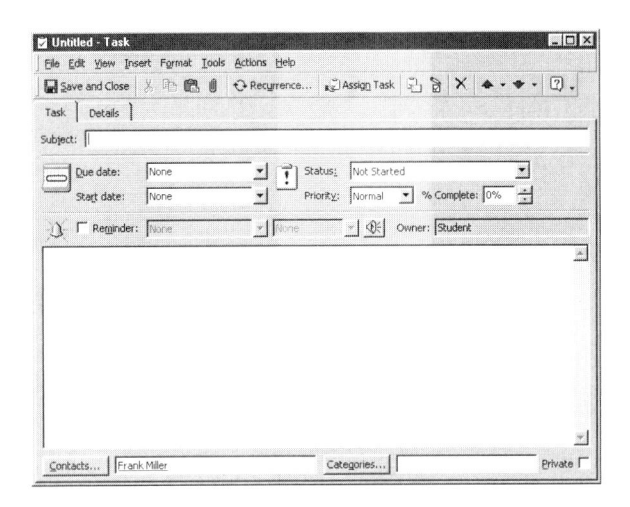

7 Type **Submit Frank's performance review**.

8 On the Standard toolbar in the task window, click the Save And Close button.

9 Display the Tasks folder.

The new task appears in the task list.

Recording a Task in the Journal

OL2000E.7.3

The Journal is a timeline that can record when you create, use, or modify Microsoft Office documents and Outlook items. As shown on the following page, the following information about tracked documents appears in the Journal: each document's type, name, and date, how long the document was open, and the path in which the document is stored on your computer. Being able to view a document path is useful if you can't remember where you stored a document.

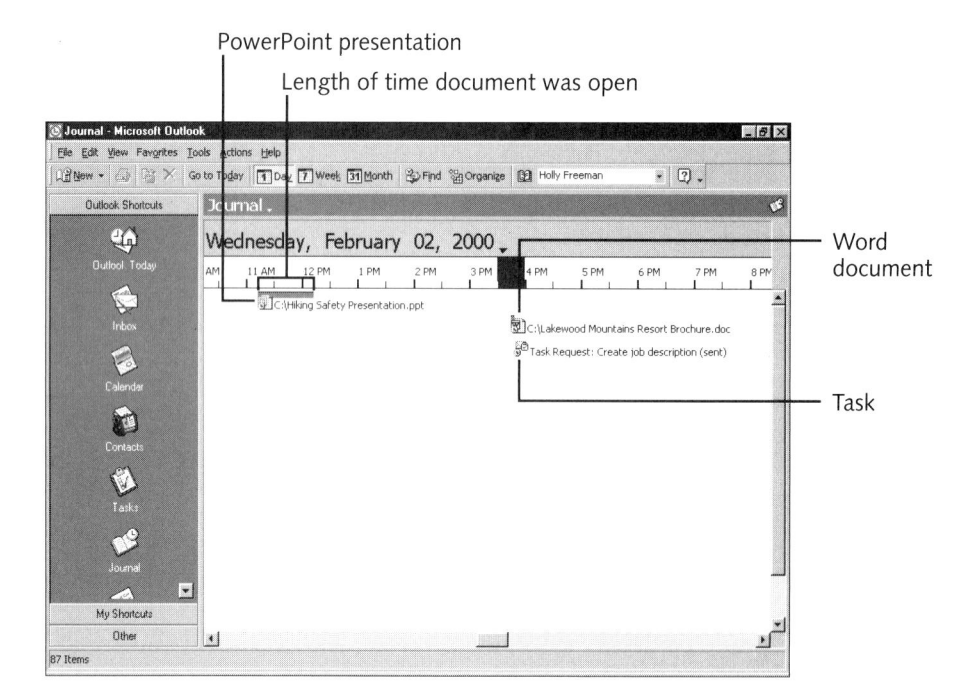

5.6 Microsoft Outlook 2000 Step by Step Courseware Expert Skills Student Guide

The gray bar above the Journal entry indicates the amount of time that the document was open. You might find it difficult to determine the actual amount of time a document was open just by glancing at the gray bar. To quickly view the length of time a document was open, double-click the Journal entry, and view the time in the Duration box.

The Journal does not automatically track Office documents and Outlook items, although you can set it up to do so. You use the Journal Options dialog box to track e-mail messages, meeting requests, responses and cancellations, and task requests and responses. For example, the marketing manager at Lakewood Mountains Resort likes to use the Journal to record task requests that she sends to her assistant. By keeping a record of task requests, she has confirmation that the task request was sent, should a dispute arise.

> **important**
> To complete the following exercise, you need to have a contact record for your class partner. This exercise will not work property if you send a task request to yourself. If you're working on this exercise at home or at your office, you can work through the steps independently by asking a coworker or friend to participate as your exercise partner.

In this exercise, you set the Journal to record task requests for your class partner and from your class partner. You also create a task and assign it to your class partner. You then accept a task request from your class partner and verify that the Journal recorded the task requests.

1 On the Tools menu, click Options.

The Options dialog box appears.

2 Click the Journal Options button.

The Journal Options dialog box appears.

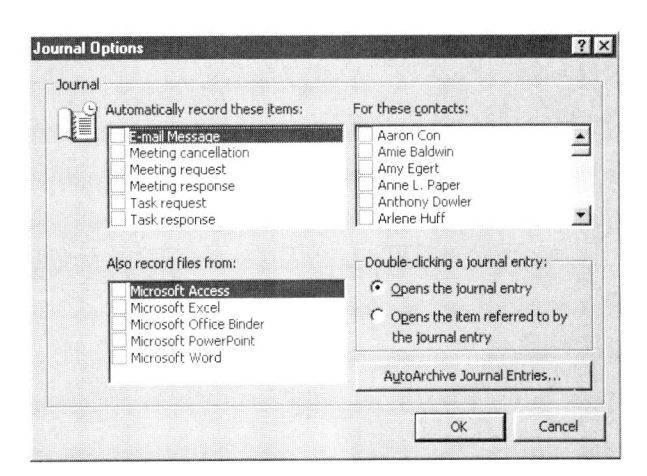

3 In the Automatically Record These Items list, select Task Request.

4 In the For These Contacts list, scroll down if necessary, select your class partner's name, and then click OK.

5 In the Options dialog box, click OK.

The Journal will record when task requests are sent to your class partner and received from your class partner.

New Task

6 On the Standard toolbar, click the New Task button.

A task window appears with the insertion point already in the Subject box.

7 In the Subject box, type **Update [your name]'s schedule**.

8 On the Standard toolbar in the task window, click the Assign Task button.

The To box appears in the task window.

9 Click the To button.

The Select Task Recipient dialog box appears.

If you know the e-mail address of the person to whom you want to assign the task, you can type the address in the To box instead of clicking the To button.

10 Click the contact record for your class partner, click the To button, and then click OK.

11 On the Standard toolbar in the task window, click the Send button.

The task is sent to your class partner.

12 Display the Inbox.

13 On the Standard toolbar, click the Send/Receive button.

A task request from your class partner appears.

14 Double-click the task request, and click the Accept button on the Standard toolbar in the task request window.

An alert box appears.

If the Environmental Net Meeting window appears, telling you that no responses have been received for the meeting, close the window.

15 Click OK to send the response.

16 On the Standard toolbar, click the Send/Receive button.

A response from your class partner appears in the Inbox.

17 Display the Journal.

18 If necessary, on the Standard toolbar, click the Day button.

The Journal appears in Day view.

19 On the left side of the Task Request gray bar, click the plus sign (+).

The time the task request was sent to your class partner appears, and the time that you received a task request from your class partner appears in the Journal.

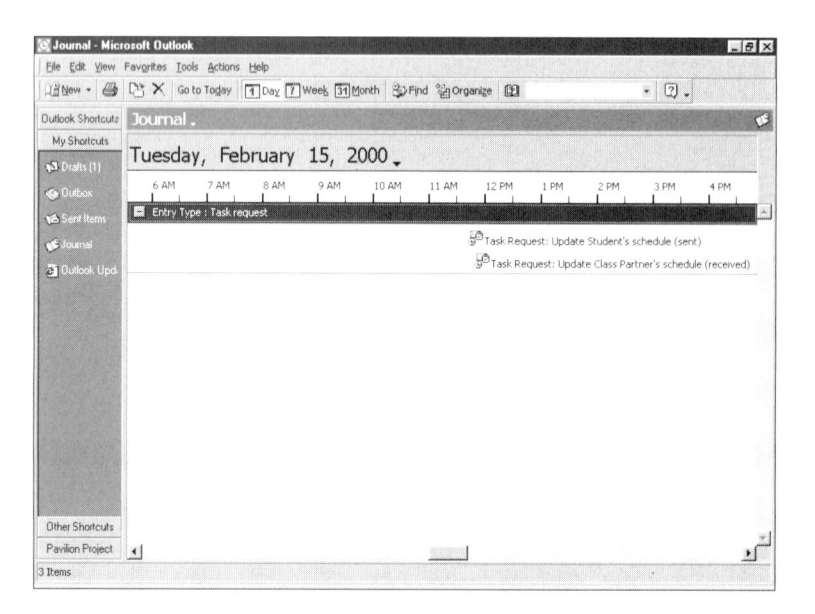

Adding Fields to the Task List

You aren't limited to the fields (columns) that appear in the task list in Detailed List view. Outlook provides dozens of additional fields that you can use to create task list columns. And if you want to remove one of the default columns (perhaps you never use it or you want to make room for a new column), you can easily delete the column. You can even create your own fields and add them as columns to the task list in Detailed List view.

Why might you want to create your own fields? Consider an example. When you create a task, you can add detailed notes for the task in the task window (as shown in the following figure). You can also double-click an existing task at any time and add notes in its task window.

Lesson 5 Using Advanced Tasks Features 5.9

You can check spelling in the task window by pressing F7 or by clicking Spelling on the Tools menu.

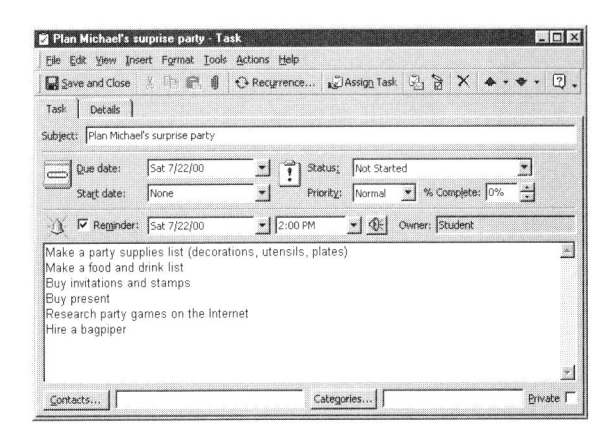

When you are in Detailed List view, you cannot see any notes that you've added to a task. However, you can add a Notes column that will partially display notes. You can also designate where you want the Notes column to appear in the task list. The Notes field is one of 14 ready-made fields that you can add to the task list.

In this exercise, you display the Notes column in the notes field and add a note to the *Submit Frank's performance review* task.

1 Display the Task folder.

2 Right-click a blank area of the task list, and click Show Fields.

The Show Fields dialog box appears.

To remove a column from Detailed List view, click the field in the Show These Fields In This Order list and click the Remove button.

3 In the Available Fields list, click Notes, and click the Add button.

The field is added to the bottom of the Show These Fields In This Order list and will be displayed in the last column of the task list in Detailed List view.

4 Click the Move Up button twice.

The position of the Notes field is changed so that it will appear before the % Complete field in Detailed List view.

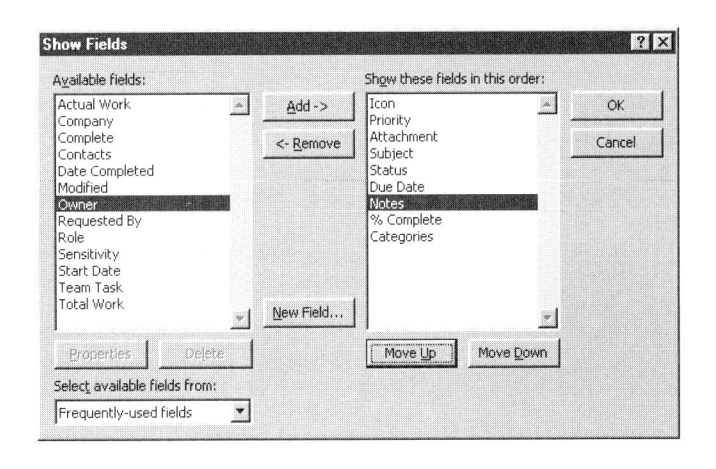

5 Click OK.

The Show Fields dialog box closes, and the Notes field appears as a column in the task list.

6 Double-click the task *Submit Frank's performance review.*

The task opens.

7 Click in the large box at the bottom of the task window, type **Frank stayed late on many occasions to help the wait staff close.**

8 On the Standard toolbar in the task window, click the Save And Close button.

The beginning of the sentence appears in the Notes column of the task *Submit Frank's performance review.*

> You can see the entire note by positioning the mouse pointer over either of the horizontal lines to the left or right of the Notes heading. When the mouse pointer changes to a resize pointer, drag the line to the left or right. You can also view the entire note by clicking Preview Pane on the View menu.

Creating Custom Columns

As mentioned earlier in the lesson, you aren't limited to the fields that Outlook provides when you add columns to the task list. You can create your own fields to suit your particular needs. For example, suppose you have created a list of tasks to prepare a marketing brochure. You might want to add columns for the writer, proofreader, graphic artist, and printer. None of these fields are provided in Outlook's ready-made list of fields.

To create a custom field and add it as a column to your task list:

1 Right-click a blank area of the task list, and click Show Fields.

2 Click the New Field button.

3 Type the name for your new field, and click OK.

4 Use the Move Up and Move Down buttons as necessary to move the field where you want it to appear in the column, and click OK.

> You can delete a custom column by right-clicking a blank area of the task list, and clicking Show Fields. In the Show These Fields In This Order list, click the column name, click the Remove button, click the Delete button, and then click OK.

Lesson Wrap-Up

This lesson covered how to create and update recurring tasks, how to create tasks while working in other Outlook folders, how to record tasks in the Journal, and how to add fields to the task list.

If you are continuing to the next lesson:

- Close any open tasks.

If you are not continuing to other lessons:

Close

- In the top-right corner of the Outlook window, click the Close button. Outlook closes.

Lesson Glossary

Journal A timeline that records when you create, use, or modify Microsoft Office documents and Outlook items.

recurring tasks Tasks that repeat on specified days for a specific amount of time.

Quick Quiz

1. How can you make an existing task recurring?
2. What is the Journal?
3. How do you create a task in the Calendar?
4. How do you add a new field to the task list?
5. What is a recurring task?
6. How do you delete all occurrences of a recurring task?

Putting It All Together

Exercise 1: Create a recurring task called Expenses that reminds you to complete an expense report by the 15th of each month. Using the contact Prasanna Samarawickrama, create a task that reminds you to ask her to collect the expense reports from the other department members. Delete all occurrences of the Expenses task.

Exercise 2: Set the Journal to automatically record task responses. Send the following task request to your class partner: Take [your name] to the airport. Accept the task *Take [class partner's name] to the airport*, and view the task response in the Journal. Remove the Notes column from the Detailed List view.

LESSON 6

Using Net Folders and Public Folders

After completing this lesson, you will be able to:

✔ Share a file folder with others.
✔ Grant others permission to use your folders.
✔ Grant a delegate access to your folders.
✔ Use Net Folders.
✔ Work offline.
✔ Synchronize folders.
✔ Create a quick synchronization group.
✔ Synchronize by message size.

Many companies use a messaging service that enables members of their organization to exchange and share information with each other on a server and on the Internet. One such messaging service is called Microsoft Exchange Server. If you use Exchange Server, you can share your Microsoft Outlook folders so that other users can view the contents. For example, the vice president at Lakewood Mountains Resort gives her assistant access to her Outlook Calendar so that he can answer questions about her schedule when she's out of the office. If your organization doesn't use Exchange Server, you can still share your folders with others over the Internet by using **Net Folders**. Net Folders are specific Outlook folders that can be accessed by other users over the Internet according to rules that you specify. For example, you could allow your customers to view your Outlook Calendar on the Internet so that they'll know when you're available to answer questions, or you could let your spouse view your Contacts folder so that he or she could access phone numbers for mutual contacts like friends, family, or doctors.

In this lesson, you will learn how to share a file folder with others and how to grant permissions to folders. You will also learn how to grant delegate access and use Net Folders. Finally you will learn how to work offline, synchronize files, create synchronization groups, and synchronize messages by message size.

Practice files for the lesson

No practice files are required to complete the exercises in this lesson.

Your Outlook folders should already contain the Outlook items (tasks and contact records) that are necessary to complete the exercises in this lesson. If you need to add these items to your Outlook folders, see the "Using the CD-ROM" section at the beginning of this book.

important

To complete some of the exercises in this lesson, you will need to exchange e-mail messages with a class partner. If you don't have a class partner or are performing the exercises alone, you can enter your own e-mail address instead of your class partner's and send the messages to yourself.

Sharing a Folder with Others

OL2000E.4.1

If you work on a network that includes Microsoft Exchange Server, you can share Outlook items with others by putting the items in a **public folder**. A public folder can contain messages or information that can be shared with designated users. For example, the human resources manager at Lakewood Mountain Resort likes to have access to the Calendars for all departmental managers so that she can see when a particular manager will be available to interview applicants.

When you share an Outlook folder, anyone on the network with the appropriate permission can make changes to the folder, and all other users will see those changes. For example, if you share a task list with others, someone can mark a task as complete as soon as he or she finishes so that everyone involved can see that the task no longer needs to be performed.

In this exercise, you create a tasks folder and share it with others.

If you want to share items with others, you don't have to make your default Outlook folders public. You can create a public folder that others can access for a specific purpose. For example, you could create a public folder that contains a task list for a project in which others are involved. If you simply make your Tasks folder a public folder, others will be able to see your personal tasks or tasks that are unrelated to them.

1 On the File menu, point to New, and click Folder.

   The Create New Folder dialog box appears.

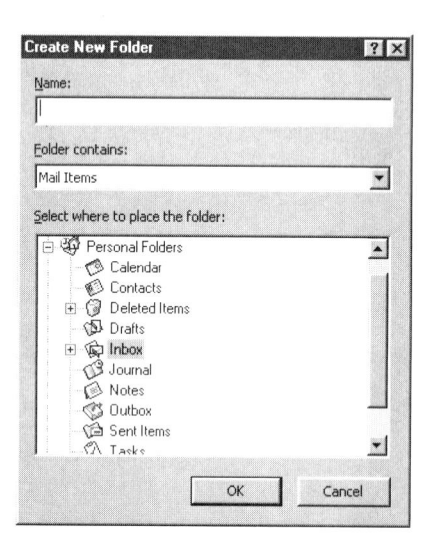

2 In the Name box, type [*Your first and last name*]'s **Company Party Tasks**.

3 Click the Folder Contains down arrow, and click Task Items.

4 In the Select Where To Place The Folder list, scroll down if necessary, click the plus sign to the left of Public Folders, click All Public Folders, and click OK.

   The Add Shortcut To Outlook Bar dialog box appears, asking if you want to add a shortcut to this new tasks folder to your Outlook Bar.

5 Click No.

6 In the Folder List, navigate to All Public Folders.

7 Scroll down, if necessary, and click your Company Party Tasks folder.

   The Company Party Tasks folder is opened.

8 Click in the box that contains the text *Click Here To Add A New Task*.

9 Type **Order invitations.**, and press Enter.

If someone else on the network opens this folder, he or she will see that this task has been completed.

You will learn how to set permissions in the next exercise.

10 Type **Book a band.**, and press Enter.

11 Type **Call caterer.**, and press Enter.

The tasks are created.

12 Select the check box to the left of the task *Book a band*.

The task is marked as complete.

13 In the Folder List, navigate to All Public Folders, and click your class partner's Company Party Tasks folder.

The task *Book a band* is already marked as complete, because your class partner, like you, marked it as complete in step 12.

14 Select the check box to the left of the task *Order invitations*.

An alert box appears, stating that you don't have permission to modify the items in this folder.

15 Click OK.

Granting Others Permission to Use Your Folders

Before anyone on the network can access a public folder that you create, you must grant each person **permission** to use the folder. When you grant permission to a person on the network, you specify what exactly this person can do to the information in the folder. For example, the events coordinator at Lakewood Mountains Resort lets her assistant view her Calendar (however, the assistant cannot create, edit or delete Calendar items), and lets her manager view and create Calendar items (however, the manager cannot delete or edit existing items). These levels of involvement are called **roles**. Outlook has nine different roles that you can assign to a user.

Role Type	Available Options
Owner	Has all permissions.
Publishing Editor	Can create, read, edit, and delete items in the folder and create subfolders.
Editor	Can create, read, edit, and delete items in the folder.
Publishing Author	Can create and read items in the folder, create subfolders, and edit and delete items that he or she created.
Author	Can create and read items in his or her folder, and edit and delete items that he or she created.
Nonediting Author	Can create and read items in the folder.
Reviewer	Can only read items.
Contributor	Can only create items; contents of the folder do not appear.
None	None.

In this exercise, you grant your class partner permission to access your Company Party Tasks folder. You also modify your class partner's Company Party Tasks folder, and then view the changes that your class partner made to your folder.

1. In the Folder List, right-click your Company Party Tasks folder.

   A shortcut menu appears.

2. On the shortcut menu, click Properties.

   The Properties dialog box appears.

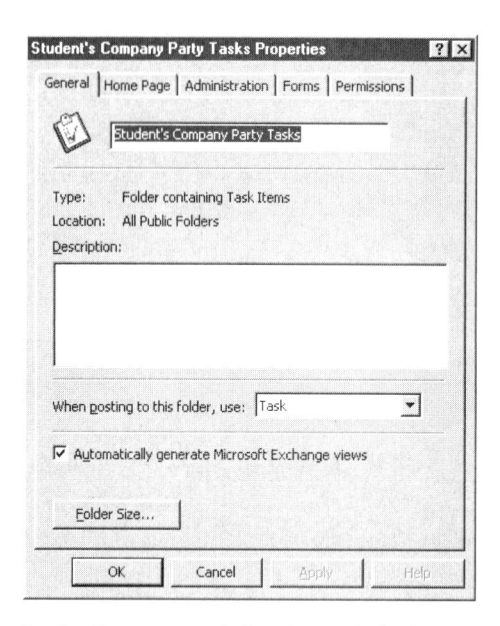

If the Permissions tab is not available on the Properties dialog box, either you are not the owner of the folder or you are not connected to the network.

3. In the Properties dialog box, click the Permissions tab.

4. Click the Add button.

   The Add Users dialog box appears.

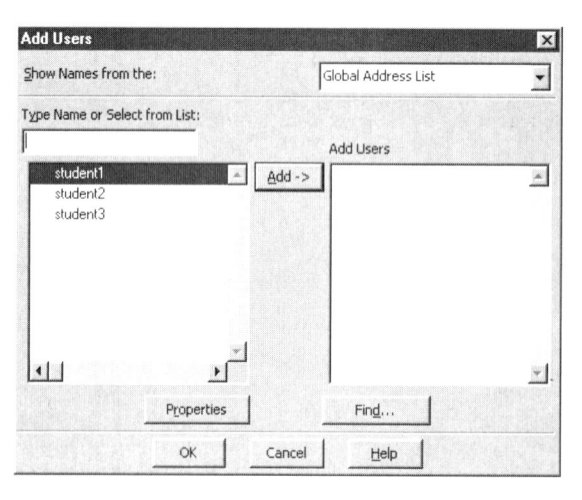

5. Scroll down if necessary, and click your class partner's name.

6. Click the Add button, and click OK.

Note that your class partner is automatically assigned the role *Author*.

7. In the Name list, click your class partner's name.

8. In the Permissions section, click the Roles down arrow, scroll up, and click Publishing Editor.

   Your class partner will be able to create, read, edit, and delete items in the folder and create subfolders.

You can set permissions to a folder for as many users as desired.

9. Click OK.

   The permissions are set.

10 In the Folder List, verify that your class partner's Company Party Tasks folder is selected.

11 Select the check box to the left of the task *Order invitations*.

You can now mark the task as complete because like you, your class partner gave you permission to edit items in his or her folder.

12 Double-click the task *Call caterer*.

A task window appears.

13 Click the Due Date down arrow, and click tomorrow's date.

14 Click the Save And Close button.

The due date appears in the task list.

15 View your Company Party Tasks folder.

The tasks in your folder have been updated by your class partner.

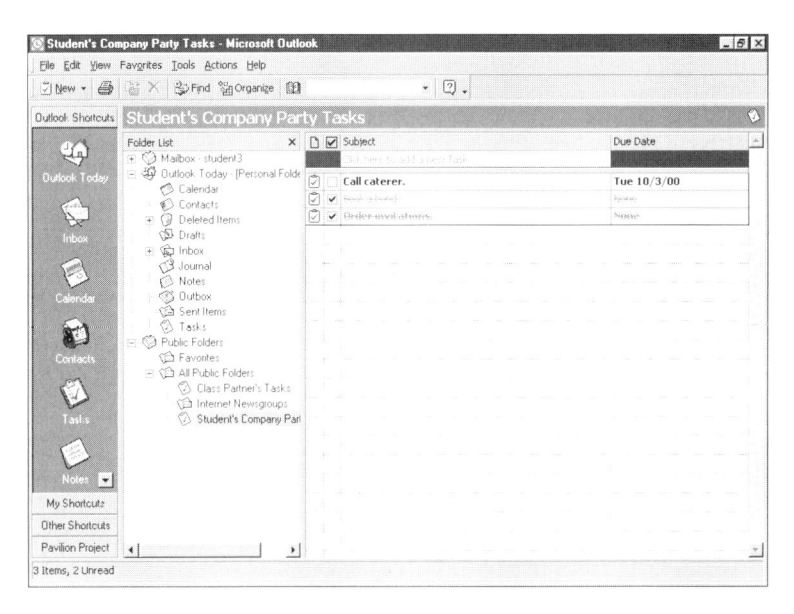

Granting a Delegate Access to Your Folders

OL2000E.4.2
OL2000E.7.4

If you go on vacation or are planning an extended business trip, you will probably need to assign one or more of your duties to someone else while you are away. If you use Outlook to manage your work activities, you'll also want to give others permission to view your appointments and make new appointments, check the status of tasks that you've assigned to others, and so on. If you are using Outlook on an Exchange Server network, you can easily provide others within your organization with the capability to view and modify your Outlook folders. Specifically, you can appoint or delegate someone to send or maintain Outlook items on your behalf. For example, the marketing director at Lakewood Mountain Resort is taking a vacation, so she has granted her assistant **delegate access** to her Inbox and Calendar folders to allow her assistant to address urgent e-mails and know when to attend appointments and meetings while she's gone.

As with granting permissions, when you specify delegate access, you can also specify what role you want the delegate to have. The following table lists the role types you can use.

Role Type	Available Options
None	None.
Reviewer	Can read items.
Author	Can read and create items.
Editor	Can read, create, and modify items.

In this exercise, you grant your class partner delegate access to your Tasks and Inbox folders. You also test delegate access privileges.

1   On the Tools menu, click Options.

    The Options dialog box appears.

2   In the Options dialog box, click the Delegates tab.

> You can delete a delegate's access by clicking the delegate's name in the Delegates list on the Delegates tab and then clicking the Remove button.

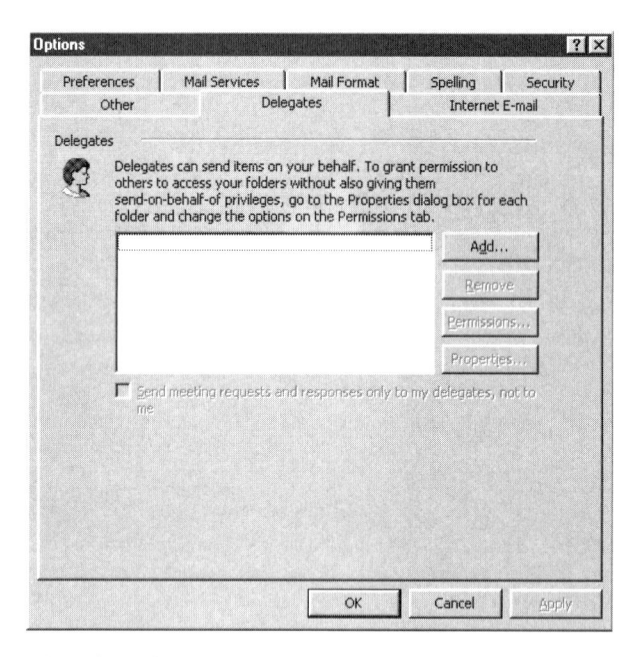

3   Click the Add button.

    The Add Users dialog box appears.

4   Click your class partner's name, and click the Add button.

    Your class partner is now a delegate.

tip

You can grant delegate access to more than one user at a time. In the Add Users dialog box, click a name, click the Add button, click another name, and click the Add button again. Repeat as necessary to add all of the desired names. Click OK, and set permissions for the desired folders.

5 Click OK.

The Delegate Permissions dialog box appears.

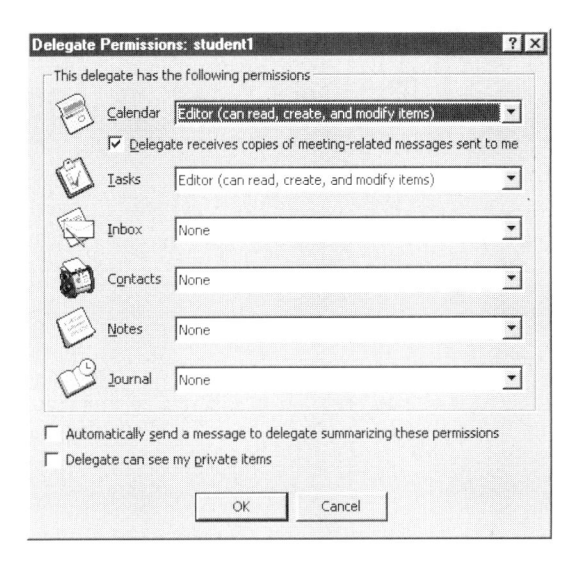

6 Click the Calendar down arrow, and click None.

Your class partner will not have access to your Calendar.

7 Click the Tasks down arrow, and click Author.

Your class partner will be able to read and create items in the Tasks folder.

8 Click the Inbox down arrow, and click Reviewer.

Your class partner will be able to read only e-mail messages in the Inbox folder.

9 Click OK twice.

The delegate's permissions are set.

10 On the File menu, point to Open, and click Other User's Folder.

The Open Other User's Folder dialog box appears.

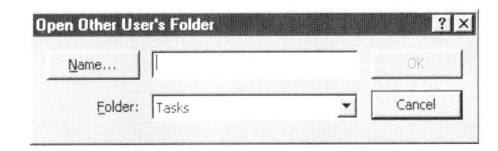

You can also select a name by clicking the Name button, clicking the name in the Select Name dialog box, and clicking OK.

11 In the Name box, type your class partner's name.

12 Click the Folder down arrow, click Inbox, and then click OK.

Your class partner's Inbox appears in its own window. Since you only have Reviewer access, you can read only the e-mail messages in the Inbox.

Close

13 In the top-right corner of your class partner's Inbox window, click the Close button.

14 Your class partner's Inbox closes.

15 On the File menu, point to Open, and click Other User's Folder.

The Open Other User's Folder dialog box appears.

16 In the Name box, type your class partner's name.

17 Click the Folder down arrow, click Calendar, and click OK.

An alert box appears, telling you that Outlook was unable to display the folder. This is because your class partner did not give you permission to view it.

18 Click OK, and click the Cancel button in the Open Other User's Folder dialog box.

Using Voting and Tracking Options

At times, you'll want to send an e-mail message to others within your organization for the specific purpose of determining whether the recipients approve or agree with the subject or question in your e-mail message. For example, you might ask managers if they would like to start a weekly casual day and then ask them to respond to your e-mail message. At other times, you might send a particularly important e-mail message and want to ensure that your recipients have received and read the message you've sent.

In Outlook, you can use the Voting And Tracking Options section of the Message Options dialog box to send a message that recipients can vote on, called **voting**, or to request a receipt when either an e-mail message has been received by a recipient or has been read, called **tracking**. You display this dialog box by clicking the Options button in a new Message window.

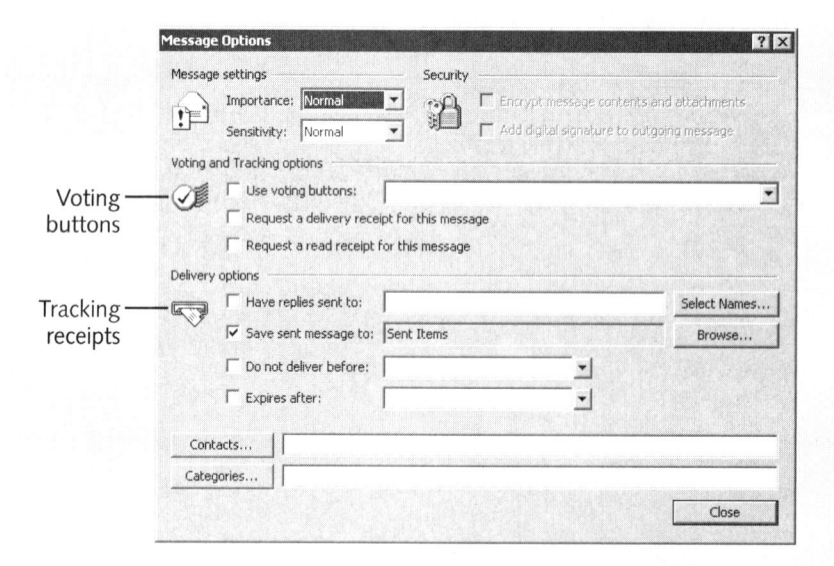

If you want others to vote on a question or issue provided in an e-mail message that you send, you select the Use Voting Buttons check box. You then use the down arrow to the right to display three sets of voting option buttons—Approve;Reject, Yes;No, or Yes;No;Maybe. Select the most appropriate set of voting buttons for your e-mail message. When a recipient receives and reads your e-mail, they will see a message window similar to the following.

(continued)

continued

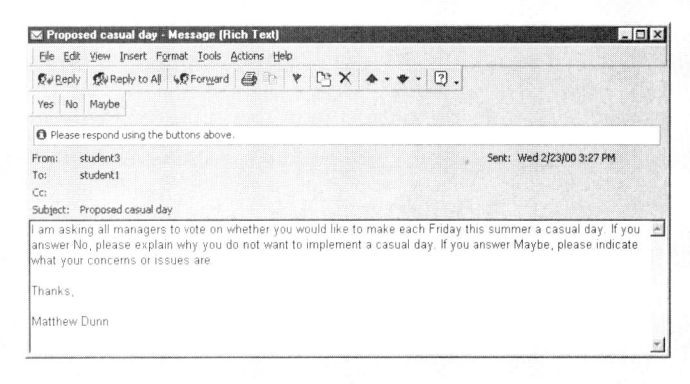

Recipients can then click the desired button, add a reply message to explain their vote if desired, and then send their reply.

important

The Voting Buttons only work if you and your recipients send and receive e-mail via an Exchange Server network.

Using Net Folders

OL2000E.4.1

Suppose that you want to give someone outside your Exchange Server network access to one of your Outlook folders. For example, the marketing assistant at Lakewood Mountains Resort wanted to give a friend access to her Calendar folder so that her friend would know what days she was available for lunch. With Outlook, you can share folders with anyone over the Internet by creating Net Folders.

You create a Net Folder by first designating a folder that you want to **publish** (or share). You then send an invitation to others to **subscribe** (or have access) to this folder. If the recipient accepts the invitation to subscribe, he or she will become a **subscriber** to the folder and the folder will be copied to the subscriber's computer. If you make any changes to the folder, the items will be updated for all subscribers.

After you publish a Net Folder, a message is automatically sent to the potential subscribers. To become a subscriber, he or she must click Accept in the message. However, recipients who do not use Outlook will only receive a notification message that they are subscribed.

You can publish a folder that you created and added items to, or you can publish Outlook folders (except the Inbox, Outbox, or Exchange folders). You can share contacts, tasks, journal entries, notes, or Calendar items. If you want to share contacts or Calendar items with a subscriber, the subscriber must also use Outlook because these items can't be viewed by other e-mail programs.

When you publish a Net Folder, you set subscriber permissions. The subscriber permissions are much like the permissions you set for a Public folder using Exchange Server. The following table lists each type of permission.

Permission	Available Options
Reviewer	Can read items and files, but cannot create, edit, or delete items or files.
Contributor	Can create and read items and files, but cannot edit or delete items or files.
Author	Can create and read items and files in a folder, and edit and delete items that he or she created.
Editor	Can create, read, edit, and delete items and files in a folder.
Minimum	Receive items as attachments to e-mail messages; changes made are not updated in other members' folders (designated for users who do not use Outlook).

important

You and a class partner must have an e-mail address, and you must have the Net Folders component installed on your computer to complete the procedures in this exercise. Normally you would create a Net Folder for someone outside your network, but for classroom purposes you will create a Net Folder for your class partner to use.

In this exercise, you publish your Calendar as a Net Folder and set a permission level for your class partner. You also send an invitation to your class partner to subscribe to your Calendar folder, and you accept an invitation from your class partner to subscribe to his or her Calendar folder. You then update your class partner's Calendar.

important

You don't need to use Microsoft Exchange Server to publish your folders as Net Folders.

1   In the Folder List, under Personal Folders, click Calendar.
2   On the File menu, point to Share, and click This Folder.

The first Net Folder Wizard dialog box appears.

If an alert box appears telling you that the add-in is not installed, click Yes and insert the Microsoft Office CD-ROM or the Microsoft Outlook CD-ROM.

Lesson 6 Using Net Folders and Public Folders   6.11

3 Click Next.

The next wizard dialog box appears, asking you to create a list of people with whom you will share the folder.

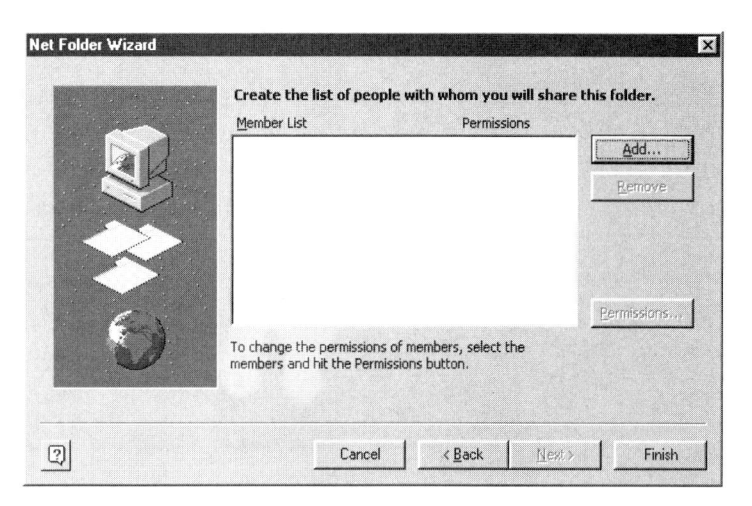

4 Click the Add button, click the Show Names From The down arrow, and then click Contacts.

Your list of contacts appears.

5 In the list, click your class partner's name, click the To button, and then click OK.

Your class partner is set up to be a potential subscriber.

You can set the same permission to multiple potential subscribers by adding their names to the Member List, selecting their names in the Member List box, and then setting a level of permission.

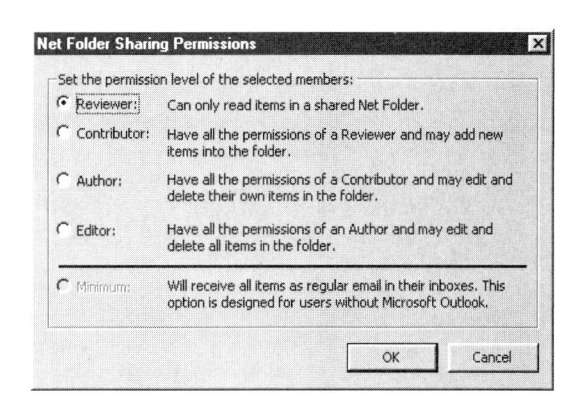

6 If necessary, in the Member List box, click your class partner's name.

7 Click the Permissions button.

The Net Folder Sharing Permissions dialog box appears.

Your class partner will only be able to read and create items in the Calendar.

8 Click the Contributor option, click OK, and then click Next.

The next wizard dialog box appears, asking you to describe the shared folder.

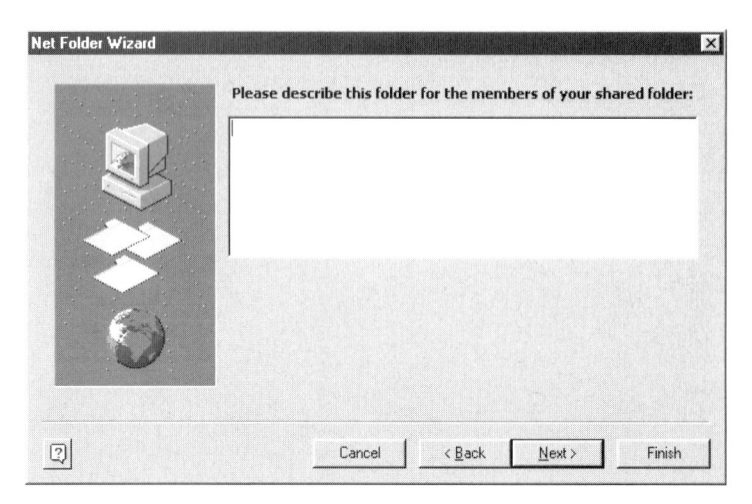

9 Type **[your name]'s Calendar**, click Next, and then click Finish.

An alert box appears, notifying you that you have sent your invitation successfully.

10 Click OK.

11 Display your Inbox, and, if necessary, click the Send/Receive button on the Standard toolbar.

12 Double-click the message *New subscription to [class partner's name]*.

A window appears, describing the subscription.

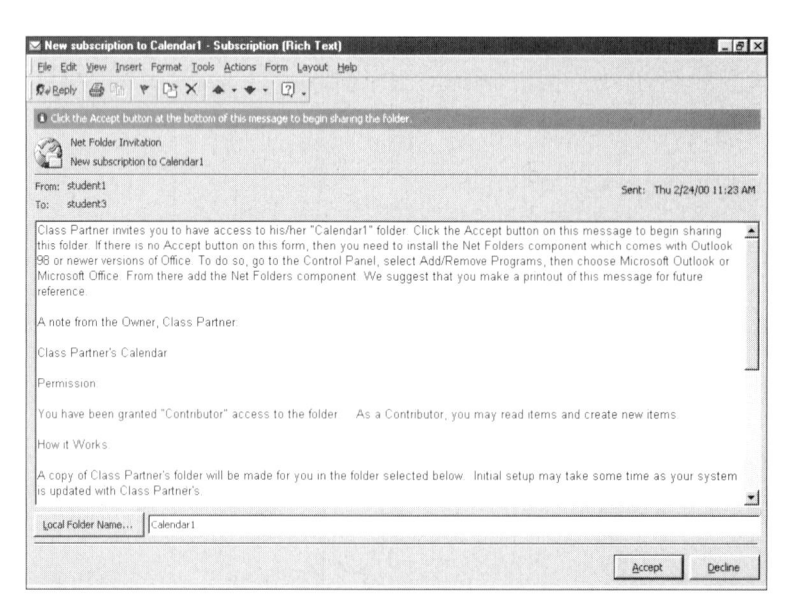

13 Click the Accept button.

Your class partner's Calendar appears in the Folder List.

Outlook will automatically display this addition in your class partner's Personal Folders Calendar in 30 minutes. For classroom purposes, you will send the update now.

14 In the Folder List, click your class partner's Calendar, and then display tomorrow's date, click the 11:00 A.M. line, type **[your name]'s meeting with the president**, and press Enter.

15 In the Folder List, right-click [your class partner]'s Calendar, and click Properties on the shortcut menu that appears.

The [your class partner]'s Calendar Properties dialog box appears.

16 Click the Sharing tab.

Note that Outlook will automatically send updates every 30 minutes.

17 Click the Send Updates Now button.

An alert box appears, informing you that the updates were sent successfully.

18 Click OK twice.

19 Under Personal Folders, click your Calendar, and display tomorrow's date.

Your Calendar displays your class partner's appointment.

> You can set up Outlook to send updates at a time interval other than 30 minutes. Click the Updates Will Be Sent Out Every down arrow, and click a time interval.

> It might take a few minutes for your class partner's appointment to appear in your Calendar.

OL2000E.5.3

New!
You can add Web site shortcuts to your Favorites folder.

Managing Your Favorite Web Sites

If you use Microsoft Internet Explorer as your Web browser, you probably already know that you can save the addresses for frequently visited sites to your Favorites folder (also called your Favorites list) within Internet Explorer. This folder is also part of Outlook. In Outlook, the Favorites folder is located in the Other Shortcuts (or Other) group on the Outlook Bar. When you add a Web site to your Favorites folder from within Internet Explorer, the name of the Web site will also appear in the Favorites folder within Outlook.

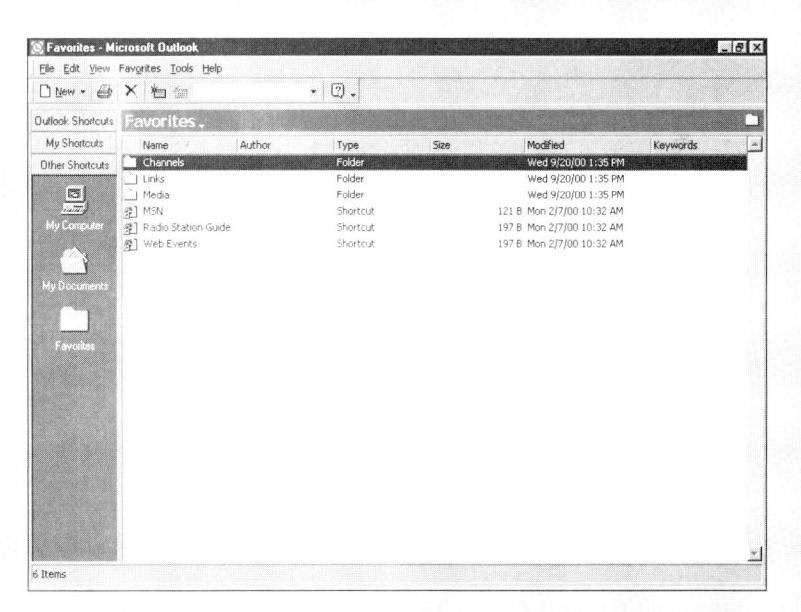

To add a Web site to the Favorites list:

1 Start Internet Explorer.

2 Type the address of a Web site you want to visit in the Address box, and press Enter.

3 After the Web page appears, click Add To Favorites on the Favorites menu.

(continued)

continued

4 Click OK to accept the default title line as the name of the Favorite, or type a new name, and click OK.

As you add more and more Web addresses to your Favorites folder, you might need to manage the Web addresses so that you can easily locate the sites that you want to see. You manage your Web addresses in the same way you manage your e-mail messages. You can sort and filter Web addresses, and you can delete Web addresses that you no longer visit. You can also change the views of the Favorites folder to Icons, Details (displays the name, author, type, size, when the file was added to the list, and keywords), By Author, By File Type, Document Timeline, and Programs view.

To sort Web addresses:

- Click the column header that you want to sort by.

To filter Web addresses:

1 On the View menu, point to Current View, and then click Customize Current View.

The Customize Current View dialog box appears.

2 Click the Filter button.

The Filter dialog box appears.

3 Specify the desired options, and click OK twice.

To delete Web addresses:

1 Click a Web address, and press Delete.

2 Click Yes to confirm the deletion.

To display different views of the Favorites folder:

- On the View menu, point to Current View, and then click a view.

Working Offline

OL2000E.1.1

If you work chiefly with Exchange Server, you probably know that sometimes you need or want to use Outlook or have access to Outlook folders **offline**—that is, when Outlook is not connected to the server, such as when the server is down for servicing or you want to use Outlook when you are traveling. The opposite of offline is **online**, which refers to the operating mode in which Outlook is connected to a server or the Internet.

To work with Outlook both in an Exchange Server environment and offline, you must enable offline use and tell Exchange Server that you want to work in Outlook without connecting to the server.

In this exercise, you enable offline use, set Outlook to work offline, and then add a task to the Tasks folder.

important

To set up Outlook to display the option to work offline, you must first perform the following steps:

1. On the Tools menu, click Services, click Microsoft Exchange Server in the list, and click the Properties button.
2. In the When Starting section, click the Manually Control Connection State option, select the Choose The Connection Type When Starting check box, and click the Work Offline And Use Dial-Up Networking option.
3. Click the Dial-Up Networking tab, and click the Display Connection Dialogs At Logon option.
4. Click OK twice.

---

1. On the Tools menu, click Services.

   The Services dialog box appears.

2. Click Microsoft Exchange Server, and click the Properties button.
3. Click the Advanced tab.

   The Microsoft Exchange Server dialog box appears.

   ![Microsoft Exchange Server dialog box showing the Advanced tab with Mailboxes, Encrypt information, Logon network security, and Enable offline use options.]

4. Select the Enable Offline Use check box.
5. Click OK twice.
6. Quit Outlook.
7. Start Outlook.

   The Microsoft Exchange Server dialog box appears.

   ![Microsoft Exchange Server dialog box with Connect, Work Offline, and Help buttons.]

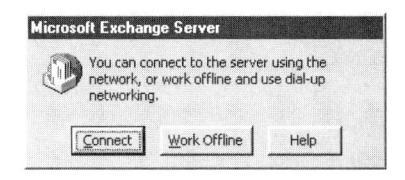

8. Click the Work Offline button.

   Outlook is now offline.

If an alert box appears, telling you that Outlook is going to synchronize your files, click OK.

If the Microsoft Exchange Server dialog box doesn't appear, restart Outlook.

9 Display the Tasks folder under Mailbox-[your name].

10 Click in the box that contains the text *Click Here To Add A New Task*, and type **Create Presentation on Mountaineering**. Press Enter.

The task is created offline.

11 Quit Outlook.

Synchronizing Folders

Outlook offers improved synchronization of offline folders.

If you make changes to a folder offline, you will then need to update the folder that's on the server (the online version of the folder) so that the offline and online versions have the same content. Depending on your settings, Outlook will automatically **synchronize** your offline folders with their online counterparts when you set Outlook to work online at startup. Outlook can synchronize one folder at a time or all folders at once.

In this exercise, you set Outlook to work online, and you synchronize the Tasks folder.

1 Start Outlook. When Outlook asks if you want to work online, click the Connect button.

2 Display the Tasks folder under Mailbox-[your name].

The task you added is not in your task list.

important

Depending on your connection speed and settings, Outlook might automatically synchronize your Tasks folder.

You can also synchronize all Outlook folders by pressing F9.

3 On the Tools menu, point to Synchronize, and click This Folder.

The Tasks folder is synchronized. The task you created in the previous exercise now appears in the task list.

OL2000E.2.6

Creating a Quick Synchronization Group

If you want to synchronize more than one folder at a time, but you don't want to synchronize every folder in Outlook, you can select a group of folders—called the **quick synchronization group**—to synchronize. When you want to synchronize the group, simply click the group name on the Synchronize submenu.

In this exercise, you create a quick synchronization group that includes the Inbox, Calendar, and Contacts; create a contact and an appointment while offline; and then use the synchronization group to synchronize the new information.

1 On the Tools menu, point to Synchronize, and click Offline Folder Settings.

The Offline Folder Settings dialog box appears.

2   Click the Quick Synchronization tab, and click the New button.

    The Quick Synchronization Group dialog box appears.

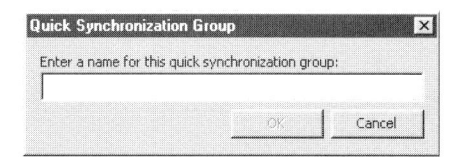

3   Type **Inbox/Cal/Contact**, and click OK.

    The new group is already selected.

4   Click the Choose Folders button.

    The Choose Folders dialog box appears.

5   If necessary, click the plus sign (+) to the left of Mailbox-[your name].

6   Select the check boxes to the left of the Calendar, Contacts, and Inbox folders.

7   Click OK twice.

    The group is created.

8   Restart Outlook, and specify that you want to work offline.

9   Create a contact (using the Contacts folder under Mailbox-[your name]), and type in the following information:

    Full name: **D.J. Cornfield**
    Company: **Duffy Vineyards**
    E-mail: **dj@dv.microsoft.com**

10 Create an appointment (using the Calendar folder under Mailbox-[your name]), and type in the following information:

    Day: **Next Saturday**
    Time: **4:00 PM**
    Subject: **Attend D. J. Cornfield's presentation**

11 Restart Outlook, and specify that you want to work online.

12 On the Tools menu, point to Synchronize, and click Inbox/Cal/Contact.

    The group is synchronized.

13 Display the Contacts folder to see that the new contact has been added.

14 Display next Saturday in the Calendar to see that the new appointment has been added.

> To see the contact you just created, you might need to display the Contacts folder in Detailed Address Cards view (on the View menu, point to Current View, and click Detailed Address Cards).

Synchronizing by Message Size

If you have a lot of large messages in your Inbox, or if you don't want to download any large messages to your computer during synchronization, you can specify a maximum number of kilobytes (KB) per message that you will allow Outlook to download. The messages that have more KB than specified will be moved to the Large Messages folder on your server.

In this exercise, you specify the maximum number of KB per message that you will allow Outlook to download.

1 On the Tools menu, point to Synchronize, and click Offline Folder Settings.

The Offline Folder Settings dialog box appears.

2 Click the Download Options button.

The Download Options dialog box appears.

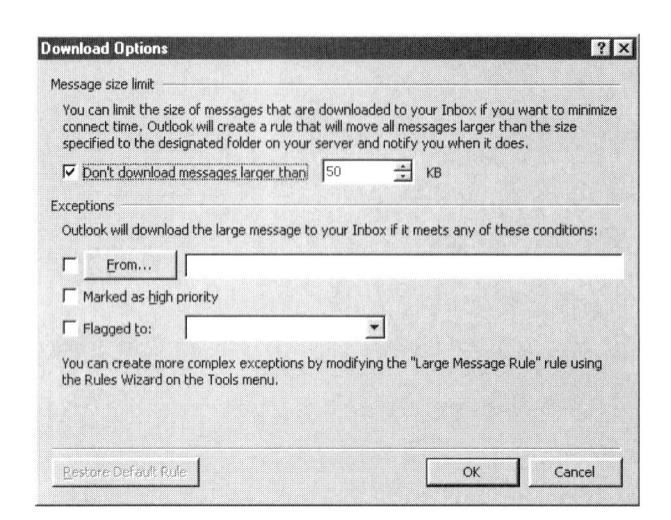

3 In the Message Size Limit section, select the current number, and type **800**.

4 Click OK twice.

Outlook will not download any messages during synchronization that are more than 800 KB.

Lesson Wrap-Up

This lesson covered how to work with files and folders using Microsoft Exchange Server. You learned how to share an Outlook folder with others, and how to grant permissions and delegate access to those folders. You also learned how to use and subscribe to Net Folders. Finally you learned how to work offline and synchronize files, and how to create synchronization groups and synchronize by message size.

If you are continuing to the next lesson:

- Display the Inbox.

If you are not continuing to other lessons:

Close

- In the top-right corner of the Outlook window, click the Close button. Outlook closes.

Lesson Glossary

delegate access Permission granted to access Outlook items belonging to another person.

Net Folders Designated Outlook folders that can be accessed by other users over the Internet according to permission rules that you specify.

offline The operating mode in which Outlook is not connected to a server or the Internet.

online The operating mode in which Outlook is connected to a server or the Internet.

permission A set of instructions set up to control who can view and modify the contents of your folders.

public folder A folder that contains messages or information that can be shared with designated users.

publish The process of making the contents of a folder available to users via a network or Internet connection.

quick synchronization group A specific group of folders designated to be updated during synchronization.

roles Levels of involvement a user is assigned when working with public folders.

subscribe To access another person's Net Folders via the Internet.

subscriber A person who has access to another person's Net Folder via the Internet.

synchronize The process of updating the folders stored on your computer (offline folders) with those stored on a server (online folders).

tracking In Outlook, the ability to request a receipt, or notification, when the recipient of an e-mail message that you send reads your message or when the message has been placed in the recipient's Inbox.

voting In Outlook on an Exchange Server network, the ability to add buttons (Approve;Reject, Yes;No, or Yes;No;Maybe) to an e-mail message that asks a question or describes an issue and a proposed solution so that recipients can select the appropriate button to send back their response.

Quick Quiz

1 How do you synchronize folders?

2 What happens when you set Outlook to work offline?

3 What are the four roles from which you can choose when setting delegate access?

4 What is a Net Folder?

5 In Outlook, what is a subscriber?

6 What is a public folder?

7 What can you do if you don't want to download large files to your computer during synchronization?

8 What happens when you synchronize offline and online folders?

Putting It All Together

Exercise 1: Make your Contacts folder a public folder. Grant your class partner delegate access to your Contacts folder and set the permission level to Editor. Create a folder called LMR Appointments, and put it in your Calendar folder (not the server's Calendar folder). Put the appointment *Attend D. J. Cornfield's presentation* in the LMR Appointments folder. Publish the LMR Appointments folder as a Net Folder, and give your class partner Contributor permission level to the folder.

Exercise 2: Restart Outlook, and set it to work offline. Create a note reminding yourself of a dentist appointment next week. Connect to the server, and synchronize the Notes folder. Create a quick synchronization group called Task/Journal, and add the Tasks and Journal folders to the group.

LESSON 7

Using the Fax Service

After completing this lesson, you will be able to:

✔ Set up the fax service.
✔ Create, send, and receive a fax.
✔ View a fax.

Transmitting documents to others and receiving copies of documents has long been possible by using fax machines and phone lines. But you can also use Microsoft Outlook to send and receive faxes by using one of Outlook's fax services. You know that you can send and receive messages via e-mail (and e-mail attachments), so you might wonder why you should fax a document instead of simply sending the document as an e-mail message attachment. If you created the attachment using a program that the recipient doesn't have, the recipient might not be able to open or read it. And because sending a fax via Outlook uses telephone lines just as a fax machine does, you can send faxes to recipients even if they do not have Internet access. When you fax documents, the fax service in Outlook essentially takes a snapshot of the document and sends it to the recipient's fax service, or fax machine. The recipient will receive either an electronic image of the document from the fax service or a paper image of the document in actual size.

Outlook provides four cover pages you can use when you send a fax. A **cover page** is a one-page document that contains a summary about the document that is being sent—such as the name of the document, number of pages, and a summary of the content—and the sender—such as the sender's name, company name, and fax number. Sometimes a cover page contains a message to the recipient and is the only document that is sent.

> Your Outlook folders should already contain the Outlook items (tasks, e-mail messages, and contact records) that are necessary to complete the exercises in this lesson. If you need to add these items to your Outlook folders, see the "Using the CD-ROM" section at the beginning of this book.
>
> **Practice files for the lesson**

In this lesson, you will learn how to set up the fax service in Outlook, create and send a fax, and receive a fax.

To complete the exercises in this lesson, you will need to use the files named Hiking and Brochure in the Outlook Expert Practice folder that is located on your hard disk.

Setting Up the Fax Service

To send faxes using Outlook, you must first install either the Microsoft Fax or Symantec WinFax Starter Edition add-in components to send and receive faxes. (These add-in components are not installed as part of the standard Outlook installation.) After the appropriate add-in component is installed, fax commands become part of the standard Outlook menus.

The steps to install a fax service will vary depending on which version of Microsoft Windows you are using and whether you have your e-mail service set up for Internet Only, or Corporate or Workgroup. If you set up Outlook for Internet Only e-mail, you can install the Symantec WinFax Starter Edition as an add-in component; the exercises in this lesson use Symantec WinFax.

If you set up Outlook for Corporate or Workgroup e-mail support, you must install Microsoft Fax from Windows, add it to your mail profile, and then reinstall Microsoft Office 2000. The sidebar after this section includes the various steps you need to follow (depending on your Windows version and e-mail service configuration) to set up Microsoft Fax.

important

You must have Windows 98 installed and have Outlook's e-mail configuration support set up for Internet Only for the steps in this exercise to work properly. If you are using a different version of Windows, or if you have Outlook's e-mail service set up for Corporate or Workgroup, follow the instructions in the sidebar following this section to set up a fax service. You must also have a modem and a fax number to properly use a fax service. If you do not, you won't be able to send and receive faxes.

In this exercise, you set up the Symantec WinFax Starter Edition.

1 If necessary, quit Outlook.

2 On the Windows taskbar, click the Start button, point to Settings, and then click Control Panel.

The Control Panel window opens.

3 Double-click the Add/Remove Programs icon.

The Add/Remove Programs Properties dialog box appears.

4 On the Install/Uninstall tab, scroll down, and click Microsoft Office 2000.

5 Click the Add/Remove button.

The Microsoft Office 2000 Setup dialog box briefly appears, and then the Microsoft Office 2000 Maintenance Mode dialog box appears.

6 Click the Add Or Remove Features button.

The Microsoft Office 2000: Update Features dialog box appears.

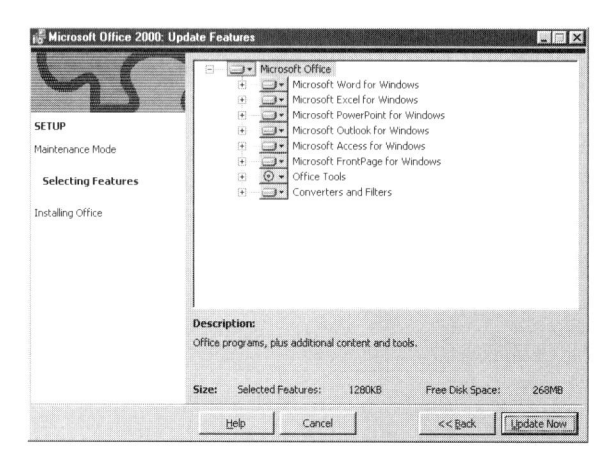

Lesson 7 Using the Fax Service 7.3

7 Click the plus sign (+) to the left of Microsoft Outlook For Windows to show the installation options, click the icon next to Symantec Fax Starter Edition (Internet Mail Only Configuration), and then click Run From My Computer.

A description of the Symantec WinFax Starter Edition appears in the bottom of the dialog box.

If a dialog box appears asking you to insert the Office 2000 CD-ROM into the disk drive, insert the CD-ROM into the disk drive, and click OK.

8 Click the Update Now button.

A progress bar appears as the fax service is installed.

9 After Symantec WinFax Starter Edition is installed, click OK, close the Add/Remove Programs Properties dialog box, and then close the Control Panel window.

10 Start Outlook.

The Symantec WinFax Starter Edition Setup Wizard appears.

If the Symantec WinFax Starter Edition Setup Wizard does not start, close Outlook and look for a file named Olfsetup.exe to start the wizard. On the Windows taskbar, click Start, point to Find, and click Files Or Folders. In the Named box, type Olfsetup.exe. In the Look In list, if necessary, click your hard disk. Select the Include Subfolders check box (if necessary), and click the Find Now button. When the file name appears in the lower pane, double-click it to start the Symantec WinFax Starter Edition Setup Wizard.

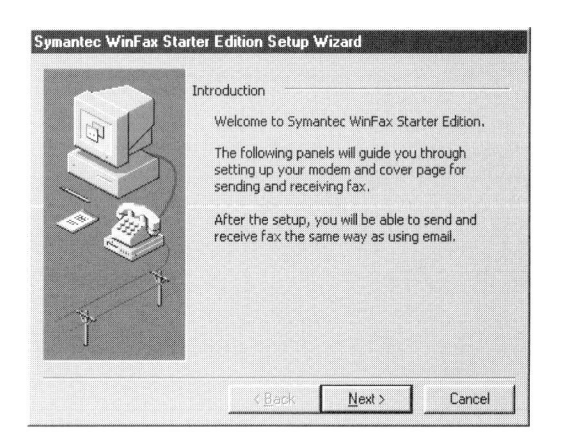

11 Click Next.

The next wizard dialog box appears, asking for user information.

12 Type your name and fax number in the appropriate boxes, and click Next.

The next wizard dialog box appears, asking for address information.

13 Type your address information in the appropriate boxes, and click Next.

The next wizard dialog box appears, asking for receiving and modem information.

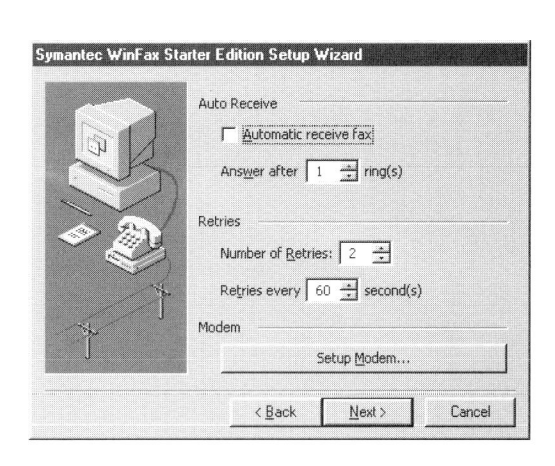

14 In the Auto Receive section, select the Automatic Receive Fax check box, and click the Setup Modem button in the Modem section.

The Modem Properties dialog box appears.

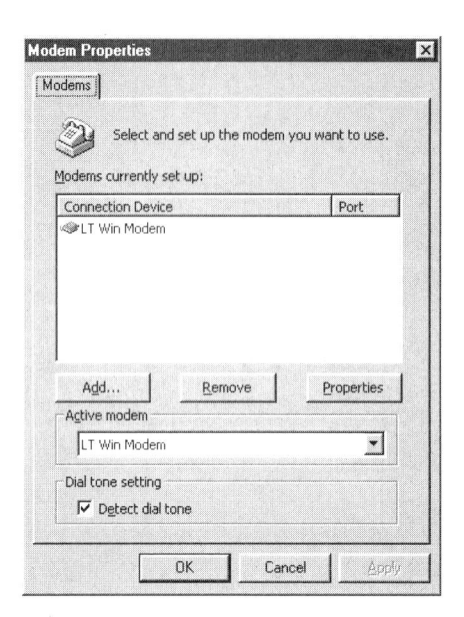

15 Click OK.

16 If an alert box appears telling you that you changed the active modem and need to restart Outlook before you use the fax service, click OK.

17 If another alert box appears telling you that you need to configure your modem to work with WinFax, click Yes, and follow the steps in the Modem Configuration Wizard. When you are finished, click Finish.

The Symantec WinFax Starter Edition Setup Wizard reappears.

18 Click Next.

The next wizard dialog box appears asking what style of template you want to use for your cover page. Notice that the Classic Bold style is already selected.

You can change the style of the cover page template after you set up the fax service.

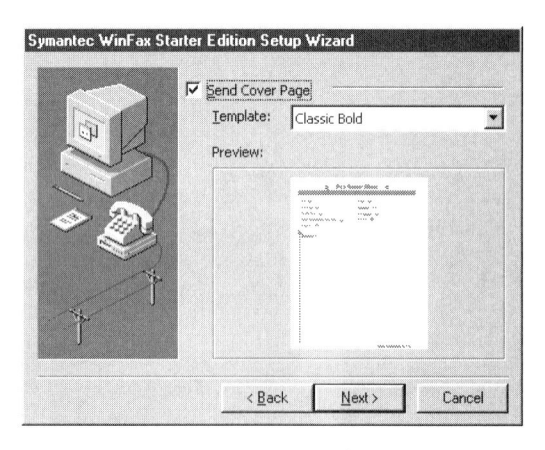

19 Click Next.

The final wizard dialog box appears, notifying you that you have successfully set up the Symantec WinFax Starter Edition.

If the Registration Wizard appears, click the Skip button to register later.

20 Click Finish, and if necessary, close the Find dialog box.

Outlook appears.

important

If you had to configure your modem during the setup process, you must restart Outlook.

Setting Up Microsoft Fax

If you set up Outlook for Corporate or Workgroup e-mail support, you must install Microsoft Fax from Windows to send and receive faxes. After you install Microsoft Fax, you must add it to your mail profile and reinstall Microsoft Office 2000.

To install Microsoft Fax on a Corporate or Workgroup installation for Windows 95:

1   On the Windows taskbar, click the Start button, point to Settings, and then click Control Panel.
2   Double-click the Add/Remove Programs icon.
3   On the Windows Setup tab, click Microsoft Fax, and click OK.

To install Microsoft Fax on a Corporate or Workgroup configuration for Windows 98:

1   Insert the Windows 98 CD-ROM into your CD-ROM drive.
2   In Windows Explorer, display the contents of your CD-ROM drive, and navigate to tools\OldWin95\message\us.
3   Double-click the file awfax.
4   Read the license agreement, and click Yes.
5   Click Yes in the alert box to restart your computer.

To add Microsoft Fax to your mail profile:

1   On the Windows taskbar, click the Start button, point to Settings, and then click Control Panel.
2   Double-click the Mail (or Mail And Fax) icon, and click Add.
3   Click Microsoft Fax, and click OK.

To reinstall Office 2000:

1   Insert the Office 2000 CD-ROM into the CD-ROM drive.
2   On the Windows taskbar, click the Start button, point to Settings, and then click Control Panel.
3   Double-click the Add/Remove Programs icon.
4   On the Install/Uninstall tab, click Microsoft Office 2000, and click the Add/Remove button.
5   Click Repair Office.
6   Click the Reinstall Office option, and click Finish.

After you install Microsoft Fax, you will be prompted to enter some basic information regarding your location and phone number. You will need a fax number and a modem.

OL2000E.9.1
OL2000E.9.2

To preview the different cover pages, click Options on the Tools menu, click the Fax tab, click the Template button, click the Template down arrow, and then click a cover page.

Creating, Sending, and Receiving a Fax

Before you send a fax, you need to select which cover page you want to send (if any), and you need to create a contact record for the recipient. If you attempt to send a fax to a recipient who is not found in your Contacts folder, the Check Names dialog box will appear, stating that there is no match for the name you have listed.

You can choose to send only a cover page that has a message on it, send a cover page and any attached files, or just send files without a cover page. Symantec WinFax Starter Edition has five ready-made cover pages that you can choose from: Classic Bold, Dot Style, Informal Basics, Modern Basics, and Strong Standard.

You create a fax in a window (as shown below) that looks almost identical to the message window you use to send e-mail messages. To create the fax, you type the name of the recipient in the To box, type a subject in the Subject box, type a message in the message area, and if necessary, click the Insert File button to send a document with your cover page.

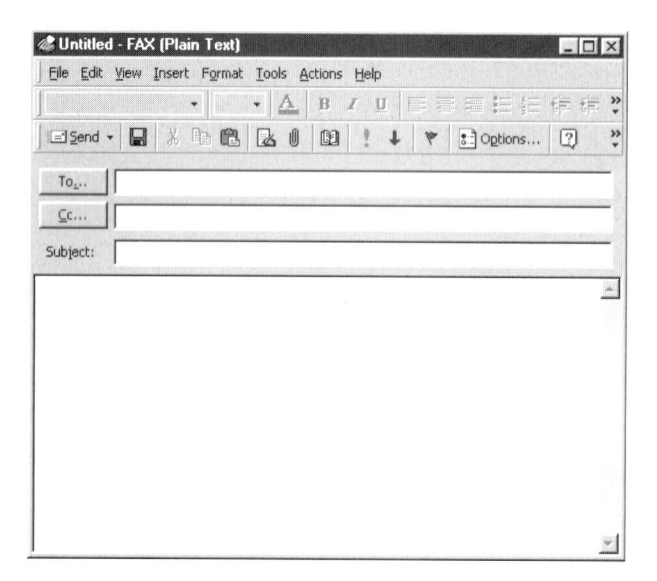

In addition to sending faxes in Outlook, you can receive faxes in Outlook. Outlook must be running for you to receive a fax. If someone sends you a fax when Outlook is not open, you will not receive the fax. The fax machine (or Outlook) either will redial your fax number until you open Outlook or will cancel the fax. If the fax is cancelled, the fax must be sent again while Outlook is open for it to appear in the Inbox. When a new fax arrives, a progress bar will appear, and then the fax header will appear in your Inbox. Faxes will automatically appear; however, you can manually receive a fax by clicking Receive Fax on the Tools menu.

In this exercise, you choose a cover sheet and send a fax to your class partner. You also receive a fax from your class partner.

Lesson 7 Using the Fax Service 7.7

> **important**
> You must know your class partner's fax number to send a fax. You also should add your class partner's fax number to the Business Fax box in the contact window.

1. If necessary, start Outlook.
2. On the Tools menu, click Options.
   The Options dialog box appears.
3. Click the Fax tab.
   The faxing information that you added when you set up the Symantec WinFax Starter Edition fax service appears.

In the Cover Page Information section, you can click the Edit button to edit your cover page information such as your address, company name, and fax number.

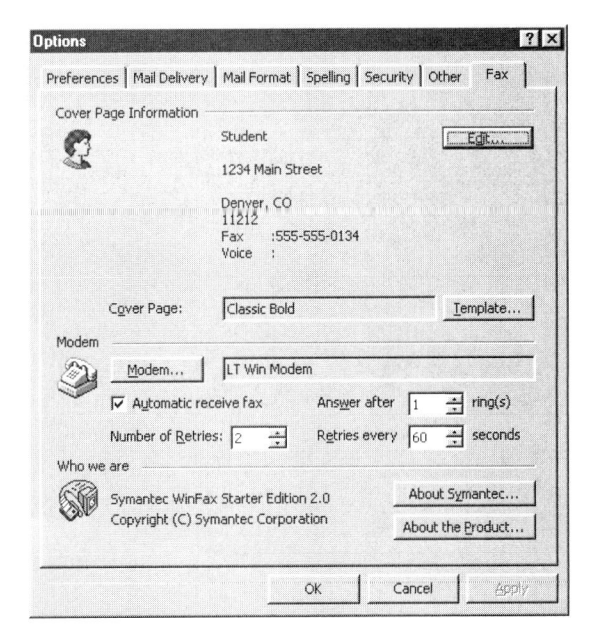

4. In the Cover Page Information section, click the Template button.
   The Cover Page Properties dialog box appears.

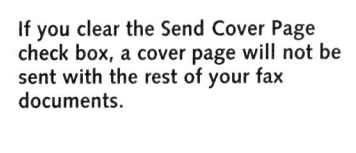

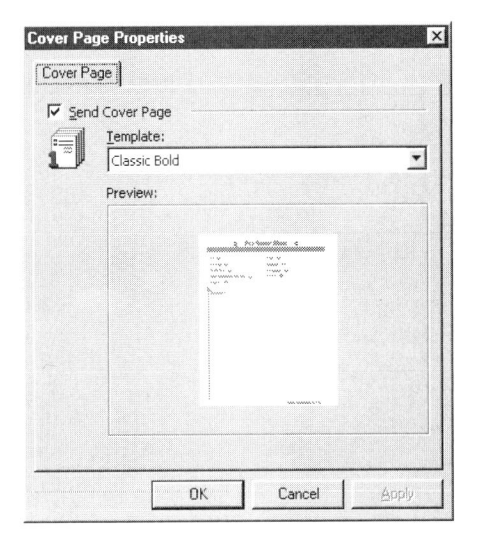

If you clear the Send Cover Page check box, a cover page will not be sent with the rest of your fax documents.

5 Click the Template down arrow, and click Modern Basics.

A preview of the Modern Basics cover page appears in the Preview section.

6 Click OK.

The Options dialog box reappears.

7 Click OK.

8 On the Standard toolbar, click the down arrow to the right of the New Mail Message button, and click Fax Message.

A fax window appears.

> You can also display a fax window by clicking New Fax Message on the Actions menu.

9 In the To box, type your class partner's name.

10 In the Subject box, type **Hiking List**.

11 In the message area, type **Here is a list of items you should bring if you're going to hike while you're staying at Lakewood Mountains Resort.**

12 On the Standard toolbar in the fax window, click the Insert File button.

Insert File

The Insert File dialog box appears.

13 Click the Look In down arrow, and navigate to the Outlook Expert Practice folder.

14 Double-click the file Hiking.

The file Hiking is inserted in the message area of the fax window.

15 On the Standard toolbar, click the Send button.

The Word document that you are faxing briefly appears in Microsoft Word as the fax service converts the document into an image. The Symantec WinFax Starter Edition dialog box appears, verifying your class partner's fax number.

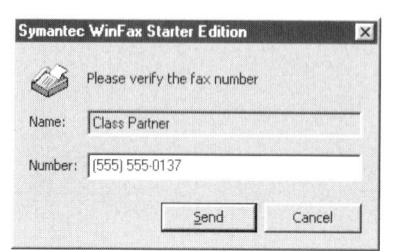

16 If necessary, in the Number box, type your class partner's fax number, and click the Send button.

> It might take a few minutes for the fax service to send and receive a fax.

A progress bar appears as the fax is sent to your class partner. Because your class partner is also sending you a fax, after a few minutes another progress bar appears as the fax service receives a fax from your class partner, and a fax header appears in the Inbox.

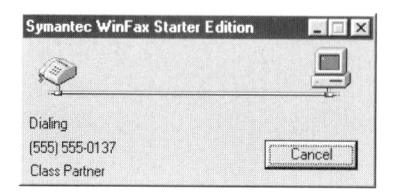

Creating a Fax Using Microsoft Fax

The steps for sending a fax using Microsoft Fax are different from the steps for sending a fax using Symantec WinFax Starter Edition. Use the following steps to send a fax using Microsoft Fax.

1. On the Actions menu, click New Fax Message.
   The Compose New Fax Wizard appears.
2. Select the desired options, and click Next.
3. In the appropriate boxes, type the name of the person that you are going to send the fax to, and the person's fax number.
4. If desired, click the Add To List button.
5. Click Next.
6. Specify whether you want to use a cover page, select the type of cover page that you want to use, and then click Next.
7. Type a subject, type a note (if desired), and then click Next.
8. If you want to include any files in the fax, click the Add File button, navigate to the location of the file that you want to add, click Open, and then click Next.
9. Click Finish.

Viewing a Fax

After you receive a fax, you can view it in Outlook. To view a fax, simply double-click the fax header in the Inbox. A window will appear with a fax status report and a fax attachment, as shown below.

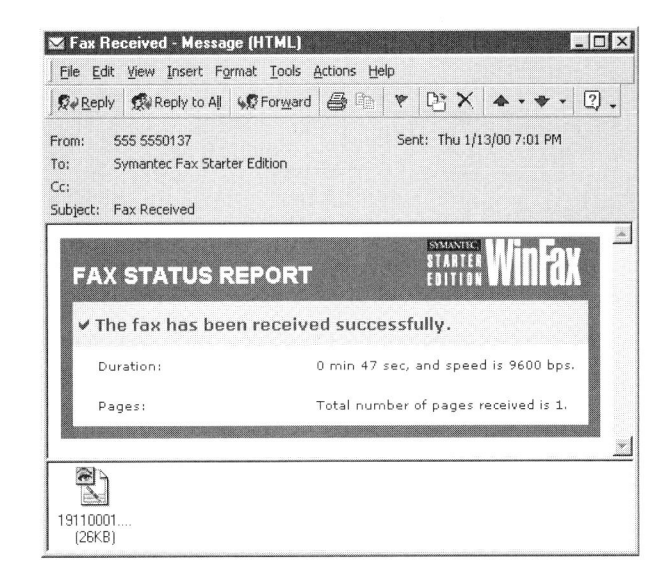

You double-click the fax icon at the bottom of the window to view it. The fax will appear in the **Quick Fax Viewer** window. You use this window to view the image of the fax, navigate through the pages of the fax, and print the fax. If you receive a fax from a fax machine, the image might come in upside down, or the details of the image might be difficult to read. You can use the Quick Fax Viewer to rotate and magnify images.

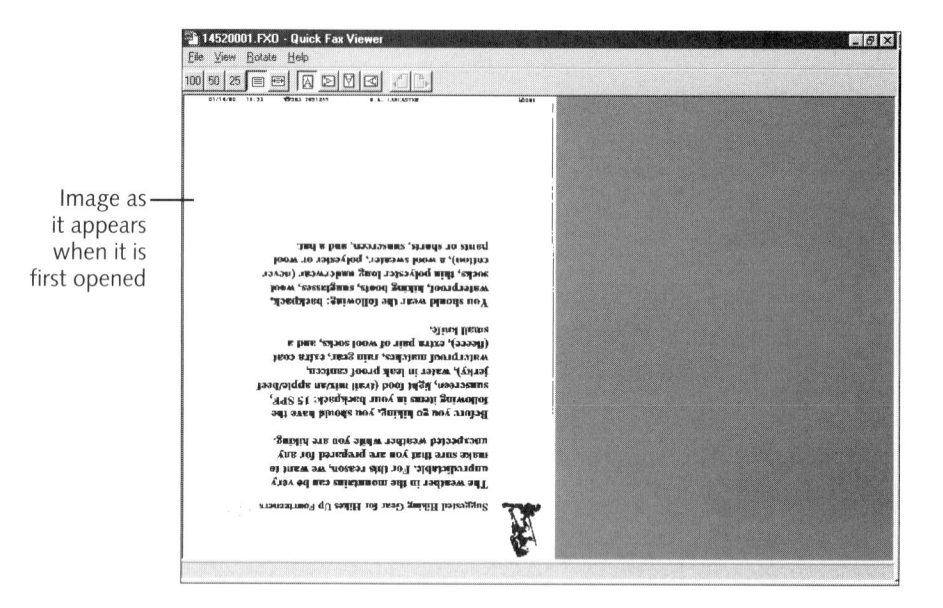

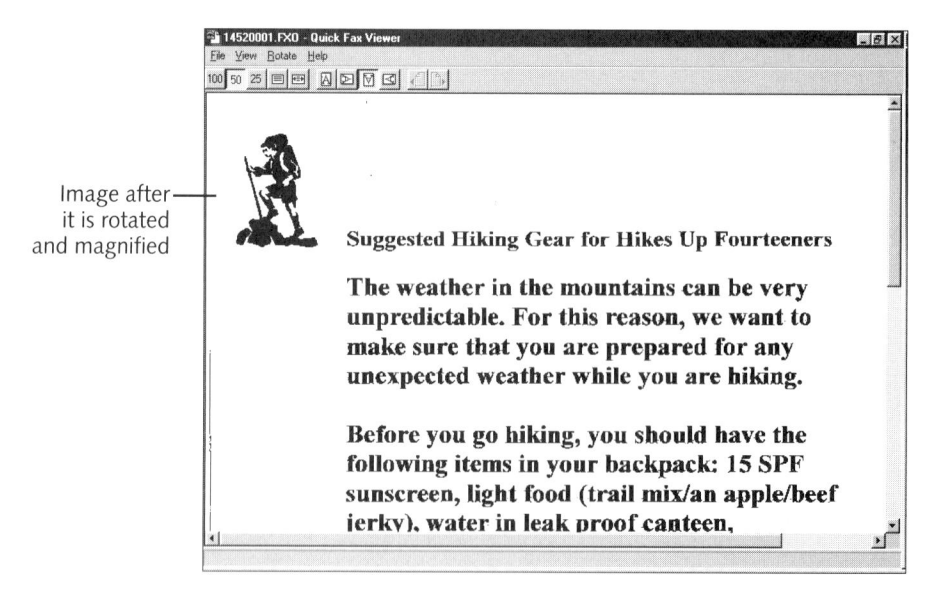

Image as it appears when it is first opened

Image after it is rotated and magnified

Lesson 7 Using the Fax Service 7.11

In this exercise, you use the Quick Fax Viewer to view the fax your class partner sent to you.

1 In the Inbox, double-click the fax.

The fax opens in a new window, the fax status report appears, and a fax icon appears at the bottom of the window.

2 Double-click the fax icon.

An alert box appears, asking if you want to open the file or save the file to the hard disk.

If necessary, in the top-right corner of the Quick Fax Viewer window, click the Maximize button.

3 Click the Open It option, and click OK.

The fax appears in the Quick Fax Viewer.

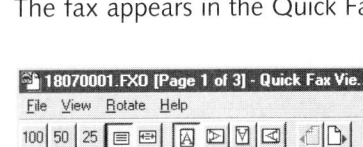

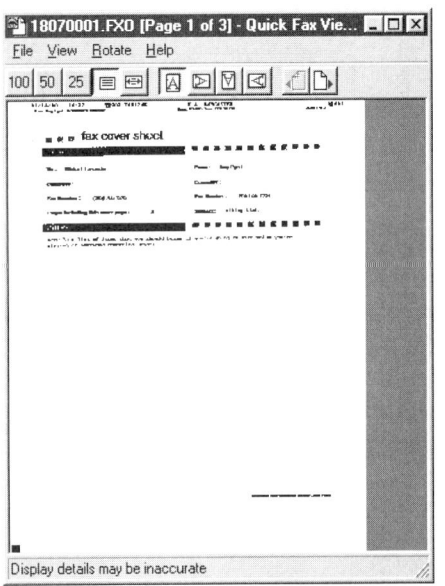

View 50%

4 On the toolbar, click the View 50% button.

The fax is magnified.

Next Page

5 On the toolbar, click the Next Page button.

The next page of the fax appears.

6 On the toolbar, click the Next Page button again.

The last page of the fax appears.

Previous Page

7 On the toolbar, click the Previous Page button twice.

The cover page of the fax reappears.

Close

8 In the top-right corner of the Quick Fax Viewer window, click the Close button.

The Quick Fax Viewer closes.

To print the fax, on the File menu, click Print.

Customizing a Fax Using Microsoft Fax

Microsoft Fax has four cover pages: Confidential!, For your information, Generic, or Urgent! To view the different types of cover pages, on the Tools menu, point to Microsoft Fax Tools, and click Options. On the Message tab in the Default Cover Page section, click one of the cover pages in the list, and click the Open button to open the cover page. You will notice that generic names such as *Sender's Company* and *Sender's Address* appear as placeholder text. When you actually send the cover page, Microsoft Fax replaces this generic information with your information. (The information that is added will depend on the information that appears on the User tab in the Microsoft Fax Properties dialog box. To view or modify this information, on the Tools menu, point to Microsoft Fax Tools, click Options, and click the User tab.)

You can use Outlook's ready-made cover pages or you can customize a cover page to suit your needs. For example, when the office manager at Lakewood Mountains Resort uses Microsoft Fax to send faxes, she sends a custom cover page with the Lakewood Mountains Resort logo at the top of the page.

You can also create a custom cover page by clicking the New button in the Microsoft Fax Properties dialog box.

You use the **Cover Page Editor** to customize a cover page. Using the Cover Page Editor, you can modify a ready-made cover page to include additional information fields as well as text and graphics. To access the Cover Page Editor, on the Tools menu, point to Microsoft Fax Tools, and click Options. On the Message tab in the Default Cover Page section, click one of the cover pages in the list, and click Open. The cover page that you want to modify will appear in the Cover Page Editor. Use the Cover Page Editor tools to modify the ready-made cover page, and then save the custom cover page with a new name. When you send a fax, simply click the name of your custom fax in the Compose New Fax Wizard.

Lesson Wrap-Up

This lesson covered how to set up a fax service, how to create and send a fax, and how to receive and view a fax.

This concludes the Microsoft Outlook Expert Skills course.

If you are going to review other lessons:

- ● In the top-right corner of the fax window, click the Close button.

  The fax window closes.

If you are not going to review other lessons:

1. In the top-right corner of the fax window, click the Close button.

   The fax window closes.

2. In the top-right corner of the Outlook window, click the Close button.

   Outlook closes.

Lesson Glossary

cover page A one-page document that contains information about additional pages that follow the cover page (such as the name of the document, number of pages, and a summary) and the sender (such as name, address, and business). Sometimes a cover page contains a message to the recipient and is the only document that is sent.

Cover Page Editor A program used to customize a cover page.

Quick Fax Viewer A program used to display, magnify, rotate the image of a fax, navigate through the pages of a fax, and print a fax.

Quick Quiz

1. Where do faxes that you receive appear?
2. How can you view the different cover pages the Symantec WinFax Starter Edition fax service has to offer?
3. What program do you use to customize a cover page?
4. What is a cover page?
5. What program do you use to view faxes?

Putting It All Together

Exercise 1: Send a fax to your class partner, using the Strong Standard cover page. Type in the following information:

Subject: **Thank You**
Message Area: **Thanks for the hiking list.**

Exercise 2: Send another fax to your class partner without sending a cover sheet. Attach the file named Brochure.

APPENDIX

Creating Forms

OL2000E.5.5

Many of the detailed windows that you see in Microsoft Outlook are actually forms. A **form** is a collection of fields and field labels for a particular record, formatted and organized for a particular use. (A **field** is a single item of data, such as a person's name, e-mail address, or phone number.) For example, the Task, Calendar, and Contacts windows are all forms; when you use any of these windows, you are essentially entering fields and records into a database that is controlled and managed by Outlook.

The ready-made forms that you use to create, view, and edit Outlook records provide plenty of flexibility, but as is true with so many components in Outlook, you can extend the capabilities of these forms. Specifically, you can modify an existing form to create a format that better matches the way you work.

You can alter an existing Outlook form in several ways: you can delete unwanted fields, add new fields, rename existing field labels, and move and resize fields. For example, in the Contact window, you might change the Company field label to Organization to accommodate government agencies and nonprofit organizations. Or you might want to lengthen the size of the E-mail and Web Page Address fields so that you can see complete addresses in the boxes. The following screen shows the form used to enter fields for a contact record. Notice that the form looks similar to the Contact window—in fact, it *is* the Contact window, but it appears in a **Design view** that allows you to modify the appearance of the window.

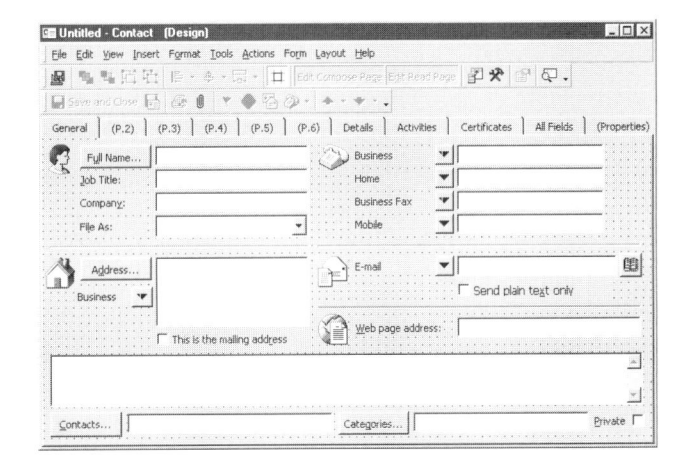

To resize a field, field label, or other object, click one of the resize handles and drag in the desired direction. To move a field, field label, or other object, click and drag until the object is positioned where you want. To delete a field, field label, or other object, click the object's border and press Delete. If you move, size, or delete an object and then change your mind, click Undo on the Edit menu to cancel the changes. To change the text for a field label, click the label, select the text, and then type the new text.

After you have finished customizing a form, you **publish** it—that is, you save the new form to a folder location that Outlook can find. The ready-made forms in Outlook are stored in the Standard Forms Library by default; you can store forms that you create in the Personal Forms Library or in a specific Outlook folder that you select. The following general steps explain how to create a form.

1 In any Outlook window, click the Tools menu, point to Forms, and then click Design A Form.

The Design Form dialog box appears. The forms in the Standard Forms Library appear in the list.

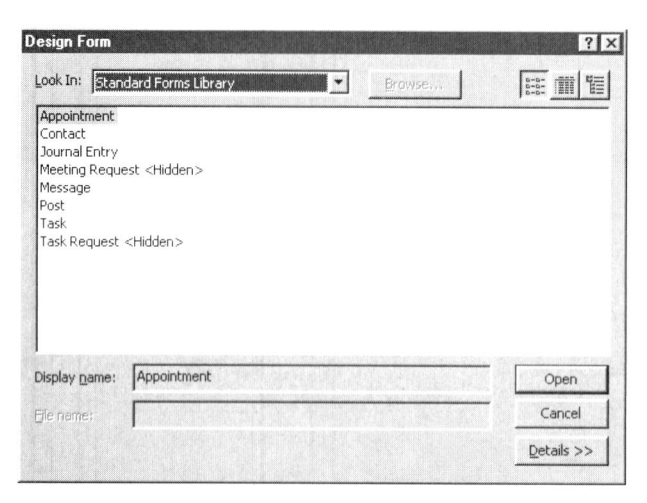

2 In the list, click the form on which you want to base your customized form, and click Open.

The Design window for the selected form appears.

3 Make changes to the layout of the form by moving, resizing, adding, or deleting field labels, fields (the boxes in which you enter data), and other objects (such as pictures or other icons).

Publish Form

4 When you are finished customizing the form, click the Publish Form button on the toolbar to display the Publish Form As dialog box as shown below.

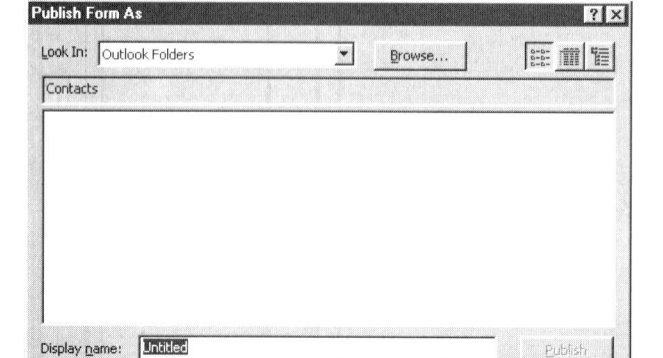

> **If you click the Save button instead of the Publish button, Outlook will attempt to save the form as a record (such as a contact record or a task item), and will probably tell you that a required field is missing. Use the Save button to save a record after you have entered data into fields; use the Publish button to save a customized form to a designated folder.**

5 Click the Look In down arrow, and click the folder where you want the form to appear.

6 Click in the Display Name box, delete the existing text, and then type a display name.

7 Click the Publish button.

8 Close the Design window without saving changes.

After you have saved a custom form, you can use it the same way you use any other Outlook form. For example, if you modify the Contact form and publish it, you can open this form and enter information whenever you create a new contact record.

To open a custom form:

1 On the Tools menu, point to Forms, and click Choose Form.

The Choose Form dialog box appears.

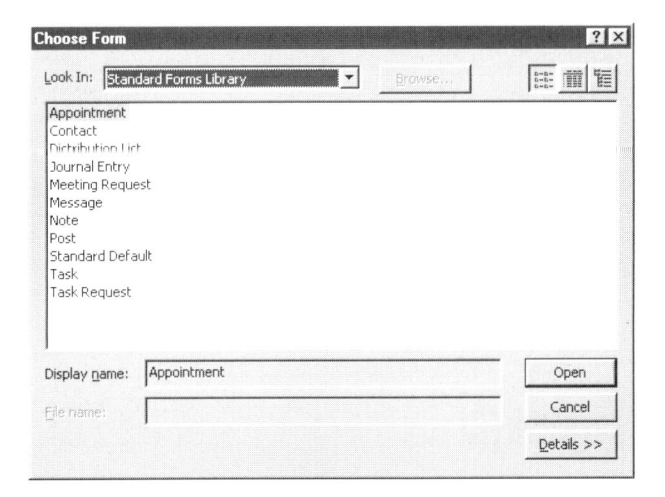

> **You can also open a custom form by clicking the form name on the Actions menu of the folder in which you put the form. For example, if you store a Contact form in the Inbox folder, you could access the form from the Inbox folder by clicking the form name on the Actions menu.**

2 Click the Look In down arrow, and navigate to the location where you saved the custom form.

3 Click the name of the form, and click Open.

tip

If you have created and saved a custom form and then decide you want to change it, open the form. On the Tools menu, point to Forms, and click Design This Form. The Design window will appear and you can then edit the form just as you did when you created it.

You can also add new fields and controls to a form. A **control** is a field or window that provides a way for users to enter data into the form. You can add controls that create text boxes (for entering fields) and field labels, lists, check boxes, option buttons, and more. For example, instead of using the lengthy list of Outlook categories, you might create a list of frequently used categories on your custom contact form. To use controls, you open the form, and click Control Toolbox on the Form menu to display the Control Toolbox.

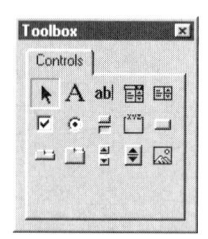

To add a control, you drag the desired control button from the Control Toolbox onto the form at the desired location. To edit a control (to change the label for a control, for example), you right-click the control on the form, and click Properties. The dialog box that appears will vary depending on the type of control you are using. A complete discussion of controls and their properties is beyond the scope of this appendix, but you can learn more about controls by experimenting with them. Create a practice form, add different controls, and change the properties of the controls to see the results.

You can also quickly add any of Outlook's ready-made fields to a form. To use ready-made fields, you open the form, and click Field Chooser on the Form menu to open the Field Chooser.

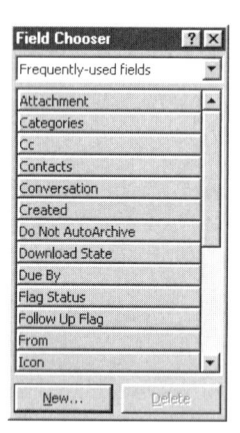

Click the down arrow to the right of the box at the top of the Field Chooser, and select the desired field category. Then scroll down (if necessary) until you see the field that you want to add, and drag the field to the desired location on the form. Outlook will add a field label and a text box (for field entry) when you drag the field onto the form.

Appendix Creating Forms   A.5

If you have created a custom form and decide that you no longer want to use it, you can use the Forms Manager to delete it. To delete a custom form:

1   On the Tools menu, click Options.

2   Click the Other tab.

3   Click the Advanced Options button.

4   Click the Custom Forms button, and click the Manage Forms button. The Forms Manager dialog box appears.

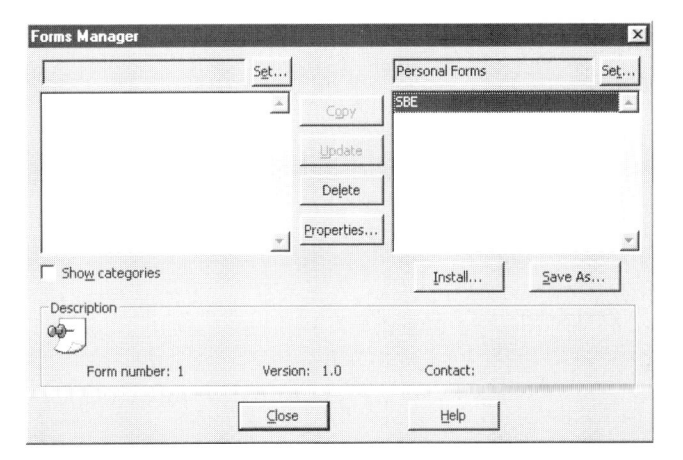

The Custom Forms button is only available if your computer is configured for Corporate or Workgroup.

5   If you published the form to a particular Outlook folder (such as the Contacts folder) click the Set button to display the Set Library To dialog box.

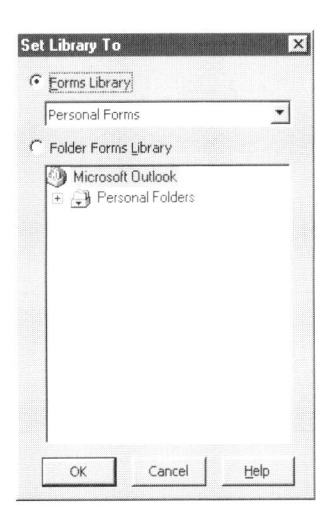

6   Click the folder in which the form is stored, and click OK.

7   In the list of forms on the left, click the form that you want to delete, and then click the Delete button.

8   Click Yes to confirm the deletion, and then close all open dialog boxes.

Or

5 If you published the form to the Personal Forms Library, click the name of the form in the list on the right side of the dialog box, and then click the Delete button.

6 Click Yes to confirm the deletion, and then close all open dialog boxes.

Glossary

control A field or window component that typically provides a way for users to enter data in a form. Lists, check boxes, option buttons, and text boxes are common types of controls.

Design view A view of a form that allows you to modify the appearance of the form.

field A single item of data, such as a person's name, e-mail address, or phone number.

form A collection of fields and field labels for a particular record, formatted and organized to support a particular use.

publish The ability to name and save a custom form to a folder that Outlook can locate when you want to use the form to create a record.

E.1

Quick Reference

Core Skills

Lesson 1: Introduction to Outlook

To start Outlook

1. On the Windows taskbar, click the Start button, point to Programs, and then click Microsoft Outlook.
2. If necessary, click the Maximize button.

Maximize

To scroll through the contents of the Outlook Bar

- Click the up arrow to scroll up through the Outlook Bar.
  Or
  Click the down arrow to scroll down through the Outlook Bar.

To expand a short menu

1. Click the desired menu.
2. Click the down arrows at the bottom of the menu.
   Or
   Wait a few seconds for the menu to expand on its own.

To use the Outlook Bar

- On the Outlook Bar, click a shortcut.

To display a different Outlook Bar group

- On the Outlook Bar, click the Outlook Shortcuts, My Shortcuts or Other Shortcuts (or Other) group bar.

To add a Web site to the list of Favorites

1. On the Windows taskbar, click the Start button, point to Programs, and then click Internet Explorer.
2. Type the address of the Web site you want to add, and press Enter.
3. Click Add To Favorites on the Favorites menu.
4. Click OK to accept the default title line as the name of the Favorite.
   Or
   Type a new name, and click OK.

To add a folder to the list of Favorites

1. On the Windows taskbar, click the Start button, point to Programs, and then click Windows Explorer.
2. Click the folder you want to add, click Add To Favorites on the Favorites menu, and then click OK to accept the default title line as the name of the Favorite.

To access a favorite Web site or folder from Outlook

1. On the Outlook bar, click the Other Shortcuts group bar (or Other group bar).
2. Click the Favorites folder, and double-click the name of the Web site or folder that you want to open.

To display a folder using the Folder List

1. If the Folder List is not already open, click the folder name that appears on the Folder Banner.
2. Click the name of the Outlook folder that you want to display.

To keep the Folder List open

Push Pin

1. Click the Folder Banner.
2. Click the Push Pin button.

Or

1. On the View menu, click Folder List.

To close the Folder List

Close

- In the Folder List, click the Close button in the top-right corner.

To use the Office Assistant

Microsoft Outlook Help

1. On the Standard toolbar, click the Microsoft Outlook Help button.
2. Type a question, and click the Search button.
3. In the list of topics that appears, click the topic that most closely matches your help request.

To hide the Office Assistant

1. Right-click the Office Assistant.
2. Click Hide.

Lesson 2: Using E-Mail in Outlook

To compose, address, and send a message

New Mail Message

1. In the Inbox, click the New Mail Message button on the Standard toolbar.
2. In the To text box, type an e-mail address.
3. Press Tab, and type another e-mail address in the Cc box if necessary.
4. Press Tab, type the message description in the Subject text box, and then press Enter.
5. Type your message, and click the Send button.

To flag a message

Flag

1. Create an e-mail message.
2. On the Standard toolbar in the message window, click the Flag button.
3. Select your options, and click OK.

To save a message as a template

1. Create the e-mail message that you want to use as a template.
2. In the message window, click Save As on the File menu.
3. In the Save As dialog box, click the Save As Type down arrow, click Outlook Template (.oft), and then click the Save button.

To open a template

1. On the Tools menu, point to Forms, and click Choose Form.
2. In the Choose Form dialog box, click the Look In down arrow, click User Templates In File System, and then double-click the name of the template.

To attach a file to a message

Insert File

1. Follow the steps for composing and addressing a message.
2. On the Standard toolbar in the message window, click the Insert File button.
3. Click the Look In down arrow, and navigate to your file.
4. Double-click the file to attach it to the e-mail message.
5. On the Standard toolbar in the message window, click the Send button.

To set message priority

Importance: High

- On the Standard toolbar in the message window, click the Importance: High button.

Or

Importance: Low

On the Standard toolbar in the message window, click the Importance: Low button.

To check for e-mail messages

1. If necessary, on the Outlook Bar, click the Outlook Shortcuts group bar, and click the Inbox shortcut.
2. On the Standard toolbar, click the Send/Receive button.

To read e-mail messages and messages with attachments

1. In the Inbox, double-click the message header of the message you want to read.
2. Double-click the attachment icon in the message (if one is included) to read the attachment.

To turn AutoPreview on or off

- On the View menu, click AutoPreview.

To turn the Preview Pane on or off

- On the View menu, click Preview Pane.

To reply to a message

1. Click the message header of the message to which you want to reply.
2. On the Standard toolbar, click the Reply button.
3. Type your message.
4. On the Standard toolbar in the message window, click the Send button.

To forward a message

1. In the Inbox, click the message header of the message that you want to forward.
2. On the Standard toolbar, click the Forward button.
3. In the To box, type an e-mail address.
4. On the Standard toolbar in the message window, click the Send button.

To print a message

1. In the Inbox, click the message header of the message that you want to print.
2. On the Standard toolbar, click the Print button.

Print

To print a message with an attachment

1. In the Inbox, click the message header of the message that you want to print.
2. On the File menu, click Print.
3. In the Print Options section in the Print dialog box, select the Print Attached Files With Item(s) check box, and click OK.

To find a message

1. On the Standard toolbar, click the Find button.
2. In the Look For box, type the search criteria.
3. Click the Find Now button.

To recall a message

1. On the Folder Banner, click the folder name Inbox.
2. In the top-right corner of the Folder List, click the Push Pin button.
3. Click Sent Items.
4. Double-click the message header of the message that you want to recall.
5. On the Actions menu, click Recall This Message.
6. Click OK.

Push Pin

To delete a message

1. In the Inbox, click the message header of the message that you want to delete.
2. On the Standard toolbar, click the Delete button.

Delete

To empty the Deleted Items folder

1. In the Folder List, click Deleted Items.
2. Select the message or messages that you want to delete.
3. Press Delete, and click Yes.

Or

1. On the Tools menu, click Empty "Deleted Items" Folder, and click Yes.

To save drafts

- In the top-right corner of the message window, click the Close button, and click Yes.

Close

Or

On the Standard toolbar in the message window, click the Save button, and click the Close button in the top-right corner of the message window.

Save

To retrieve a draft

1. Display the Folder List, and click the Drafts folder.
2. Double-click the desired message to open it.
3. Complete or edit the message, and send it just as you normally would.

Lesson 3: Customizing E-Mail

To specify e-mail options

1. On the Standard toolbar, click the New Mail Message button.
2. On the Standard toolbar in the message window, click Options.
3. Select the options you want.
4. Click the Close button.

New Mail Message

To change message format

1. On the Tools menu, click Options.
2. Click the Mail Format tab.
3. In the Message Format section, click the Send In This Message Format down arrow, select the desired format, and then click OK.

To use stationery

1. On the Actions menu, click New Mail Message Using, and click More Stationery.
2. Select the stationery you want, and click OK.

To add a signature to e-mail messages

1. On the Tools menu, click Options.

2 Click the Mail Format tab.
3 Click the Signature Picker button.
4 Click the New button.
5 Type the name of your signature, and select the method you want to use to create the signature.
6 Click the Next button.
7 Type the text you want to include in your signature.
8 Click Finish, and click OK twice.

To set viewing options

1 On the Standard toolbar, click the Organize button.
2 Click the Using Views link.
3 Select the view option you want.
4 On the Standard toolbar, click the Organize button.

To sort messages

1 On the View menu, point to Current View.
2 Click Customize Current View.
3 Click the Sort button.
4 Select your options, and click OK twice.

To filter a view

1 On the View menu, point to Current View.
2 Click Customize Current View.
3 Click the Filter button.
4 Select the filter options that you want, and click OK twice.

To create folders

1 On the Standard toolbar, click the Organize button.
2 Click the Using Folders link.
3 In the top of the Organize pane, click the New Folder button.
4 In the Name box, type a folder name.
5 In the Select Where To Place The Folder list, select where to place the folder, and click OK.

To move messages between folders

1 Highlight the desired message.
2 On the Standard toolbar, click the Organize button.
3 Click the Using Folders link.
4 In the first line, select the folder to which you want to move the message.
5 Click the Move button.

To color-code message headers

1 On the Standard toolbar, click the Organize button.
2 In the Organize pane, click the Using Colors link.
3 Click or type an e-mail address.
4 Select your color options.
5 Click the Apply Colors button.

To filter junk e-mail

1 On the Standard toolbar, click the Organize button.

2   In the Organize pane, click the Junk E-Mail link.
3   Select the desired filter options.
4   Click the Turn On button.

To archive messages

1   On the File menu, click Archive.
2   Select your options, and click OK twice.

Lesson 4: Using the Contacts Folder

To view a contact

1   On the Outlook Bar, click the Contacts shortcut.
2   In the Contacts pane, double-click the title bar for the desired contact.

To create or edit a contact

1   On the Standard toolbar, click the New Contact button.
2   Type in the information you have about the person or company or both.
3   On the Standard toolbar, click the Save And New button.

New Contact

Save And New

To enter multiple contacts for the same company

1   In the Contacts folder, click the existing contact from the same company.
2   On the Actions menu, click New Contact From Same Company.
3   Type in the information you have about the new contact.
4   On the Standard toolbar in the Contact window, click the Save And Close button.

To use the Office Clipboard

1   Double-click a contact.
2   On the View menu, click Toolbars, and click Clipboard.
3   Highlight the items you want to copy.
4   On the Clipboard toolbar, click the Copy button .
5   Start the application you want to copy the information to.
6   Click either the Paste All icon or the icon containing the specific information you want to copy.

Copy

To delete a contact

1   Click the contact record you want to delete.
2   On the Standard toolbar, click the Delete button.

Delete

To restore a contact

●   Drag the contact record from the Deleted Items folder to the Contacts shortcut on the Outlook Bar.

To create folders

1   On the Standard toolbar, click the Organize button.
2   In the Organize pane, click the Using Folders link.
3   In the top-right corner of the Organize pane, click the New Folder button.
4   In the Name box, type a name for the new folder.
5   Select the desired folder options, and click OK.

To move contacts into a folder

1   On the Standard toolbar, click the Organize button.

2 In the Organize pane, click the Using Folders link.
3 Click the contact you want to move.
4 In the Organize pane, click the Move button.

To display the Contacts folder using views

1 On the Standard toolbar, click the Organize button.
2 In the Organize pane, click the Using Views link.
3 In the Change Your View list, choose the view you want from the Change Your View list.

To create a new category

1 On the Standard toolbar, click the Organize button.
2 Click the Using Categories link.
3 In the Create New Category Called box, type the name of the new category.
4 Click the Create button.

To assign a contact to a category

1 In the Contacts folder, click the desired contact.
2 In the Organize pane, select the desired category, and click the Add button.

To sort information using categories

1 On the Standard toolbar, click the Organize button.
2 In the Organize pane, click the Using Views link.
3 In the Change Your View list, click By Category.

To assign a contact to multiple categories

1 In the Contacts folder, double-click the desired contact.
2 In the Contact window, click the Categories button.
3 In the Categories dialog box, select the desired categories, and click OK.

To add a category to the Master Category List

1 On the Edit menu, click Categories.
2 Click the Master Category List button.
3 In the New Category box, type the new category name.
4 Click the Add button.

To delete a category from the Master Category List

1 On the Edit menu, click Categories.
2 Click the Master Category List button.
3 In the Master Category List, click the desired contact.
4 Click the Delete button.

To reset the Master Category List

1 On the Edit menu, click Categories.
2 Click the Master Category List button.
3 In the Master Category List, click the Reset button.
4 Click OK.

To sort contacts

1 On the Standard toolbar, click Organize.
2 Click the Using Views link

3 In the Change Your View list, click the desired view.
4 At the top of the Organize pane, click the Customize Current View button.
5 Click the Sort button.
6 In the Sort Items By section, select the desired options.
7 Click OK twice.

To use the Address Book to send e-mail

Address Book

1 On the Standard toolbar, click the Address Book button.
2 Select a recipient.
3 On the toolbar, click the Action button, and click Send Mail.
4 Compose and send an e-mail message as you normally would.

To use contacts to send e-mail

1 In the Contacts folder, double-click the desired contact.
2 On the Standard toolbar in the message window, click the New Message To Contact button.
3 Compose and send an e-mail message as you normally would.

To send contact information via e-mail

1 In the Contacts folder, right-click the desired contact record.
2 On the shortcut menu that appears, click Forward As vCard.
3 In the To text box, type the address of the recipient.
4 Click the Send button.

To insert a vCard into a signature

1 On the Tools menu, click Options.
2 Click the Mail Format tab, and click the Signature Picker button.
3 Select an existing signature, and click the Edit button.
4 At the bottom of the dialog box, click the New vCard From Contact button.
5 Click a desired vCard, click the Add button, and then click OK.

To receive contact information via e-mail

1 On the Outlook Bar, click the Inbox shortcut.
2 Double-click the message containing the vCard.
3 Double click the vCard.
4 On the Contact pane, click the Save And Close button.

To create a letter using the Letter Wizard

1 In the Contacts folder, click the desired contact.
2 On the Actions menu, click New Letter To Contact.
3 In the Letter Wizard dialog boxes, fill in the information as requested in Microsoft Word.
4 Click the Finish button.
5 Complete the letter and save or print it or both.

Lesson 5: Using the Calendar

To navigate within the Calendar

1 On the Outlook Bar, click the Calendar shortcut.
2 In the Appointment Area, drag the scroll bar up or down to display the times of the day you wish to view.
3 Click the desired date in the Date Navigator.

Quick Reference E.9

4 At the top of the Date Navigator, click the arrows to display previous and future months.

5 In the Date Navigator, click and hold the name of the current month to display a menu of months.

6 On the Standard toolbar, click the Go To Today button to display the current day.

To change the Calendar view

1 On the Standard toolbar, click the Work Week button to display the work week.

2 On the Standard toolbar, click the Week button to display the week.

3 On the Standard toolbar, click the Month button to display the month.

4 On the View menu, click Preview Pane to split the window and display the Preview Pane.

5 On the View menu, click Preview Pane to close the Preview Pane.

6 On the Standard toolbar, click the Day button to display the day view.

To schedule an appointment

1 In the Date Navigator, click the date for which you want to make the appointment.

2 In the Appointment Area, click the time slot for which you want to schedule the appointment.

3 Enter the name of the appointment, and press Enter.

To schedule an event

1 In the Date Navigator, click the first day of the event you want to schedule.

2 On the Standard toolbar, click the New Appointment button.

New Appointment

3 In the Subject box, type the name of the event, and press Tab.

4 In the Location box, type the location of the event.

5 Select the All Day Event check box.

6 Click the End Time down arrow.

7 In the mini-calendar, click the end date for the event.

8 Click the Show Time As down arrow, and click the option that suits your event.

9 On the Standard toolbar in the event window, click the Save And Close button.

To create recurring appointments

1 In the Date Navigator, click the date of the recurring appointment.

2 In the Appointment Area, click the time slot in which you want the appointment to occur.

3 Type the name of the appointment, and press Enter.

4 Double-click the appointment.

5 On the Standard toolbar, click the Recurrence button.

6 In the Recurrence Pattern section, click the option that suits the appointment.

7 Click the check box of the day on which you want the appointment to occur.

8 In the Range Of Recurrence section, click the End After option.

9 In the End After box, type the number of weeks you want the appointment to recur.

10 Click OK.

To set reminders

1 In the Date Navigator, click the date on which you want to remind yourself of an appointment.

2   Double-click the appointment for which you want a reminder.
3   If necessary, click the Reminder check box.
4   Click the Reminder down arrow, scroll up, and click the time at which you want to remind yourself of the appointment.
5   Click the Reminder button.
6   Click OK.
7   On the Standard toolbar in the appointment window, click the Save And Close button.

To edit appointments

1   Double-click the appointment that you want to edit.
2   Click in the Location box to change the location of the appointment.
3   Click the first Start Time down arrow.
4   In the mini-calendar, click another date to change the date of the appointment.
5   Click the Show Time As down arrow, and select the option that best suits your appointment.
6   On the Standard toolbar, in the appointment window, click to change the importance of the appointment.
7   In the bottom-right corner of the window, select the Private check box to make the appointment private.
8   On the Standard toolbar, in the appointment window, click the Save And Close button.

To delete normal appointments

1   Click the appointment that you want to delete.
2   On the Standard toolbar, click the Delete button.

Delete

To delete recurring appointments

1   Click the recurring appointment you want delete.
2   On the Standard toolbar, click the Delete button.
3   In the alert box that appears, click OK.

Delete

To restore a deleted appointment

1   On the Outlook Bar, scroll to the Deleted Items shortcut.
2   Drag the appointment that you want to restore onto the Calendar shortcut on the Outlook Bar.
3   On the Outlook Bar, click the Calendar shortcut.
4   In the Date Navigator, click the date on which you want to restore the appointment.

To organize appointments by using categories

1   On the Standard toolbar, click the Organize button.
2   In the Organize pane, type a category name in the Create A New Category Called box.
3   Click the Create button.
4   In the Date Navigator, click a date, and in the Appointment window, scroll down and click an appointment.
5   In the Organize pane, click the Add button.

To organize appointments by using views

1   In the Organize pane, click the Using Views link.
2   In the Change Your View list, scroll to the bottom, and click By Category.
3   If necessary, click the plus sign (+) on the Planning gray bar.

Quick Reference E.11

4 In the Organize pane, click Recurring Appointments in the Change Your View list.
5 In the Change Your View list, click Active Appointments.
6 In the Change Your View list, scroll up to the top, and click Day/Week/Month.
7 On the Standard toolbar, click the Organize button.

To plan meetings

1 On the Navigation Bar, click a future date.
2 Click the time at which you want to have the meeting.
3 On the Standard toolbar, click the down arrow to the right of the New Appointment button, and click Meeting Request.
4 Click the To button.
5 Scroll down if necessary, click the names of the people you want to attend the meeting, and click the Required button.
6 Click OK.
7 Click in the Subject box, type the subject of the meeting, and press Tab.
8 In the Location box, type the location of the meeting.
9 Click in the Memo box, and type a memo.
10 On the Standard toolbar in the meeting window, click the Send button.

To accept an invitation to a meeting

1 On the Outlook Bar, scroll up if necessary, and click the Inbox shortcut.
2 On the Standard toolbar, click the Send/Receive button.
3 Double-click the meeting request.
4 On the Standard toolbar in the meeting request window, click the Accept button.
5 Click OK in the alert box that appears.
6 On the Standard toolbar, click the Send/Receive button.

To print a Calendar

Print

1 On the Standard toolbar, click the Print button.
2 In the Print Style section, scroll down, and click a style.
3 In the Print Range section, click the Start down arrow.
4 Click the first day of the month you want to print.
5 In the Print Range section, click the End down arrow.
6 Click the last day on the calendar that you want to print.
7 Click OK.

To save a Calendar as a Web page

1 On the File menu, click Save As Web Page.
2 In the Duration section, click the Start Date down arrow, and click the first day of the month you want to save.
3 In the Duration section, click the End Date down arrow, and click the last day of the month you want to save.
4 In the Calendar Title box, type your name (if necessary), press the Spacebar, and type the title of the calendar.
5 Click the Browse button.
6 Click the Save In down arrow, and navigate to the folder in which you want to save the Web page.
7 In the File Name box, type the name of the page.

8 Click the Select button.
9 Click the Save button.

To integrate the Calendar with other Outlook components

1 In the Calendar, click the box that contains the text *Click Here To Add A New Task* in the TaskPad.
2 Type the name of the task, and press Enter.

Lesson 6: Using Tasks

To create a task

1 On the Outlook Bar, click the Tasks shortcut.
2 Click in the box that contains the text *Click Here To Add A New Task*, and type the name of the new task.
3 To the right of the task that you just created, click in the Due Date column.
4 Click the down arrow.
5 Click the button for the date on which the task is due.
6 Press Enter.

To change task views

- On the View menu, point to Current View, and click the desired view.

To add task details

1 Double-click the task to which you want to add details.
2 Enter information in the Task and Details tabs.
3 On the Standard toolbar in the task window, click the Save And Close button.

To sort tasks

- Click the column heading by which you want to sort.

To print a task list

1 On the Standard toolbar, click the Print button.
2 Select the print style and, if you want, click the Page Setup button to choose options, such as text formatting and different paper sizes and types.
3 When you are finished selecting options, click OK.

Print

To organize tasks by using folders

1 On the Standard toolbar, click the Organize button.
2 Click the Using Folders link.
3 In the task list, select the tasks that you want to move.
4 In the Organize pane, click the Move Task Selected Below To down arrow, and select the desired folder.
5 Click the Move button.

To organize tasks by using categories

1 On the Standard toolbar, click the Organize button.
2 Click the Using Categories link.
3 In the task list, select the tasks that you want to move.
4 In the Organize pane, click the Add Tasks Selected Below To down arrow, and select the desired category.
5 In the Organize pane, click the Add button.

To assign a task

1. Select the task that you want to assign.
2. On the Standard toolbar in the task window, click the Assign Task button.
3. Click the To button.
4. In the Select Task Recipient dialog box, click the name of the person you're assigning the task to, and click the To button.
5. Click OK.
6. On the Standard toolbar in the task window, click the Send button.

To accept or decline a task

1. In the Inbox, double-click the task request that you want to accept or decline.
2. On the Standard toolbar in the task request window, click the Accept button or the Decline button.
3. Click OK to send the response now, and in the top-right corner of the task request window, click the Close button.

   Or

   Click the Edit The Response Before Sending option, click OK to edit the response, type comments in the memo area, and then click the Send button.

To mark a task as complete

1. Open the task that you want to mark as complete.
2. Click the Details tab, and click the Date Completed down arrow.
3. Click the date on which the task was completed.

   Or

   Click the Status down arrow, and click Completed.
4. On the Standard toolbar in the task window, click the Save And Close button.

To manually record a task in the journal

1. Drag the task that you want to record to the Journal folder in the Folder list or to the Journal shortcut on the Outlook Bar.
2. Enter the desired information in the Journal Entry window.
3. On the Standard toolbar in the journal entry window, click the Save And Close button.

To delete a task

1. Select the task that you want to delete.
2. On the Standard toolbar, click the Delete button.

Lesson 7: Using Notes

To create notes

1. On the Outlook Bar, click the Notes shortcut.
2. On the Standard toolbar, click the New Note button.
3. Type the text for the note.
4. In the top-right corner of the note, click the Close button.

To edit notes

1. In the Notes window, double-click the note.
2. Change the text in the note.
3. In the top-right corner of the note, click the Close button.

To copy a note to a folder or to the desktop

1. Click the note that you want to copy.
2. Drag it to a folder or to the Windows desktop.

To move notes

1. Click the note you want to move.
2. On the Standard toolbar, click the Move To Folder button.
3. Click the folder name from the Folder List, and complete the information as necessary.

To forward notes

1. Right-click the note that you want to forward.
2. On the shortcut menu that appears, click Forward.
3. In the To box, type an e-mail address, and complete the message as necessary.
4. Click the Send button.

To change the Notes view

1. On the Standard toolbar, click the Organize button.
2. In the Organize pane, click the Using Views link.
3. In the Change Your View list, click the desired view.

To change the color of notes

1. Right-click the desired note.
2. On the Shortcut menu that appears, click Color.
3. Click the color that you want the note to appear.

To delete a note

1. Click the note that you want to delete.
2. On the Standard toolbar, click the Delete button.

Delete

Appendix

To install Outlook over a previous version

1. In the first Outlook 2000 Startup Wizard dialog box, click Next.
2. Click Next.
3. Click None Of The Above, and click Next.
4. Select the Internet Only (if the only e-mail connection you have is with an ISP) or Corporate Or Workgroup (if your e-mail system works with a network) option, and click Next.
5. If necessary, click Yes.
6. Click No to register later.

To install Outlook over a different e-mail program

1. In the first Outlook 2000 Startup Wizard dialog box, click Next.
2. Click None Of The Above, and click Next.
3. Select the Internet Only (if the only e-mail connection you have is with an ISP) or Corporate Or Workgroup (if your e-mail system works with a network) option, and click Next.
4. If necessary, click Yes.
5. Type your name, and click Next.
6. Type your e-mail address, and click Next.

Quick Reference   E.15

7 Type the address for your incoming mail server, and press Tab.
8 Type the address for your outgoing mail server, and click Next.
9 Type your e-mail account name (if it is different than the one Outlook inserts), and press Tab. Your e-mail account name is usually the portion of your e-mail address that precedes the @ symbol.
10 Type your e-mail account password, verify that the Remember Password check box is selected, and then click Next.
11 Verify that the Connect Through My Local Area Network (LAN) option is selected, and click Next.
12 Click Finish.
13 If the Internet Accounts dialog box appears, click the Close button.

Close

14 To use Outlook as the default e-mail manager, click Yes.
15 Click No to register later.

To create a user profile

1 On the Windows taskbar, click the Start button, point to Settings, and then click Control Panel.
2 Double-click the Mail icon, and click the Show Profiles button in the dialog box.

Mail

3 In the Mail dialog box, click the Add button.
4 Select the information services that you want to use with the profile, and click Next.
5 In the Profile Name box, type a name, and click Next.
6 If necessary, in the next wizard dialog box, click Next.
7 In the last wizard dialog box, click Finish.
8 Click the Close button to close the Mail dialog box.
9 In the top-right corner of the Control Panel, click the Close button to close it.

Close

To add an information service

1 On the Tools menu, click Services.
2 Click the Add button.
3 Select the service that you want to add, and click OK.
4 Insert the CD-ROM, and click OK.
5 Click OK to close the Services dialog box.

To modify an information service

1 On the Tools menu, click Services.
2 Click the name of the service you want to change, and then click the Properties button. The dialog box that appears next will depend on which service you selected.
3 Change the properties as needed, and click OK.
4 Click OK to close the Services dialog box.

To remove an information service

1 On the Tools menu, click Services.
2 Click the name of the service that you no longer want, and click the Remove button.
3 Click Yes to confirm the removal of the service, and click OK to close the Services dialog box.

To select a user profile when Outlook starts

1 On the Tools menu, click Options, and click the Mail Services tab in the Options dialog box.

2. In the Startup Settings section of the dialog box, click either the Prompt For A Profile To Be Used option or the Always Use This Profile option. If you select the Always Use This Profile option, you must select a profile from the list that appears.
3. Click OK.

Expert Skills

Lesson 1: Customizing Outlook

To change the size of icons on the Outlook Bar

- Right-click the Outlook Bar, and click Small Icons or Large Icons on the shortcut menu that appears.

To change the width of the Outlook Bar

1. Position the mouse pointer on the right border of the Outlook Bar until a re-size pointer appears.
2. Drag to the left or right.

To add a new group to the Outlook Bar

1. Right-click the Outlook Bar, and click Add New Group on the shortcut menu that appears.
2. Type the name of the new group, and press Enter.

To create a shortcut to a file

1. On the Outlook Bar, click the Other Shortcuts group bar (or the Other group bar).
2. On the Outlook Bar, click the My Computer shortcut.
3. Navigate to the desired file.
4. On the Outlook Bar, click the desired group bar.
5. Drag the file to the Outlook Bar.

To open a file from within Outlook

1. On the Outlook Bar, click the Other Shortcuts group bar (or the Other group bar).
2. On the Outlook Bar, click the My Computer shortcut.
3. In the My Computer pane, navigate to the desired file, and then double-click the file.

To display the Folder List

- On the View menu, click Folder List.
  Or
  Click the name that appears on the Folder Banner.

To display the contents of the My Computer window using the Folder List

1. Display the Folder List.
2. On the Outlook Bar, click the Other Shortcuts group bar (or the Other group bar), and click the My Computer shortcut.
3. If necessary, click the plus sign (+) to the left of the My Computer icon.

To assign an item to a category

1. Right-click the item, and click Categories on the shortcut menu that appears.
2. Select the check box of the desired category.
3. Click OK.

To redisplay Simple List view

- On the View menu, point to Current View, and click Simple List.

To add a category to the Master Category List

1. Select the items that you want to add to the Master Category List.
2. Right-click the selected items, and click Categories on the shortcut menu that appears.
3. Click the Master Category List button.
4. Type the name for the new category.
5. Click the Add button.
6. Click OK.
7. Select the check box of the new category.
8. Click OK.

To customize the Outlook Today page

1. On the Outlook Bar, click the Outlook Today shortcut.
2. In the top-right corner of the Outlook Today folder, click the Customize Outlook Today button.
3. Make the desired changes.
4. In the top-right corner of the Customize Outlook Today pane, click Save Changes.

To import an item

1. On the File menu, click Import And Export.
2. Click an action to perform, and click Next.
3. Select the program where the file originated, and click Next.
4. If necessary, click the Browse button to navigate to the file, and double-click the file.
5. Click Next.
6. If necessary, select a folder in which to store the file, and click Next.
7. Click OK, and click Finish.

To export an item to a file

1. On the File menu, click Import And Export.
2. Click Export To A File, and click Next.
3. Select the type of file you want to be exported, and click Next.
4. Select the folder from which to export, and then click Next.
5. If desired, click the Browse button to navigate to a folder in which to save the file.
6. If desired, type a new name for the file, and click OK.
7. Click Next, and click Finish.

Lesson 2: Using Advanced E-Mail Features

To format the text in an e-mail message

1. Create a message.
2. On the Format menu, click HTML or Rich Text.
3. Select the desired text.
4. Use the Formatting toolbar to format text.

To create a message using stationery

1. On the Format menu, point to Background, and click Picture.

2. Click the File down arrow to scroll through the list, and select a background picture.
3. Click OK.
4. Type your message, and send the e-mail as you normally would.

To create a message template

1. Create a message without addressing it.
2. On the File menu in the message window, click Save As.
3. Click the Save As Type down arrow, and click Outlook Template.
4. In the File Name box, type the desired file name.
5. Click Save.

To use a message template

1. On the File menu, point to New, and click Choose Form.
2. Click the Look In down arrow, and click User Templates In File System.
3. Click the desired template, and click Open.
4. Address the message, and make any other modifications as needed.
5. Click the Send button.

To display the Office Clipboard

1. Open an e-mail message.
2. On the View menu, point to Toolbars, and click Clipboard.

To copy text to the Clipboard

Copy

1. Select the text to be copied, and click the Copy button on the Clipboard toolbar.
2. An icon representing the copied item appears on the Clipboard toolbar.

To paste an individual item from the Clipboard

- Position the insertion point at the desired location, and then click the icon for the item you want to paste.

To paste all items on the Clipboard

- On the Office Clipboard, click the Paste All button.

To attach a vCard to a message

1. Display the Contacts folder.
2. Right-click the desired contact, and click Forward As vCard on the shortcut menu that appears.
3. Address the message as necessary, and click the Send button.

To read a vCard received in a message

1. Double-click the message that contains the vCard.
2. Double-click the vCard attachment.

To create a rule

1. On the Tools menu, click Rules Wizard.
2. Click the New button.
3. Select the type of rule to be created, click an underlined value in the Rule Description list to edit it if necessary, and then click Next.
4. Select the desired conditions, click an underlined value in the Rule Description list to edit it if necessary, and then click Next.

5   Select the desired actions to be taken, click an underlined value in the Rule Description list to edit it if necessary, and then click Next.
6   Select the desired exceptions, click an underlined value in the Rule Description list to edit it if necessary, and then click Next.
7   Type the name for the rule.
8   Click Finish, and click OK.

To track when messages are delivered and read

1   Create a message.
2   On the Standard toolbar in the message window, click the Options button.
3   In the Tracking options section, select the Request A Read Receipt For This Message check box, and click Close.
4   On the Standard toolbar, click the Send button.

To create a Personal Address Book

1   On the Tools menu, click Services.
2   Click the Add button.
3   Scroll down, click Personal Address Book, and then click OK.
4   Click OK three times.
5   On the Windows taskbar, click the Start button, point to Programs, and then click Microsoft Outlook.
6   On the Tools menu, click Services.
7   Click the Addressing tab, and click the Add button.
8   Click Personal Address Book, and click the Add button.
9   Click the Close button.
10 Click the Keep Personal Addresses In down arrow, click Personal Address Book, and then click OK.

To add a contact to your Personal Address Book

Address Book

1   On the Standard toolbar, click the Address Book button.
2   Click the desired contact.
3   Click the Add To Personal Address Book button.

To display the Personal Address Book

Address Book

1   Click the Address Book button.
2   Click the Show Names From The down arrow.
3   Click Personal Address Book.

To create a personal distribution list

1   On the File menu, point to New, and click Distribution List.
2   Type a name.
3   Click the Select Members button.
4   Click the name of the desired contact, and click the Add button.
5   Repeat step 4 as necessary.
6   If necessary, click the New Contact button to add a new contact.
7   Click OK.
8   On the Standard toolbar in the distribution list window, click the Save And Close button.

To send a message to a personal distribution list

New Mail Message

1   On the Standard toolbar, click the New Mail Message button.
2   Click the To button.

3   Click the desired personal distribution list, click the To button, and then click OK.

4   Type a message as necessary, and click the Send button.

To import data between Outlook and other e-mail applications

1   On the File menu, click Import And Export.

2   Scroll down, click Import Internet Mail And Addresses, and then click Next.

3   Follow the steps in the Import And Export Wizard. These steps will vary depending on the e-mail application from which you want to import.

To export data from Outlook

1   On the File menu, click Import And Export.

2   Click Export To A File, and click the Next button.

3   Click the desired file type, and click the Next button.

4   Click the desired folder that contains the data that you want to export, and click the Next button.

5   Select the location to which you want the file exported.

6   Click in the File Name box, type the desired name, and then click OK.

7   Click the Next button.

8   Click the Finish button.

To import data into Outlook Express

1   On the File menu, point to Import, and click the desired file type.

2   Click the desired file options, and click the Import button.

3   Click the Browse button, navigate to the location in which the file is stored, click the desired file, and then click the Open button.

4   Click the Next button.

5   Click the Finish button.

6   Click OK, and click the Close button.

To send e-mail attachments with other Office applications

1   Start the Office application, and open the file you wish to send as an attachment.

2   On the File menu, point to Send To, and click Mail Recipient (As Attachment).

3   Type an address in the To box.

4   Write the message as necessary.

5   On the Standard toolbar of the message window, click the Send button.

To set up a news account

1   On the View menu, point to Go To, and click News.

2   If necessary, click the Outlook Express icon on the Folders list.

3   In the Newsgroups section in the Outlook Express pane, click the Set Up A Newsgroups Account link. (You only have to do this once.)

4   In the Display Name box, type your name (if necessary), and then click Next.

5   In the E-mail Address box, type your e-mail address (if necessary), and click Next.

6   Type the news server name provided by your Internet service provider, click Next, and then click Finish.

7   Click Yes.

To view a newsgroup and newsgroup messages

1. In Outlook Express, in the Folders list, click the news account.
2. On the toolbar, click the Newsgroups button.
3. In the Newsgroup Subscriptions dialog box, type a subject of a newsgroup in the Display Newsgroups Which Contain box.
4. Click the desired newsgroup, and click the Go To button.
5. Click a post header to read a message.
6. Click the minus sign to the left of a post to hide responses.
7. Click a post that has a plus sign to the left of it that shows all posts sent in response to the original post.

To subscribe to a newsgroup

- In Outlook Express in the Folders list, right-click a newsgroup, and click Subscribe on the shortcut menu that appears.

Or

1. Click the Newsgroups button on the toolbar.
2. Select the newsgroup's name in the list.
3. Click the Subscribe button.

To unsubscribe to a newsgroup

1. In the Folders list, right-click the newsgroup, and click Unsubscribe on the shortcut menu that appears.
2. Click OK.

Lesson 3: Using Advanced Calendar Features

To customize Calendar options

1. On the Tools menu, click Options.
2. Click the Calendar Options button.
3. Select the desired options, and click OK twice.

To change time zone settings

1. On the Tools menu, click Options.
2. Click the Calendar Options button.
3. Click the Time Zone button.
4. Select the Show An Additional Time Zone check box.
5. In the Show Additional Time Zone section, type the name of the country that is in a different time zone in the Label box.
6. Click the Time Zone down arrow, scroll down, and click the desired time zone.
7. Click OK three times.

To schedule online meetings using NetMeeting

1. On the Calendar, display the desired day that you want to schedule the NetMeeting.
2. On the Calendar, click the time that the NetMeeting will start.
3. On the Standard toolbar, click the down arrow to the right of the New Appointment button.
4. Click Meeting Request.

5 Click the To button.
6 Click the name of a meeting attendee.
7 Click the Required or Optional button.
8 Repeat steps 6 and 7 as desired.
9 Click OK.
10 Type a subject, choose an end date and end time.
11 Select the This Is An Online Meeting Using check box.
12 Make any other desired selections.
13 Click the Send button.

To start a NetMeeting using an ILS directory

1 If necessary, go to ils.microsoft.com (in NetMeeting, on the Call menu, click Log On To ils.microsoft.com.
2 On the Call menu, click Directory, select the person you're calling from the list, and then click the Call button.

To start a NetMeeting using an IP address

1 Exchange IP address information with your contact. (To find your IP address, start NetMeeting, on the Help menu, click About Windows NetMeeting. Your IP Address will be listed at the bottom of the About Windows NetMeeting dialog box after the text IP Addresses.)
2 Type your contact's IP address in the Address text box, and click the Place Call button. Your contact will have to answer the call.

To schedule a NetShow

1 To the right of the New Appointment button, click the down arrow, and click Meeting Request.
2 Click the To button.
3 Select attendees, clicking the Required button after each one, and click OK.
4 In the Subject box, type the meeting subject.
5 Select the This Is An Online Meeting Using check box, click the This Is An Online Meeting Using down arrow, and click NetShow Services.
6 In the Event address box, type the Web address of the NetShow.
7 Click the first Start Time down arrow, and click a start date. Click the second Start Time down arrow and click a time.
8 Click the first End Time down arrow, and click an end date (if necessary). Click the second End Time down arrow, and click an end time.

To send a meeting request over the Internet

1 On the Calendar, display the desired day that you want to schedule the NetMeeting.
2 On the Calendar, click the time the NetMeeting will start.
3 On the Standard toolbar, click the down arrow to the right of the New Appointment button, and click Meeting Request.

New Appointment

4 Click the To button.
5 Select a name of a meeting attendee.
6 Click the Required button.
7 Repeat steps 5 and 6 as desired.
8 Click OK.
9 Click the Required button, and click OK.
10 Type a subject, location, and choose an end date and end time.
11 In the meeting window, on the Actions menu, click Forward As iCalendar.

Close

12 Click the Send button.
13 In the top-right corner of the message window, click the Close button.
14 Click Yes.

To accept or decline a meeting request

1 Open the attachment of the message that contains the meeting request.
2 On the Standard toolbar, click the Accept button or the Decline button.
3 In the alert box, click the desired option.
4 Click OK.

To use the Calendar on the Web

1 Add appointments to the Calendar as necessary.
2 On the File menu, click Save As Web Page.
3 In the Duration section, specify a start date and an end date.
4 In the Options section, specify any additional options.
5 In the Calendar Title box, select the current text, and type a title for the Calendar.
6 Click the Browse button to navigate to a location in which to store the file, type a file name in the File Name box, and then click Save.

Lesson 4: Using Advanced Contacts Features

To flag contacts for follow up

Flag For Follow Up

1 Select or open a contact.
2 On the Standard toolbar, click the Flag For Follow Up button.
3 Click the Flag To down arrow, and click an option.
  Or
  Type an action.
4 Click the Due By down arrow, and click a date.
5 Click OK.

To mark a flag as complete

1 Right-click the flagged contact.
2 On the shortcut menu, click Flag Complete.

To clear a flag

1 Right-click the flagged contact.
2 On the shortcut menu, click Clear Flag.

To sort contacts

● Click the column heading that you want to sort by to toggle between ascending and descending order.
  Or
1 Right-click a blank area of the contact list and click Sort.
2 Click the Sort Items By down arrow, click an item, and then click the Ascending or Descending option.
3 If desired, click the Then By down arrow, click an item, and then click the Ascending or Descending option.
4 If desired, to change the field sets displayed in the Sort Items By and Then By lists, click the Select Available Fields From down arrow, and then click a new field set.
5 Click OK.

To link contacts to other Outlook items

1. Display the Contacts folder.
2. Right-click the contact to which you want to link, point to Link on the shortcut menu that appears, and then click Items.
3. In the Link Items To Contact dialog box, click the type of item to which you want to link.
4. In the Items list, click the item to which you want to link, and click the Apply button.

To apply a filter

1. Right-click a blank area of the window of the folder that appears.
2. On the shortcut menu, click Filter.
3. Set the desired options.
4. Click OK.

To remove a filter

1. Right-click a blank area of the window of the folder that appears.
2. On the shortcut menu, click Filter.
3. Click the Clear All button, and click OK.

To add or remove fields in the current view

1. Right-click a blank area of the Contacts list.
2. On the shortcut menu, click Show Fields.
3. In the Show These Fields In This Order list, click a field and click the Remove button.
   Or
   In the Available fields list, click a field, and click the Add button.
4. Repeat step 3 as necessary.
5. Click OK.

To use contacts to create mailing labels

1. Display Contacts. If desired, filter your contacts or select contacts or do both.
2. On the Tools menu, click Mail Merge.
3. In the Contacts section, click the desired option.
4. In the Fields To Merge section, click the desired option.
5. In the Document File section, click the desired option.
6. In the Contact Data File section, click the desired option.
7. In the Merge Options section, click the Document Type down arrow, click Mailing Labels, click the Merge To down arrow, click an option, and then click OK.
8. Click the Complete Setup option in the Office Assistant dialog box.
9. If an alert box appears, click OK.
10. Click the Setup button to display the Label Options dialog box.
11. Select options as desired, and click OK.
12. Click the Insert Merge Field button, and select the first field name for the label.
13. Repeat step 12 until all the fields are entered. (Make sure you add any necessary spaces and punctuation.)
14. Click OK.
15. Click the Merge button.
16. In the Merge dialog box, click the Merge button.
17. Print or save the completed labels.

Lesson 5: Using Advanced Tasks Features

To create recurring tasks

1. On the Standard toolbar, click the New Task button.
2. In the Subject box, type a subject.
3. Select options as desired.
4. On the Standard toolbar, click the Recurrence button.
5. Specify the recurrence pattern.
6. Select desired options, and click OK.
7. On the Standard toolbar, click the Save And Close button.

New Task

To update recurring tasks

1. Display the task list in Detailed List view.
2. Click in the Status field of the recurring task to display a list.
3. In the Status list, click an item.
   Or
   In the % Complete field, select the text, and type a new percent.

To create tasks in Calendar

1. Display the Calendar.
2. On the TaskPad, click in the box that contains the text *Click Here To Add A New Task*.
3. Type the name of the task.

To create tasks from a contact

1. Right-click the desired contact, and click New Task For Contact.
2. Enter the desired task information.
3. On the Standard toolbar in the task window, click the Save And Close button.

To record tasks in the Journal

1. On the Tools menu, click Options.
2. Click the Journal Options button.
3. In the Automatically Record These Items list, select the type of task actions desired.
4. Select other options as necessary, and click OK.

To add fields to the task list

1. Display the Tasks folder.
2. Right-click a blank area of the task list, and click Show Fields.
3. In the Available Fields list, click Notes, and click the Add button.
4. Click OK.

To create custom columns

1. Right-click a blank area of the task list, and click Show Fields.
2. Click the New Field button.
3. Type the name of the new field, and click OK.
4. Use the Move Up and Move Down buttons as necessary to move the field where you want it to appear in the column, and click OK.

Lesson 6: Using Net Folders and Public Folders

To share a folder with others

1. From any private folder, on the File menu, point to New, and click Folder.
2. In the Name box, type a name.
3. Click the Folder Contains down arrow, and click the type of item the folder will contain.
4. In the Select Where To Place The Folder box, click the plus sign (+) to the left of Public Folders, click All Public Folders, and then click OK.
5. In the alert box that appears, click Yes or No.

To grant others permission to use your folders

1. Display the Folder List.
2. Right-click the folder.
3. On the shortcut menu, click Properties.
4. In the Properties dialog box, click the Permissions tab.
5. Click the Add button.
6. Type or click the name of the person to be added to the permissions list.
7. Click the Add button, and click OK.
8. In the Name list, click the name.
9. Click the Roles down arrow, click a role to determine the level of permission for the user, and then click OK.

To grant a delegate access to your folders

1. On the Tools menu, click Options.
2. Click the Delegates tab.
3. Click the Add button.
4. Type or click the name of the delegate, and click the Add button.
5. Click OK.
6. Select the appropriate permissions for the desired folders, and click OK twice.

To use Net Folders

1. Display the Folder List.
2. If desired, create a folder that you want to share in the Personal Folders file.
   Or
   Copy an existing folder to your Personal Folders file.
3. Click the folder that you want to share.
4. On the File menu, point to Share, and click This Folder.
5. Click Next.
6. Click the Add button.
7. Click the Show Names From The down arrow, and click Contacts.
8. In the Type Name Or Select From List box, type the name of the potential subscriber.
   Or
   Select the name from the list.
9. Click the To button, and click OK.
10. In the Member List box, click a name, if necessary.
11. Click the Permissions button, and assign a level of permission to the potential subscriber in the Net Folder Sharing Permissions dialog box.

Quick Reference   E.27

12 Click Next.
13 If desired, type a description of the Net Folder, click Next, and then click Finish.
14 Click OK.

To add a Web site to the Favorites list

1 In Internet Explorer, type the address of a Web site you want to visit in the Address box, and press Enter.
2 After the Web page appears, click Add To Favorites on the Favorites menu.
3 Click OK to accept the default title line as the name of the Favorite.
Or
Type a new name.
4 Click OK.

To sort Web addresses

- Click the column header that you want to sort by.

To filter Web addresses

1 On the View menu, point to Current View, and then click Customize Current View.
2 Click the Filter button.
3 Specify the desired options, and click OK twice.

To delete Web addresses

1 Click a Web address, and press Delete.
2 Click Yes.

To display different views of the Favorites folder

- On the View menu, point to Current View, and then click a view.

To enable offline use

1 Display the Inbox.
2 On the Tools menu, click Services.
3 If necessary, in the The Following Information Services Are Set Up In This Profile box, click Microsoft Exchange Server.
4 Click the Properties button.
5 Click the Advanced tab.
6 Click the Enable Offline Use check box.
7 Click OK twice.

To work offline

1 If necessary, set up an offline folder file.
2 Quit Outlook.
3 Start Outlook.
4 In the Microsoft Exchange Server dialog box, click the Work Offline button.
5 Use Outlook as you would normally.

To synchronize a folder

1 Set Outlook to work online.
2 Display the Folder List.
3 Click the folder that you want to synchronize.
4 On the Tools menu, point to Synchronize, and click This Folder.

To synchronize all folders

1. Set Outlook to work online.
2. On the Tools menu, point to Synchronize, and click All Folders.

To create a quick synchronization group

1. On the Tools menu, point to Synchronize, and click Offline Folder Settings.
2. Click the Quick Synchronization tab, and click the New button.
3. Type the name for the group, and click OK.
4. Click the Choose Folders button.
5. If necessary, click the plus sign (+) to the left of the folder type.
6. Select the check box to the left of each folder you want to include in the group.
7. Click OK twice.

To synchronize by message size

1. On the Tools menu, point to Synchronize, and click Offline Folder Settings.
2. Click the Download Options button.
3. In the Message Size Limit section, specify the maximum number of kilobytes in a message that you want to download.
4. Click OK twice.

Lesson 7: Using the Fax Service

To install the Symantec WinFax Starter Edition with an Internet Only installation

1. On the Windows taskbar, click the Start button, point to Settings, and then click Control Panel.
2. Double-click the Add/Remove Programs icon.
3. Click Microsoft Office 2000.
4. Click the Add/Remove button.
5. Click the Add Or Remove Features button.
6. Click the plus sign (+) to the left of Microsoft Outlook For Windows to show the installation options, click the icon next to Symantec Fax Starter Edition, and then click Run From My Computer.
7. Click the Update Now button.
8. After Symantec Fax Starter Edition is installed, start Outlook, and follow the steps in the Symantec Fax Starter Edition Setup Wizard.

To install Microsoft Fax with a Corporate or Workgroup installation for Windows 95

1. On the Windows taskbar, click the Start button, point to Settings, and then click Control Panel.
2. Double-click the Add/Remove Programs icon.
3. On the Windows Setup tab, click Microsoft Fax, and click OK.

To install Microsoft Fax with a Corporate or Workgroup installation for Windows 98

1. Insert the Windows 98 CD-ROM.
2. In Windows Explorer, display your CD-ROM drive and navigate to tools\OldWin95\message\us.
3. Double-click the file awfax.
4. Read the license agreement, and click Yes.
5. Click Yes in the alert box to restart your computer.

To add Microsoft Fax to your mail profile

1. On the Windows taskbar, click the Start button, point to Settings, and click Control Panel.
2. Double-click the Mail (or Mail and Fax) icon, and click Add.
3. Click Microsoft Fax, and click OK.

To reinstall Office 2000

1. Insert the Office 2000 CD-ROM into the CD-ROM drive.
2. On the Windows taskbar, click the Start button, point to Settings, and then click Control Panel.
3. Double-click the Add/Remove Programs icon.
4. On the Install/Uninstall tab, click Microsoft Office 2000, and click the Add/Remove button.
5. Click Repair Office.
6. Click Reinstall Office 2000, and click Finish.

To create a fax cover page

1. On the Tools menu, click Options.
2. Click the Fax tab.
3. In the Cover Page Information section, click the Template button.
4. Click the Template down arrow, and select a template.
5. Click OK twice.

To create and send a fax

New Mail Message

1. Display the Inbox.
2. On the Standard toolbar, click the down arrow to the right of the New Mail Message button, and click Fax Message.
3. In the To box, type the name of the recipient.
4. In the Subject box, type a subject.
5. In the message area, type a message.
6. If necessary, on the Standard toolbar in the fax window, click the Insert File button, click the Look In down arrow, navigate to the folder that contains the document that you want to fax, and then double-click the file.
7. On the Standard toolbar, click the Send button.
8. If necessary, in the alert box that appears in the Number box, type the fax recipient's number, and click Send.

Creating a fax using Microsoft Fax

1. On the Actions menu, click Fax New Message.
2. Select the desired options, and click Next.
3. In the appropriate boxes, type the name of the person that you are going to send the fax to, and the person's number.
4. If desired, click the Add To List button.
5. Click Next.
6. Specify whether you want to use a cover page, select the type of cover page that you want to use, and then click Next.
7. Type a subject, type a note (if desired), and then click Next.
8. If you want to include any files in the fax, click the Add File button, navigate to the location of the file that you want to add, click Open, and then click Next.
9. Click Finish.

To view a fax

1. Display the Inbox.
2. Double-click the fax.
3. Click the Open It option, and click OK.

Appendix

To create a form

1. In any Outlook window, click the Tools menu, point to Forms, and then click Design A Form.
2. In the list, click the form on which you want to base your customized form, and click Open.
3. Make changes to the layout of the form by moving, resizing, adding, or deleting field labels, fields, and other objects.
4. When you are finished customizing the form, click the Publish Form button on the toolbar.

Publish Form

5. Click the Look In down arrow, and click the folder in which you want the form to appear.
6. Click in the Display Name box, delete the existing text, and then type a display name.
7. Click the Publish button.
8. Close the Design window without saving changes.

To open a custom form

1. On the Tools menu, point to Forms, and click Choose Form.
2. Click the Look In down arrow, and navigate to the location where you saved the custom form.
3. Click the name of the form, and click Open.

To delete a custom form

1. On the Tools menu, click Options.
2. Click the Other tab.
3. Click the Advanced Options button.
4. Click the Custom Forms button, and click the Manage Forms button.
5. If you published the form to a particular Outlook folder, click the Set button.
6. Click the folder in which the form is stored, and click OK.
7. In the list of forms on the left, click the form that you want to delete, and click the Delete button.
8. Click Yes to confirm the deletion, and close all open dialog boxes.

Or

5. If you published the form to the Personal Forms Library, click the name of the form in the list on the right side of the dialog box, and click the Delete button.
6. Click Yes to confirm the deletion, and close all open dialog boxes.

Index

Special Characters

– (minus sign), 1.7
+ (plus sign), 1.7

A

accepting
    invitations, E.11
    meeting requests, 3.11
    tasks, E.13
accessing Web sites from Outlook, E.1
actions, defined, 2.10, 2.32
Add to Personal Address Book button, 2.18
adding
    categories to Master Category List, 1.11–1.12, E.7, E.17
    contacts to Personal Address Book, 2.16–2.18, E.19
    controls to forms, A.4
    fields, E.24
    fields to forms, A.4
    fields to task list, 5.8–5.10, E.25
    folders to Favorites, E.1
    groups to Outlook Bar, E.16
    information services, E.15
    signatures to messages, E.4–E.5
    task details, E.12
    vCards to messages, 2.8–2.10, E.18
    Web sites to Favorites, E.1
Address Book
    button, 2.18
    sending e-mail with, E.8
addressing messages, E.2
applying filters, E.24
appointments
    creating recurring, E.9
    deleting, E.10
    editing, E.10
    organizing, E.10–E.11
    restoring, E.10
    scheduling, E.9
    scheduling for broadcasts with NetShow, 3.9–3.10, E.22
archiving messages, E.6
assigning
    contacts to categories, E.7
    contacts to multiple categories, E.7
    items to categories, 1.9–1.11, E.16
    tasks, E.13
attaching
    files to messages, E.2
    vCards to messages, E.18
attachments, printing, E.3
AutoPreview, turning on or off, E.3

B

backgrounds in messages, 2.2–2.5
broadcasts
    defined, 3.9, 3.13
    scheduling with NetShow, 3.9–3.10, E.22

C

Calendar
    changing view, E.9
    customizing options, 3.1–3.4, E.21
    deleting holidays, 3.4
    integrating with Outlook compononents, E.12
    navigating within, E.8–E.9
    options list, 3.2
    printing, E.11
    publishing with Net Folders, 6.9–6.13, E.26
    saving as Web page, 3.12, E.11–E.12, E.23
    sharing over Internet, 3.10–3.12
    using on Web, 3.12
categories
    adding to Master Category List, 1.11–1.12, E.7, E.17
    assigning contacts to multiple, E.7
    assigning items to, 1.9–1.11, E.16
    creating, E.7
    defined, 1.9, 1.22
    deleting from Master Category List, E.7
    resetting defaults, 1.12
    sorting with, E.7
changing
    Calendar view, E.9
    message formats, E.4
    note colors, E.14
    Notes view, E.14
    task views, E.12
    time zone settings, 3.5–3.6, E.21
chat window, defined, 3.6, 3.13
checking for e-mail messages, E.3
check spelling, 2.5, 5.9

Index

clearing
flags, E.23
time zones, 3.5
Clipboard, using, 2.8, E.18
Close button, 1.8
closing Folder List, E.2
color-coding message headers, E.5
colors, changing in notes, E.14
column headings, 4.4
columns, creating custom, 5.10, E.25
comma-separated text file, defined, 2.24, 2.32
composing messages, E.2
conditions, defined, 2.10, 2.32
connections. *See* offline; online meetings, scheduling with NetMeeting
contacts
adding to Personal Address Book, 2.16–2.18, E.19
assigning to categories, E.7
creating, E.6
creating letters for, 4.16
deleting and editing, E.6
entering multiples for companies, E.6
exporting to other e-mail programs, 2.24–2.26, E.20
filtering for mail merge, 4.10–4.12
flagging for follow up, 4.2–4.3, E.23
importing from other e-mail programs, 2.21–2.23, E.20
linking with other items, 4.7–4.9
moving, E.6–E.7
restoring, E.6
sending via e-mail, E.8
sorting, 4.4–4.6, E.7–E.8, E.23
using in mail merge, 4.10
viewing, E.6
Contacts folder, displaying, E.7
controls
adding to forms, A.4
defined, A.4, A.6
Copy button, 2.8
copying
notes, E.14
to Clipboard, 2.8, E.18
Cover Page Editor, 7.12, 7.13
cover pages
creating, 7.12
defined, 7.1, 7.13
creating
categories, E.7
contacts, E.6
cover pages, 7.12
custom columns, 5.10, E.25
custom fields, 5.10

creating, *continued*
faxes, 7.6–7.8, E.29
faxes with Microsoft Fax, 7.9
folders, E.5, E.6
forms, A.1–A.3, E.30
letters with Letter Wizard, E.8
mailing labels, 4.12–4.16, E.24
notes, E.13
Personal Address Book, 2.16–2.18, E.19
personal distribution lists, 2.18–2.20, E.19
quick synchronization groups, 6.16–6.17, E.28
recurring appointments, E.9
recurring tasks, 5.1–5.3, E.25
rules, 2.10–2.13, E.18–E.19
shortcuts, 1.4–1.6, E.16
tasks, E.12
tasks from other folders, 5.4–5.5, E.25
templates, 2.5–2.8, E.18
user profiles, E.15
custom forms. *See* forms
customizing
Calendar options, 3.1–3.4
faxes with Microsoft Fax, 7.12
message appearance, 2.2–2.5, E.17–E.18
Outlook Today, 1.13–1.15, E.17

D

data source, defined, 4.10, 4.17
data
exporting to other programs, 2.24–2.26, E.20
importing from other programs, 2.21–2.23, E.20
databases. *See* Microsoft Access, importing databases from
dates, displaying, 3.4
declining
meeting requests, 3.11, E.23
tasks, E.13
default
Calendar options, 3.3
categories, 1.9
delegate access
defined, 6.5, 6.18
granting to folders, 6.5–6.8, E.26
Deleted Items folder, emptying, E.4
deleting
appointments, E.10
categories from Master Category List, E.7
columns in Excel, 1.21
contacts, E.6
forms, A.5–A.6, E.30
groups, 1.3
messages, E.4
notes, E.14

deleting, *continued*
tasks, E.13
Web addresses, 6.14, E.27
delivery tracking, 2.13–2.16
Design view, defined, A.1, A.6
displaying
Clipboard toolbar, 2.8
Contacts folder, E.7
Contacts window, 4.9
current date, 3.4
Distribution List window, 2.19
Favorites, 6.14, E.27
Flag For Follow Up dialog box, 4.2
Folder List, 1.8, E.16
Inbox, 1.11
Master Category List, 1.11
My Computer, 1.8, E.16
Office Clipboard, E.18
Outlook Bar groups, 1.3, E.1
Personal Address Book, 2.18, E.19
posts, 2.31
Distribution List, displaying, 2.19
drafts, saving, E.4

E

editing
appointments, E.10
contacts, E.6
forms, A.3
notes, E.13
e-mail. *See also* messages
filtering junk, E.5–E.6
integrating with other Office applications, 2.26–2.28
sending contacts via, E.8
sending with Address Book, E.8
specifying options, E.4
emptying Deleted Items folder, E.4
enabling offline use, E.27
entering multiple contacts for same company, E.6
events
defined, 3.4, 3.13
scheduling, 3.4, E.9
exceptions, defined, 2.10, 2.32
expanding menus, E.1
export, defined, 1.1, 1.22, 2.24, 2.32
exporting
data to other e-mail programs, 2.24–2.26, E.20
Outlook data, 1.19–1.21, E.17

F

Favorites
adding folders to, E.1
adding Web sites to, 6.13–6.14, E.1, E.27
deleting, 6.14, E.27

Index E.33

faxes. *See also* Microsoft Fax
    creating, 7.6–7.8, E.29
    creating with Microsoft Fax, 7.9
    customizing with Microsoft Fax, 7.12
    printing, 7.11
    sending, 7.6–7.8, E.29
    setting up service, 7.1–7.5
    viewing, 7.6–7.8, E.30
fields
    adding to forms, A.4
    adding to task list, 5.8–5.10, E.25
    creating custom, 5.10, E.25
    defined, 4.10, 4.17, A.1, A.6
    removing, E.24
files
    attaching to messages, E.3
    opening in Outlook, E.16
filtering
    contacts for mail merge, 4.10–4.12, E.24
    defined, 4.1, 4.10, 4.17
    junk e-mail, E.5–E.6
    Web addresses, E.27
filters, applying, E.24
Find feature, 4.9
finding messages, E.3
Flag For Follow Up
    button, 2.14
    displaying dialog box, 4.2
flagging
    contacts for follow up, 4.2–4.3, E.23
    defined, 4.1, 4.17
    messages, E.2
    removing, 4.3
flags
    clearing, E.23
    marking complete, E.23
Folder Banner, 1.7
Folder List
    closing, E.2
    defined, 1.6, 1.22
    displaying, E.16
    opening, E.2
    using, 1.6–1.8, E.1
folders
    adding to Favorites, E.1
    creating, E.5, E.6
    granting delegate access to, 6.5–6.8, E.26
    granting permission for, 6.3–6.5, E.26
    moving between, 1.8
    sharing, 6.2–6.3, E.26
    synchronizing, 6.16, E.27–E.28
Font Color button, 2.3
formatting messages, 2.2–2.5, E.4, E.17

Formatting toolbar, 2.3
forms
    adding controls to, A.4
    adding fields to, A.4
    creating, A.1–A.3, E.30
    defined, A.1, A.6
    deleting, A.5–A.6, E.30
    editing, A.3
    opening, A.3, E.30
    publishing, A.2–A.3
    saving, A.3
Forms Manager, using, A.5–A.6
forwarding
    messages, E.3
    notes, E.14

G

granting
    delegate access to folders, 6.5–6.8, E.26
    permission for folders, 6.3–6.5, E.26
groups
    defined, 1.2, 1.22
    deleting, 1.3

H

help. *See* Office Assistant
hiding
    labels, 4.11–4.12
    Office Assistant, E.2
holidays
    deleting, 3.4
    selecting in Calendar, 3.4
HTML
    defined, 2.2, 2.32, 3.12, 3.13
    formatting in messages, 2.2–2.5

I

iCalendar
    defined, 3.10, 3.13
    sending as attachment, 3.10–3.12
icons, resizing, 1.3, E.16
ILS directory
    defined, 3.8, 3.13
    starting NetMeeting with, 3.8, E.22
Import/Export, installing, 1.15
importants
    Calendar options and Corporate Or Workgroup, 3.2
    choosing newsgroups, 2.30
    class partner, 2.2, 3.1, 6.1
    contact record for exercises, 5.6

importants, *continued*
    iCalendar requirements, 3.10
    installing Net Folders, 6.10
    installing NetMeeting, 3.7
    Microsoft Exchange Servers and Personal Address Book, 2.16
    Net Folders and Exchange Server, 6.10
    offline work set up, 6.15
    personal distribution lists vs. Personal Address Book, 2.18
    synchronizing and connection speeds, 6.16
    voting buttons and Exchange Server, 6.9
    Windows 98 and fax service, 7.2
importing
    data from other e-mail programs, 2.21–2.23, E.20
    defined, 1.1, 1.15, 1.22, 2.21, 2.32
    from word processing programs, 1.15
    Microsoft Access databases, 1.15–1.19, E.17
Inbox, displaying, 1.11
information services
    adding, E.15
    modifying, E.15
Insert File button, 7.8
inserting vCards into signature, E.8
installing
    fax service, 7.1–7.5, E.28
    Import/Export, 1.15
    Microsoft Fax, 7.5, E.28
    NetMeeting, 3.7
    Outlook 2000 over different e-mail programs, E.14–E.15
    Outlook 2000 over previous versions, E.14
    Symantec WinFax, 7.1–7.5, E.28
Internet, sharing Calendar on, 3.10–3.12
invitations, accepting, E.11
IP address
    defined, 3.8, 3.13
    starting NetMeeting with, 3.9, E.22
items
    assigning to categories, 1.9–1.11, E.16
    linking contacts to, 4.7–4.8
    selecting multiple, 4.8

J

Journal
    defined, 5.1, 5.11
    recording tasks in, 5.5–5.8, E.13
junk e-mail, filtering, E.5–E.6

L

labels
    creating, 4.14–4.16
    hiding, 4.11–4.12
letters
    creating letters for contacts in Word, 4.16
    creating with Letter Wizard, E.8
linking
    contacts with other items, 4.7–4.9
    defined, 4.7, 4.17

M

mail merge
    defined, 4.1, 4.17
    filtering contacts, 4.10–4.12
    performing, 4.12–4.16
    using contacts in, 4.10
mailing labels, 4.14–4.16, E.24
main document, defined, 4.10, 4.17
map, 1.15, 1.22
marking
    flags complete, E.23
    tasks complete, E.13
Master Category List
    adding categories to, E.7
    default categories, 1.9
    defined, 1.9, 1.22
    deleting categories from, E.7
    modifying, 1.11–1.12
    resetting, E.7
meetings
    accepting requests, 3.11, E.23
    planning, E.11
    scheduling with NetMeeting, 3.6–3.8, E.21–E.22
    sending requests over Internet, E.22–E.23
menus, expanding, E.1
messages
    adding signatures to, E.4–E.5
    adding vCards to, 2.8–2.10
    addressing, E.2
    archiving, E.6
    attaching files, E.2
    checking for, E.3
    checking spelling in, 2.5
    color-coding, E.6
    composing, E.2
    creating with stationery, E.17–E.18
    creating templates in, 2.5–2.8, E.18
    deleting, E.4
    finding, E.3
    flagging, 2.14, E.2
    formatting, 2.2–2.5, E.4, E.17
    forwarding, E.3
    moving, E.5
    printing, E.3
    printing with attachments, E.3

messages, *continued*
    reading, E.3
    recalling, E.4
    replying to, E.3
    sending, E.2
    sending with Address Book, E.8
    sending to newsgroups, 2.31
    sending from other Office applications, 2.27–2.28, E.20
    sending with personal distribution lists, 2.18–2.20, E.19–E.20
    setting priority, E.3
    sorting, E.5
    tracking, 2.13–2.16, E.19
message size, synchronizing by, 6.17–6.18, E.28
Microsoft Access, importing databases from, 1.15–1.19, E.17
Microsoft Excel
    deleting columns, 1.21
    exporting Outlook data to, 1.19–1.21
Microsoft Exchange Server, with Personal Address Book, 2.16
Microsoft Fax. *See also* Symantec Winfax Starter Edition
    creating faxes with, 7.9
    customizing faxes, 7.12
    setting up, 7.5, E.28
Microsoft Word, creating letters to contacts with, 4.16
minus sign (-), 1.7
moving
    contacts, E.6–E.7
    messages, E.5
    notes, E.14
multimedia, defined, 3.9, 3.13

N

navigating in Calendar, E.8–E.9
Net Folders
    defined, 6.1, 6.18
    permission options, 6.10
    using, 6.9–6.13
NetMeeting
    defined, 3.1, 3.6, 3.13
    installing, 3.7
    scheduling online meetings, 3.6–3.8, E.21–E.22
    starting with ILS directory, 3.8, E.22
    starting with IP address, 3.9, E.22
    using, 3.8–3.9
NetShow
    defined, 3.9, 3.13
    scheduling appointments for, 3.9–3.10, E.22

New Contact button, 2.9
New in Outlook 2000
    Office Clipboard, 2.8
    Outlook Express newsreader, 2.29
    sending e-mail from other Office applications, 2.26
    synchronizing offline folders, 6.16
    Web site shortcuts in Favorites, 6.13
New Mail Message button, 2.3
New Task button, 5.2
news accounts, setting up, 2.28–2.29, E.20
newsgroups
    defined, 2.28, 2.33
    displaying posts, 2.31
    sending messages to, 2.31
    subscribing to, 2.31, E.21
    viewing, 2.30–2.31, E.21
newsreader, defined, 2.29, 2.33
news servers, defined, 2.29, 2.33
Next Page button, 7.11
notes
    changing colors, E.14
    changing views, E.14
    copying, E.14
    creating, E.13
    deleting, E.14
    editing, E.13
    forwarding, E.14
    moving, E.14

O

Office 2000, reinstalling, 7.5, E.29
Office Assistant
    hiding, E.2
    using, E.2
Office Clipboard
    using, 2.8, E.6, E.18
offline
    enabling use, E.27
    synchronizing folders, 6.16
    working, 6.14–6.16, E.27
online meetings, scheduling with NetMeeting, 3.6–3.8, E.21–E.22
opening
    files from Outlook, E.16
    Folder List, E.2
    forms, A.3, E.30
    templates, E.2
options
    Calendar, 3.1–3.4, E.21
    changing view, E.5
    clearing sorts, 4.6
    Mail Merge Contacts, 4.13
    Net Folders, 6.10
    Outlook Bar, 1.2–1.4
    roles, 6.3, 6.6

Index E.35

options, *continued*
   tracking, 6.8–6.9
   voting, 6.8–6.9
organizing
   appointments, E.10–E.11
   shortcuts, 1.6
   tasks, E.12
Outlook 2000
   accessing Web sites from, E.1
   installing over different e-mail programs, E.14–E.15
   installing over previous versions, E.14
   starting, E.1
Outlook Bar
   adding groups to, E.16
   creating shortcuts on, 1.4–1.6
   customizing, 1.2–1.4
   displaying groups with, E.1
   organizing shortcuts, 1.6
   resizing, E.16
   scrolling, E.1
   using, E.1
Outlook data, exporting to Excel, 1.19–1.21
Outlook Today
   defined, 1.22
   using and customizing, 1.13–1.15, E.17

P

pasting, 2.8, E.18
performing mail merge, 4.12–4.16
permission
   defined, 6.3, 6.19
   granting for folders, 6.3–6.5, E.26
   Net Folder options, 6.10
Personal Address Book
   adding contacts to, 2.17–2.18, E.19
   creating, 2.16–2.18, E.19
   defined, 2.16, 2.33
   displaying, 2.18, E.19
personal distribution list
   creating, 2.18–2.20, E.19
   selecting names in, 2.19
   sending messages with, 2.18–2.20, E.19–E.20
Place Call button, 3.9
plain text, defined, 2.2, 2.33
planning meetings, E.11
plus sign (+), 1.7
posts
   defined, 2.29, 2.33
   displaying, 2.31
Preview Pane, turning on or off, E.3
Previous Page button, 7.11
Print button, 4.16

printing
   calendars, E.11
   faxes, 7.11
   messages, E.3
   messages with attachments, E.3
priority, setting in messages, E.3
public folder, defined, 6.2, 6.19
Publish Form button, A.2
publishing
   defined, A.2, A.6
   forms, 6.9, 6.19, A.2–A.3
   as Net Folder, 6.9–6.13, E.26
Push Pin button, 1.7

Q

Quick Fax Viewer, defined, 7.10, 7.13
quick synchronization groups
   creating, 6.16–6.17, E.28
   defined, 6.16, 6.19

R

reading
   messages, E.3
   tracking in messages, 2.13–2.16
   vCards, 2.10, E.18
read receipt, defined, 2.13, 2.33
recalling messages, E.4
receiving vCards, E.8
recording tasks in Journal, 5.5–5.8, E.13
recurring events, scheduling, 3.4
recurring tasks
   creating and updating, 5.1–5.3, E.25
   defined, 5.1, 5.11
reinstalling Office 2000, 7.5, E.29
Reminder
   selecting, 3.8
   setting, E.9–E.10
removing
   fields, E.24
   flags, 4.3
   information services, E.15
replying to messages, E.3
requests, accepting for meetings, 3.11, E.23
resetting
   default categories, 1.12
   Master Category List, E.7
resizing
   icons, 1.3, E.16
   Outlook Bar, E.16

restoring
   appointments, E.10
   contacts, E.6
rich text, defined, 2.2, 2.33
roles
   defined, 6.3, 6.19
   types of, 6.3, 6.6
rules
   creating, E.18–E.19
   defined, 2.10, 2.33
Rules Wizard, using, 2.10–2.13
running rules, 2.12

S

saving
   Calendar as Web page, 3.12, E.11–E.12, E.23
   drafts, E.4
   forms, A.3
   templates, 2.6, E.2
scheduling
   appointments, E.9
   events, 3.4, E.9
   NetShow, 3.9–3.10, E.22
   online meetings with NetMeeting, 3.6–3.8, E.21–E.22
ScreenTip, 4.4
searching text, 2.11–2.12
selecting
   multiple items, 4.8
   names in distribution list, 2.19
   Reminder, 3.8
   user profiles when Outlook starts, E.15–E.16
sending
   contacts via e-mail, E.8
   e-mail from other Office applications, 2.27–2.28, E.20
   e-mail with Address Book, E.8
   faxes, 7.6–7.8, E.29
   meeting requests over Internet, E.22
   messages, E.2
   messages to newsgroups, 2.31
   messages with personal distribution lists, 2.18–2.20, E.19–E.20
service, setting up for fax, 7.1–7.5
setting
   message priority, E.3
   reminders, E.9–E.10
   time zones, 3.5–3.6, E.21
setting up
   Microsoft Fax, 7.5, E.28
   news accounts, 2.28–2.29, E.20
   Symantec WinFax, 7.1–7.5
sharing
   Calendar over Internet, 3.10–3.12
   folders, 6.2–6.3, E.26

shortcuts
  creating, 1.4–1.6, E.16
  organizing, 1.6
signatures
  adding to messages, E.4–E.5
  inserting vCards into, E.8
Simple List view, redisplaying in, E.17
sorting
  with categories, E.7
  clearing options, 4.6
  contacts, 4.4–4.6, E.7–E.8, E.23
  defined, 4.1, 4.17
  messages, E.5
  tasks, E.13
  Web addresses, 6.14, E.27
spelling, checking, 2.5, 5.9
starting
  NetMeeting with ILS directory, 3.8, E.22
  NetMeeting with IP address, 3.9, E.22
  Outlook 2000, E.1
stationery
  creating messages with, E.17–E.18
  defined, 2.2, 2.33
  using, E.4
subscriber, defined, 6.9, 6.19
subscribing
  defined, 2.31, 2.33
  newsgroups, 2.31, E.21
Symantec WinFax Starter Edition
  installing, 7.1–7.5, E.28
synchronizing
  defined, 6.16, 6.19
  folders, 6.16, E.27–E.28
  by message size, 6.17–6.18, E.28
  quick groups, 6.16–6.17, E.28

T

task list, adding fields to, 5.8–5.10, E.25
Task Recurrence dialog box, 5.3
tasks
  accepting or declining, E.13
  adding details, E.12
  assigning, E.13

tasks, *continued*
  creating, E.12
  creating from other folders, 5.4–5.5, E.25
  creating recurring, 5.1–5.3, E.25
  deleting, E.13
  marking complete, E.13
  organizing, E.12
  recording in Journal, 5.5–5.8, E.13
  sorting, E.12
  updating recurring, 5.1–5.3, E.25
templates
  creating, 2.5–2.8, E.18
  defined, 2.5, 2.33
  opening, E.2
  saving, 2.6
  saving messages as, E.2
Tentative button, 3.11
text
  formatting in messages, 2.3–2.4, E.17
  searching, 2.11–2.12
text formats, defined, 2.2, 2.33
threads, defined, 2.30, 2.33
time zones
  changing settings, 3.5–3.6, E.21
  clearing, 3.5
tips
  creating letters for contacts in Word, 4.16
  customizing Outlook Bar, 1.2
  deleting holidays from Calendar, 3.4
  displaying Inbox, 1.11
  editing forms, A.3
  Find feature, 4.9
  flagging messages, 2.14
  granting delegate access to multiple users, 6.6
  hiding Outlook Bar, 1.3
  moving between folders, 1.8
  resetting default categories, 1.12
  sending messages to newsgroups, 2.31
tracking
  button, 6.8
  defined, 6.8, 6.19
  messages, 2.13–2.16, E.19
  using options, 6.8–6.9

U

unsubscribing, newsgroups, E.21
updating recurring tasks, 5.1–5.3, E.25
user profiles
  creating, E.15
  selecting when Outlook starts, E.15–E.16

V

vCards
  adding to messages, 2.8–2.10, E.18
  defined, 2.8, 2.33
  inserting into signature, E.8
  reading, 2.10, E.18
  receiving, E.8
View 50% button, 7.11
viewing
  Calendar, E.9
  changing options, E.5
  contacts, E.6
  faxes, 7.6–7.8, E.30
  newsgroups, 2.30–2.31, E.21
  tasks, E.12
voting
  button, 6.8
  defined, 6.8, 6.19
  using options, 6.8–6.9

W

Web addresses
  accessing from Outlook, E.1
  adding to Favorites, 6.13–6.14, E.1, E.27
  filtering, 6.14, E.27
  saving Calendar as, 3.12, E.11–E.12, E.23
  sorting, 6.14, E.27
  using Calendar on, 3.12
Whiteboard, defined, 3.6, 3.13
Word, creating letters for contacts with, 4.16
word processing programs, importing from, 1.15
working, offline, 6.14–6.16, E.27

ActiveEducation and Microsoft Press

Microsoft Outlook 2000 Step by Step Courseware has been created by the professional trainers and writers at ActiveEducation, Inc., to the exacting standards you've come to expect from Microsoft Press. Together, we are pleased to present this training guide.

ActiveEducation creates top-quality information technology training content that teaches essential computer skills for today's workplace. ActiveEducation courses are designed to provide the most effective training available and to help people become more productive computer users. Each ActiveEducation course, including this book, undergoes rigorous quality control, instructional design, and technical review procedures to ensure that the course is instructionally and technically superior in content and approach.

ActiveEducation (*www.activeeducation.com*) courses are available in book form and on the Internet.

Microsoft Press is the book publishing division of Microsoft Corporation, the leading publisher of information about Microsoft products and services. Microsoft Press is dedicated to providing the highest quality computer books and multimedia training and reference tools that make using Microsoft software easier, more enjoyable, and more productive.

About the Author

Holly Freeman is the author of *Microsoft Word 2000 Intermediate* and *Microsoft Outlook 2000 Intermediate*, published for ActiveEducation. She was the project editor for *Microsoft Internet Explorer 5 Step by Step*, published for Microsoft Press. Holly is currently a project editor and staff writer for ActiveEducation.

MICROSOFT LICENSE AGREEMENT

Book Companion CD

IMPORTANT—READ CAREFULLY: This Microsoft End-User License Agreement ("EULA") is a legal agreement between you (either an individual or an entity) and Microsoft Corporation for the Microsoft product identified above, which includes computer software and may include associated media, printed materials, and "online" or electronic documentation ("SOFTWARE PRODUCT"). Any component included within the SOFTWARE PRODUCT that is accompanied by a separate End-User License Agreement shall be governed by such agreement and not the terms set forth below. By installing, copying, or otherwise using the SOFTWARE PRODUCT, you agree to be bound by the terms of this EULA. If you do not agree to the terms of this EULA, you are not authorized to install, copy, or otherwise use the SOFTWARE PRODUCT; you may, however, return the SOFTWARE PRODUCT, along with all printed materials and other items that form a part of the Microsoft product that includes the SOFTWARE PRODUCT, to the place you obtained them for a full refund.

SOFTWARE PRODUCT LICENSE

The SOFTWARE PRODUCT is protected by United States copyright laws and international copyright treaties, as well as other intellectual property laws and treaties. The SOFTWARE PRODUCT is licensed, not sold.

1. **GRANT OF LICENSE.** This EULA grants you the following rights:
   a. **Software Product.** You may install and use one copy of the SOFTWARE PRODUCT on a single computer. The primary user of the computer on which the SOFTWARE PRODUCT is installed may make a second copy for his or her exclusive use on a portable computer.
   b. **Storage/Network Use.** You may also store or install a copy of the SOFTWARE PRODUCT on a storage device, such as a network server, used only to install or run the SOFTWARE PRODUCT on your other computers over an internal network; however, you must acquire and dedicate a license for each separate computer on which the SOFTWARE PRODUCT is installed or run from the storage device. A license for the SOFTWARE PRODUCT may not be shared or used concurrently on different computers.
   c. **License Pak.** If you have acquired this EULA in a Microsoft License Pak, you may make the number of additional copies of the computer software portion of the SOFTWARE PRODUCT authorized on the printed copy of this EULA, and you may use each copy in the manner specified above. You are also entitled to make a corresponding number of secondary copies for portable computer use as specified above.
   d. **Sample Code.** Solely with respect to portions, if any, of the SOFTWARE PRODUCT that are identified within the SOFTWARE PRODUCT as sample code (the "SAMPLE CODE"):
      i. **Use and Modification.** Microsoft grants you the right to use and modify the source code version of the SAMPLE CODE, *provided* you comply with subsection (d)(iii) below. You may not distribute the SAMPLE CODE, or any modified version of the SAMPLE CODE, in source code form.
      ii. **Redistributable Files.** Provided you comply with subsection (d)(iii) below, Microsoft grants you a nonexclusive, royalty-free right to reproduce and distribute the object code version of the SAMPLE CODE and of any modified SAMPLE CODE, other than SAMPLE CODE, or any modified version thereof, designated as not redistributable in the Readme file that forms a part of the SOFTWARE PRODUCT (the "Non-Redistributable Sample Code"). All SAMPLE CODE other than the Non-Redistributable Sample Code is collectively referred to as the "REDISTRIBUTABLES."
      iii. **Redistribution Requirements.** If you redistribute the REDISTRIBUTABLES, you agree to: (i) distribute the REDISTRIBUTABLES in object code form only in conjunction with and as a part of your software application product; (ii) not use Microsoft's name, logo, or trademarks to market your software application product; (iii) include a valid copyright notice on your software application product; (iv) indemnify, hold harmless, and defend Microsoft from and against any claims or lawsuits, including attorney's fees, that arise or result from the use or distribution of your software application product; and (v) not permit further distribution of the REDISTRIBUTABLES by your end user. Contact Microsoft for the applicable royalties due and other licensing terms for all other uses and/or distribution of the REDISTRIBUTABLES.

2. **DESCRIPTION OF OTHER RIGHTS AND LIMITATIONS.**
   - **Limitations on Reverse Engineering, Decompilation, and Disassembly.** You may not reverse engineer, decompile, or disassemble the SOFTWARE PRODUCT, except and only to the extent that such activity is expressly permitted by applicable law notwithstanding this limitation.
   - **Separation of Components.** The SOFTWARE PRODUCT is licensed as a single product. Its component parts may not be separated for use on more than one computer.
   - **Rental.** You may not rent, lease, or lend the SOFTWARE PRODUCT.
   - **Support Services.** Microsoft may, but is not obligated to, provide you with support services related to the SOFTWARE PRODUCT ("Support Services"). Use of Support Services is governed by the Microsoft policies and programs described in the user manual, in "online" documentation, and/or in other Microsoft-provided materials. Any supplemental software code provided to you as part of the Support Services shall be considered part of the SOFTWARE PRODUCT and subject to the terms and conditions of this EULA. With respect to technical information you provide to Microsoft as part of the Support Services, Microsoft may use such information for its business purposes, including for product support and development. Microsoft will not utilize such technical information in a form that personally identifies you.
   - **Software Transfer.** You may permanently transfer all of your rights under this EULA, provided you retain no copies, you transfer all of the SOFTWARE PRODUCT (including all component parts, the media and printed materials, any upgrades, this EULA, and, if applicable, the Certificate of Authenticity), **and** the recipient agrees to the terms of this EULA.
   - **Termination.** Without prejudice to any other rights, Microsoft may terminate this EULA if you fail to comply with the terms and conditions of this EULA. In such event, you must destroy all copies of the SOFTWARE PRODUCT and all of its component parts.

3. **COPYRIGHT.** All title and copyrights in and to the SOFTWARE PRODUCT (including but not limited to any images, photographs, animations, video, audio, music, text, SAMPLE CODE, REDISTRIBUTABLES, and "applets" incorporated into the SOFTWARE PRODUCT) and any copies of the SOFTWARE PRODUCT are owned by Microsoft or its suppliers. The SOFTWARE PRODUCT is protected by copyright laws and international treaty provisions. Therefore, you must treat the SOFTWARE PRODUCT like any other copyrighted material **except** that you may install the SOFTWARE PRODUCT on a single computer provided you keep the original solely for backup or archival purposes. You may not copy the printed materials accompanying the SOFTWARE PRODUCT.

4. **U.S. GOVERNMENT RESTRICTED RIGHTS.** The SOFTWARE PRODUCT and documentation are provided with RESTRICTED RIGHTS. Use, duplication, or disclosure by the Government is subject to restrictions as set forth in subparagraph (c)(1)(ii) of the Rights in Technical Data and Computer Software clause at DFARS 252.227-7013 or subparagraphs (c)(1) and (2) of the Commercial Computer Software—Restricted Rights at 48 CFR 52.227-19, as applicable. Manufacturer is Microsoft Corporation/One Microsoft Way/Redmond, WA 98052-6399.

5. **EXPORT RESTRICTIONS.** You agree that you will not export or re-export the SOFTWARE PRODUCT, any part thereof, or any process or service that is the direct product of the SOFTWARE PRODUCT (the foregoing collectively referred to as the "Restricted Components"), to any country, person, entity, or end user subject to U.S. export restrictions. You specifically agree not to export or re-export any of the Restricted Components (i) to any country to which the U.S. has embargoed or restricted the export of goods or services, which currently include, but are not necessarily limited to, Cuba, Iran, Iraq, Libya, North Korea, Sudan, and Syria, or to any national of any such country, wherever located, who intends to transmit or transport the Restricted Components back to such country; (ii) to any end user who you know or have reason to know will utilize the Restricted Components in the design, development, or production of nuclear, chemical, or biological weapons; or (iii) to any end user who has been prohibited from participating in U.S. export transactions by any federal agency of the U.S. government. You warrant and represent that neither the BXA nor any other U.S. federal agency has suspended, revoked, or denied your export privileges.

DISCLAIMER OF WARRANTY

NO WARRANTIES OR CONDITIONS. MICROSOFT EXPRESSLY DISCLAIMS ANY WARRANTY OR CONDITION FOR THE SOFTWARE PRODUCT. THE SOFTWARE PRODUCT AND ANY RELATED DOCUMENTATION ARE PROVIDED "AS IS" WITHOUT WARRANTY OR CONDITION OF ANY KIND, EITHER EXPRESS OR IMPLIED, INCLUDING, WITHOUT LIMITATION, THE IMPLIED WARRANTIES OF MERCHANTABILITY, FITNESS FOR A PARTICULAR PURPOSE, OR NONINFRINGEMENT. THE ENTIRE RISK ARISING OUT OF USE OR PERFORMANCE OF THE SOFTWARE PRODUCT REMAINS WITH YOU.

LIMITATION OF LIABILITY. TO THE MAXIMUM EXTENT PERMITTED BY APPLICABLE LAW, IN NO EVENT SHALL MICROSOFT OR ITS SUPPLIERS BE LIABLE FOR ANY SPECIAL, INCIDENTAL, INDIRECT, OR CONSEQUENTIAL DAMAGES WHATSOEVER (INCLUDING, WITHOUT LIMITATION, DAMAGES FOR LOSS OF BUSINESS PROFITS, BUSINESS INTERRUPTION, LOSS OF BUSINESS INFORMATION, OR ANY OTHER PECUNIARY LOSS) ARISING OUT OF THE USE OF OR INABILITY TO USE THE SOFTWARE PRODUCT OR THE PROVISION OF OR FAILURE TO PROVIDE SUPPORT SERVICES, EVEN IF MICROSOFT HAS BEEN ADVISED OF THE POSSIBILITY OF SUCH DAMAGES. IN ANY CASE, MICROSOFT'S ENTIRE LIABILITY UNDER ANY PROVISION OF THIS EULA SHALL BE LIMITED TO THE GREATER OF THE AMOUNT ACTUALLY PAID BY YOU FOR THE SOFTWARE PRODUCT OR US$5.00; PROVIDED, HOWEVER, IF YOU HAVE ENTERED INTO A MICROSOFT SUPPORT SERVICES AGREEMENT, MICROSOFT'S ENTIRE LIABILITY REGARDING SUPPORT SERVICES SHALL BE GOVERNED BY THE TERMS OF THAT AGREEMENT. BECAUSE SOME STATES AND JURISDICTIONS DO NOT ALLOW THE EXCLUSION OR LIMITATION OF LIABILITY, THE ABOVE LIMITATION MAY NOT APPLY TO YOU.

MISCELLANEOUS

This EULA is governed by the laws of the State of Washington USA, except and only to the extent that applicable law mandates governing law of a different jurisdiction.

Should you have any questions concerning this EULA, or if you desire to contact Microsoft for any reason, please contact the Microsoft subsidiary serving your country, or write: Microsoft Sales Information Center/One Microsoft Way/Redmond, WA 98052-6399.

Proof of Purchase 0-7356-0982-9

Do not send this card with your registration.
Use this card as proof of purchase if participating in a promotion or
rebate offer on *Microsoft® Outlook® 2000 Step by Step Courseware
Expert Skills Student Guide*. Card must be used in conjunction with
other proof(s) of payment such as your dated sales receipt—see offer details.

Microsoft® Outlook® 2000 Step by Step Courseware Expert Skills Student Guide

_____
WHERE DID YOU PURCHASE THIS PRODUCT?

_____
CUSTOMER NAME

Microsoft®
mspress.microsoft.com

Microsoft Press, PO Box 97017, Redmond, WA 98073-9830

OWNER REGISTRATION CARD   *Register Today!*   0-7356-0982-9

Return the bottom portion of this card to register today.

Microsoft® Outlook® 2000 Step by Step Courseware Expert Skills Student Guide

_____ _____ _____
FIRST NAME   **MIDDLE INITIAL** **LAST NAME**

_____
INSTITUTION OR COMPANY NAME

_____
ADDRESS

_____ _____ _____
CITY   **STATE**   **ZIP**

_____ (   ) _____
E-MAIL ADDRESS   **PHONE NUMBER**

U.S. and Canada addresses only. Fill in information above and mail postage-free.
Please mail only the bottom half of this page.

start faster go farther

For information about Microsoft Press® products, visit our Web site at
mspress.microsoft.com

Microsoft®

BUSINESS REPLY MAIL
FIRST-CLASS MAIL   PERMIT NO. 108   REDMOND WA

POSTAGE WILL BE PAID BY ADDRESSEE

NO POSTAGE
NECESSARY
IF MAILED
IN THE
UNITED STATES

MICROSOFT PRESS
PO BOX 97017
REDMOND, WA 98073-9830